Global Environmental Institutions

Global warming, the ozone hole, toxic chemicals, endangered species – such topics are now part of our daily news. There has been a concurrent growth in interest in the institutions that deal with global environmental issues. A vast number of international organizations address these matters; this volume provides an overview of the major global institutions attempting to protect the natural environment.

It first considers the United Nations Environment Programme and the other entities within the United Nations that play important roles in global environmental governance. It then examines institutions clustered by issue area, introducing institutions that focus on protecting endangered species and biodiversity, those that govern the ocean environment, those focusing on the atmosphere, and a recent set of institutions that regulate the transboundary movement of hazardous substances. It concludes with current debates on financing international environmental action, gaining widespread participation by states, and the question of whether the institutional structure of global environmental governance can, and should, be fundamentally reformed. The volume as a whole focuses on:

- the underlying causes of global environmental problems;
- the creation of global environmental institutions;
- the effectiveness of action undertaken by these institutions.

Written by an acknowledged expert in the field, *Global Environmental Institutions* is essential reading for students of environmental politics and international organizations.

Elizabeth R. DeSombre is Frost Associate Professor of Environmental Studies and Associate Professor of Political Science at Wellesley College. Her previous books include: *Flagging Standards: Globalization and Environmental, Safety, and Labor Regulations at Sea* (2006), *The Global Environment and World Politics* (2002, second edition 2007), and *Domestic Sources of International Environmental Policy: Industry, Environmentalists, and U.S. Power* (2000), the latter of which won the 2001 Chadwick F. Alger Prize for the best book published in 2000 in the area of international organization and the 2001 Lynton Caldwell Award for the best book published on environmental policy.

Global Institutions Series

Thomas G. Weiss
The CUNY Graduate Center, New York, USA
and Rorden Wilkinson
University of Manchester, UK

About the series

The "Global Institutions Series" is edited by Thomas G. Weiss (The CUNY Graduate Center, New York, USA) and Rorden Wilkinson (University of Manchester, UK) and designed to provide readers with comprehensive, accessible, and informative guides to the history, structure, and activities of key international organizations. Every volume stands on its own as a thorough and insightful treatment of a particular topic, but the series as a whole contributes to a coherent and complementary portrait of the phenomenon of global institutions at the dawn of the millennium.

Books are written by recognized experts, conform to a similar structure, and cover a range of themes and debates common to the series. These areas of shared concern include the general purpose and rationale for organizations, developments over time, membership, structure, decision-making procedures, and key functions. Moreover, current debates are placed in historical perspective alongside informed analysis and critique. Each book also contains an annotated bibliography and guide to electronic information as well as any annexes appropriate to the subject matter at hand.

The volumes currently under contract include:

The United Nations and Human Rights (2005)
by Julie A. Mertus (American University)

The UN Secretary-General and Secretariat (2005)
by Leon Gordenker (Princeton University)

United Nations Global Conferences (2005)
by Michael G. Schechter (Michigan State University)

The UN General Assembly (2005)
by M.J. Peterson (University of Massachusetts, Amherst)

Internal Displacement
Conceptualization and Its Consequences (2006)
by Thomas G. Weiss (The CUNY Graduate Center) and David A. Korn

The World Intellectual Property Organization
Resurgence and the Development Agenda (2006)

UNHCR
The Politics and Practice of Refugee
Protection into the Twenty First
Century
*by Gil Loescher (University of
Oxford), James Milner (University of
Oxford), and Alexander Betts
(University of Oxford)*

The World Health Organization
*by Kelley Lee (London School of
Hygiene and Tropical Medicine)*

The World Trade Organization
*by Bernard Hoekman (World Bank)
and Petros Mavroidis (Columbia
University)*

**The International Organization for
Standardization and the Global
Economy**
Setting Standards
*by Craig Murphy (Wellesley College)
and JoAnne Yates (Massachusetts
Institute of Technology)*

For further information regarding the series, please contact:

Craig Fowlie, Publisher, Politics & International Studies
Taylor & Francis
2 Park Square, Milton Park, Abingdon
Oxford OX14 4RN, UK

+44 (0)207 017 6665 Tel
+44 (0)207 017 6702 Fax

Craig.Fowlie@tandf.co.uk
www.routledge.com

Global Environmental Institutions

Elizabeth R. DeSombre

Routledge
Taylor & Francis Group

LONDON AND NEW YORK

First published 2006
by Routledge
2 Park Square, Milton Park, Abingdon, Oxon OX14 4RN

Simultaneously published in the USA and Canada
by Routledge
270 Madison Ave, New York, NY 10016

*Routledge is an imprint of the Taylor & Francis Group, an
informa business*

Typeset in Times New Roman by Taylor & Francis Ltd
Printed and bound in Great Britain by Antony Rowe Ltd,
Chippenham, Wiltshire

British Library Cataloguing in Publication Data
A catalogue record for this book is available from the British
Library

Library of Congress Cataloging in Publication Data
A catalog record for this book has been requested

ISBN10: 0-415-35894-9 (hbk)
ISBN10: 0-415-35895-7 (pbk)
ISBN10: 0-203-96934-0 (ebk)

ISBN13: 978-0-415-35894-1 (hbk)
ISBN13: 978-0-415-35895-8 (pbk)
ISBN13: 978-0-203-96934-2 (ebk)

Contents

List of illustrations

Tables

Figures

Boxes

Series editors' foreword

The current volume is the eighth in a new and dynamic series on "global institutions." The series strives (and, based on the initial volumes, we believe succeeds) to provide readers with definitive guides to the most visible aspects of what we know as "global governance." Remarkable as it may seem, there exist relatively few books that offer in-depth treatments of prominent global bodies and processes, much less an entire series of concise and complementary volumes. Those that do exist are either out of date, inaccessible to the non-specialist reader, or seek to develop a specialized understanding of particular aspects of an institution or process rather than offer an overall account of its functioning. Similarly, existing books have often been written in highly technical language or have been crafted "in house" and are notoriously self-serving and narrow.

The advent of electronic media has helped by making information, documents, and resolutions of international organizations more widely available, but it has also complicated matters. The growing reliance on the Internet and other electronic methods of finding information about key international organizations and processes has served, ironically, to limit the educational materials to which most readers have ready access – namely, books. Public relations documents, raw data, and loosely refereed websites do not make for intelligent analysis. Official publications compete with a vast amount of electronically available information, much of which is suspect because of its ideological or self-promoting slant. Paradoxically, the growing range of purportedly independent websites offering analyses of the activities of particular organizations have emerged, but one inadvertent consequence has been to frustrate access to basic, authoritative, critical, and well-researched texts. The market for such has actually been reduced by the ready availability of varying quality electronic materials.

For those of us that teach, research, and practice in the area, this access to information has been at best frustrating. We were delighted, then, when Routledge saw the value of a series that bucks this trend and provides key reference points to the most significant global institutions. They are betting that serious students and professionals will want serious analyses. We have assembled a first-rate line-up of authors to address that market. Our intention, then, is to provide one-stop shopping for all readers – students (both undergraduate and postgraduate), interested negotiators, diplomats, practitioners from non-governmental and intergovernmental organizations, and interested parties alike – seeking information about most prominent institutional aspects of global governance.

Global environmental institutions

When we first sat down to think about the line-up for our series, a book on global environmental institutions was high on our list. The editors of the series, however, struggled to identify precisely what was required. Like many others, we were only too well aware that moves to regulate aspects of human behavior to protect the global environment had all too frequently been piecemeal, the result of purely economic pressures or stumbled upon almost by accident. Moreover, while a good many institutions, agreements, and conventions had appeared to deal specifically (and, in some cases, tangentially) with the global environment, there existed no one central body.[1]

Whereas institutions such as the World Bank, the UN Security Council, or World Health Organization, among many others, had almost chosen themselves, we struggled to identify a core institution that would be the focus of a book. Our first thought was a book on the UN Environment Programme (UNEP) or on UN environmental conferences, conventions, and programs. We thought this the easiest and most sensible way to introduce our readers to the topic. We approached Beth DeSombre to write this book for the series. We knew her well as a leading expert on the institutional politics of the global environment, prize-winning author (for her first book, *Domestic Sources of International Environmental Policy*),[2] and friend. Beth was quick to put us right. A book centered on either UNEP or the various UN-based initiatives would sketch a skewed picture. It would focus only on a narrow range of institutional responses to environmental problems. Instead, we needed to broaden our horizons and consider the full range of institutions involved in governing the global environment.

Here again, however, we hit a problem. We knew only too well that the congested institutional terrain of global environmental governance was such that a book attempting to cover the area in its entirety would be either too long or too brief to be satisfactory. An answer was, nevertheless, at hand. Beth suggested that she focus on global environmental institutions in a more thematic way, drawing attention not only to the UN's environmental machinery but also to those aspects of regulation within and beyond the UN that deal with species and conservation, oceans, the atmosphere, the transboundary movement of hazards, and future directions.

We have come to trust our authors; Beth proved to be no different. We were delighted when she accepted our offer of contributing this book to the series; and we are proud of the result. She has produced a volume that charts a path through the congested terrain of global environmental governance in a clear, concise and measured fashion. It is a first-rate book: informative, knowledgeable, and considered. We know those that have come to expect the highest standards from our books will not be disappointed. *Global Environmental Institutions* deserves to become the standard introduction to global environmental governance. We are pleased to recommend it to all. As always, comments and suggestions from readers are welcome.

Thomas G. Weiss,
The CUNY Graduate Center, New York, USA
Rorden Wilkinson,
University of Manchester, UK
April 2006

Notes

1 See Lorraine Elliott, "Global Environmental Governance," in Rorden Wilkinson and Steve Hughes, eds., *Global Governance: Critical Perspectives* (London: Routledge, 2002), 57–58.

2 See Elizabeth R. DeSombre, *Domestic Sources of International Environmental Policy: Industry, Environmentalists and US Power* (Cambridge, Mass.: MIT Press, 2000). The book was awarded the 2001 Chadwick F. Alger prices for the best book published in the area of international organization and the 2001 Lynton Caldwell award for the best book published on environmental policy.

Acknowledgments

The field of global environmental politics has become a real community of scholars willing to provide guidance and feedback on each other's work. Two loci of this community are the Environmental Studies Section of the International Studies Association and the Teaching Global Environmental Politics (gep-ed) listserve, run by Mike Maniates, both of which help to create and maintain a cooperative environment that makes me optimistic about my profession and about our ability to have an impact on the global environment.

Within this community a number of scholars have been gracious enough to provide feedback and suggestions on one or more chapters in this volume: Henrik Selin, Peter Haas, Wil Burns, Chris Joyner, M.J. Peterson, Pam Chasek, Michele Betsill, Ted Parson, Tammi Gutner and Barbara Connolly. Others – Geoffrey Wandesforde-Smith, Kate O'Neill, Miranda Schreurs, and Ken Wilkening – helped me track down obscure bits of information. I appreciate the help from all of them. Wellesley College students Katie Clifford and Hana Freymiller assisted with some of the research for this volume. I also benefited from the research and discussion of the Wellesley students in my International Environmental Law course over the last several years, who have helped me hone my understandings of global environmental institutions.

I appreciate the excellent support I received from the University of Florida Department of Political Science while writing this book during my sabbatical sojourn in Gainesville, and am grateful to Leann Brown, who graciously let me use her UF office while she was on sabbatical.

Thanks as well to Tracy Grammer, the late Dave Carter (the best songwriter ever), Richard Shindell, and Crooked Still for the music, and to Sophie (and Michael) for the bowling.

Finally, the greatest thanks go to Sammy Barkin, who reads everything I write. There is no greater joy than to share your life with someone who shares your passions, both academic and otherwise, and can seamlessly integrate them day-to-day.

Elizabeth R. DeSombre
Wellesley College
June 2006

List of abbreviations

ACFR	Advisory Committee on Fishery Research
AIA	advanced informed agreement
AQA	Agreement between the Government of Canada and the Government of the United States of America on Air Quality
CBD	Convention on Biological Diversity
CCAMLR	Convention (or Commission) for the Conservation of Antarctic Marine Living Resources
CCD	Convention to Combat Desertification
CCOL	Coordinating Committee on the Ozone Layer
CCSBT	Commission for the Conservation of Southern Bluefin Tuna
CDM	Clean Development Mechanism
CFCs	chlorofluorocarbons
CITES	Convention on International Trade in Endangered Species of Wild Fauna and Flora
CMS	Convention on the Conservation of Migratory Species
COLREG	Convention on the International Regulations for Preventing Collisions at Sea
COP	Conference of the Parties
CPRs	common pool resources
CSD	Commission on Sustainable Development
DDT	dichlorodiphenyltrichloroethane
DEWA	Division of Early Warning and Assessment (of UNEP)
DGD	Decision Guidance Document
DNAs	Designated National Authorities
EANET	East Asian Acid Deposition Monitoring Network
ECOSOC	Economic and Social Council
EEZ	Exclusive Economic Zone

EMEP	Cooperative Program for Monitoring and Evaluation of Long-Range Transmission of Air Pollutants in Europe
ExCom	Executive Committee
FAO	Food and Agriculture Organization
GEF	Global Environment Facility
GEMS	Global Environmental Monitoring System
GEO	Global Environmental Outlook (Yearbook)
GFCM	General Fisheries Commission for the Mediterranean
GHG	greenhouse gas
GMOs	genetically modified organisms
GNP	gross national product
GPS	global positioning system
GRID	Global Resource Information Database
HBFCs	hydrobromofluorocarbons
HCFCs	hydrochlorofluorocarbons
IATTC	Inter-American Tropical Tuna Commission
IBSFC	International Baltic Sea Fisheries Commission
ICCAT	International Commission for the Conservation of Atlantic Tunas
ICES	International Council for the Exploration of the Sea
ICPD	International Conference on Population and Development
ICP	International Cooperative Program
IFCS	Intergovernmental Forum on Chemical Safety
IIASA	International Institute for Applied Systems Analysis
IISD	International Institute for Sustainable Development
IJC	International Joint Commission
ILO	International Labour Organization
IMO	International Maritime Organization
INC	Intergovernmental Negotiating Committee
INFOTERRA	International Referral System of UNEP
IOMC	Inter-Organization Program on the Sound Management of Chemicals
IOTC	Indian Ocean Tuna Commission
IPCC	Intergovernmental Panel on Climate Change
IPEN	International POPs Elimination Network
IRPTC	International Register of Potentially Toxic Chemicals
ISA	International Seabed Authority
ISM Code	International Safety Management Code
ISPS Code	International Ship and Port Facility Security Code
ITLOS	International Tribunal for the Law of the Sea

IUCN	World Conservation Union (formerly International Union for the Conservation of Nature and Natural Resources)
IWC	International Whaling Commission
LMOs	living modified organisms
LRTAP	Long-Range Transboundary Air Pollution (Convention)
LULUCF	land use, land-use change, and forestry
MAP	Mediterranean Action Plan
MARPOL	International Convention for the Prevention of Pollution from Ships
MeBr	methyl bromide
MEPC	Maritime Environment Protection Committee
MOP	Meeting of the Parties
MoU	memorandum of understanding
MSC	Maritime Safety Committee
NAFO	Northwest Atlantic Fisheries Organization
NASA	National Aeronautics and Space Administration
NASCO	North Atlantic Salmon Conservation Organization
NEAFC	Northeast Atlantic Fisheries Commission
NGOs	non-governmental organizations
NOx	nitrogen oxides
NPACF	North Pacific Anadramous Fish Commission
OAU	Organization of African Unity (now African Union)
ODP	ozone-depletion potential
ODS	ozone-depleting substance
OECD	Organization for Economic Cooperation and Development
OEWG	Open-Ended Working Group
PCBs	polychlorinated biphenyls
PIC	prior informed consent
PICES	North Pacific Marine Science Organization
POPs	persistent organic pollutants
RFMO	regional fishery management organization
ROPME	Regional Organization for the Protection of the Marine Environment (the Kuwait Region)
SAICM	Strategic Approach to International Chemicals Management
SBSTTA	Subsidiary Body on Scientific, Technical, and Technological Advice (of the CBD)
SOLAS	Convention for the Safety of Life at Sea
STCW	International Convention on Standards of Training, Certification, and Watchkeeping for Seafarers

SSC	Species Survival Commission (of IUCN)
TCC	Technical Cooperation Committee (of IMO)
TEAP	Technology and Economic Assessment Panel
UN	United Nations
UNCED	United Nations Conference on Environment and Development
UNCHE	United Nations Conference on the Human Environment
UNCLOS	United Nations Convention on the Law of the Sea
UNCTAD	United Nations Conference on Trade and Development
UNDP	United Nations Development Programme
UNECE	United Nations Economic Commission for Europe
UNEP	United Nations Environment Programme
UNESCO	United Nations Educational, Scientific and Cultural Organization
UNFCCC	United Nations Framework Convention on Climate Change
UNIDO	United Nations Industrial Development Organization
VOCs	volatile organic compounds
WCED	World Commission on Environment and Development
WCMC	World Conservation Monitoring Centre
WCPFC	West and Central Pacific Fisheries Commission
WCS	World Conservation Strategy
WHC	World Heritage Convention (Convention Concerning the Protection of the World Cultural and Natural Heritage)
WHO	World Health Organization
WMO	World Meteorological Organization
WSSD	World Summit on Sustainable Development
WTO	World Trade Organization
WWF	World Wide Fund for Nature

1 Introducing global environmental institutions

The global environment is threatened. As the Millennium Ecosystem Assessment in 2005 pointed out, "nearly two thirds of the services provided by nature to humankind are found to be in decline worldwide."[1] Species are becoming extinct at levels not experienced except during major global catastrophes. Most major commercial fisheries are depleted, and ocean ecosystems disrupted. The problem of acid rain is spreading to newly industrializing areas, and the seasonal thinning in the Antarctic ozone layer has not yet abated. Generation of toxic waste is increasing worldwide. The environmental impact of a range of chemicals is becoming better understood at the same time it is discovered how environmentally mobile and pervasive they can be. Global climate change threatens to intensify many existing environmental problems and cause new ones, with rising sea levels and changing patterns of temperature and precipitation that will affect ecosystems worldwide.

Many of the efforts to address these problems have taken place within international institutions, the focus of this book. An examination of institutions that govern the protection of the global environment is a daunting task. Unlike some issues, such as international trade, in which one large centralized organization provides most of the governance internationally, there is no centralized governance on international environmental issues. The United Nations (UN) plays an important role; the United Nations Environment Programme (UNEP) has facilitated the negotiation of many international environmental agreements, acts as the secretariat for some, and plays a role in coordinating international scientific research. But even the organizations UNEP oversees have their own internal governing processes, and there are numerous institutions without UNEP involvement.

The number of international institutions addressing global environmental issues is large and rapidly growing. One study identified 125 distinct international environmental regimes (most of them creating organizations) existing in 1992, and others have estimated that an additional five have been created annually since then.[2] This volume focuses on a subset of these institutions. It first considers UNEP and the other institutional entities within the United Nations that play important roles in global environmental governance. It then examines institutions clustered by issue area, roughly in the order that the central institutions addressing these issues were created. These chapters introduce institutions that focus on protecting endangered species and biodiversity, those that govern the ocean environment, those focusing on the atmosphere, and a recent set of institutions that focus on the transboundary movement of hazardous substances. The volume concludes with a discussion of the Global Environment Facility, an institution that provides funding to address international environmental problems, as well as some current debates: how to gain widespread participation, especially by the United States, in global environmental institutions, and whether the institutional structure of global environmental governance can, and should, be fundamentally reformed. In a world with so many institutions providing governance on environmental issues there is inevitably overlap, duplication of effort, and even the possibility of institutions working at cross-purposes. Reform of such a complex system is difficult, however.

The number and variety of existing global environmental institutions also makes impossible a consideration of all of them in one volume. The ones examined here are those deemed particularly important and also those that fit into thematically organized chapters. There are some important emerging issues, such as forest management and desertification, that have nascent institutional structures that are not discussed here, despite their increasing prominence.

A word should also be said about what is considered an "institution." Though there are some free-standing organizations, such as UNEP or the International Maritime Organization, that focus on multiple issues, most of the issue-specific entities discussed in this volume are based on a specific international agreement. The agreements designate secretariats, and have headquarters and voting procedures for making decisions within their area of competence. The focus here is also on multilateral institutions. By that broad definition there are hundreds of global environmental institutions in existence. In choosing ones to examine here, priority was given to those institutions that are empowered with independent decision making ability. Fisheries commissions set annual quotas and policies for the fisheries they oversee. The Conference of the Parties for the Convention on Migratory Species decides which species will be listed for protection. The Meeting of the Parties to the Montreal Protocol on Substances that Deplete the Ozone Layer can adjust the control measures parties have to follow. Weaker institutions such as the Convention on Wetlands of International Importance Especially as Waterfowl Habitat have no provision for changing the obligations of the parties. The independence of the stronger institutions should not be overstated: most regional fishery management organizations have a process by which states may opt out of commission rules they do not wish to follow, and states may always choose not to ratify an amendment or may even withdraw from an agreement altogether. But it is this ability to act to govern the issue areas on which they focus that makes these institutions especially important.

Examining institutions, the focus of the series in which this book appears, of necessity leaves out some important action on international environmental issues. Perhaps more than in other international issue areas, much of what happens of relevance to environmental protection happens alongside, and sometimes completely apart from, institutions. Action undertaken by non-governmental organizations, national or multinational industry actors, and national or sub-national governments has a dramatic effect on the issues examined in this volume. In some cases this extra-institutional activity helps motivate the creation of institutions or influences action within existing institutions. And in some cases, such as the innovative non-state action currently undertaken on climate change,[3] this activity occurs because international institutions appear unlikely to succeed in addressing the problem. Those interested in global environmental politics would be wise to pay attention to these types of actors and the broader issue of global environmental governance, which is of necessity slighted in a book devoted to explaining global environmental institutions.

These institutions do, however, play a major role in addressing environmental issues on the global level. International cooperation is both necessary and difficult for mitigating environmental problems, and the institutions described in this volume work to address the specific types of difficulties faced in international environmental cooperation.

On the one hand, cooperation to address some environmental issues has structural advantages. Most environmental resources regenerate, so in many cases successfully managing the environment can benefit everyone involved. If fishers can cooperate in limiting the number of fish they catch to a sustainable level, they can continue to fish indefinitely. Pollutants put into ecosystems are eventually removed or made inaccessible by natural processes, so eliminating the source of damage can often improve an environmental amenity. Moreover, environmental harms often are externalities of other activities: almost no one sets out to destroy the environment. But a set of incentive structures, some inherent and others the result of political and economic processes, can result in environmental degradation if international action is not taken.

The fact that environmental damage is not intentionally created ironically provides some of the difficulties in preventing it. Because there is often no direct economic cost to harming the environment (at least to the actors undertaking the harm), changing behavior to avoid doing so may be costly. Those whose behavior would have to change are likely to resist action, and important economic actors whose behavior damages the environment tend to have a disproportionate influence politically.[4] States, as sovereign entities under international law, do not have to accept international agreements or join international institutions they do not wish to participate in. But environmental damage is often experienced internationally regardless of the location of the activity that causes it, so many problems require widespread participation to be addressed successfully. Moreover, even when states know they benefit from cooperative action to protect the environment, they may prefer to let others undertake costly action, and gain from the environmental benefits generated by others without having to bear the costs themselves. If enough states take this approach, international cooperation will fail.

These difficulties are augmented by two additional problems that face efforts to sustain cooperation on environmental issues: time horizons and uncertainty. Environmental protection works to ensure long-run benefits for those who sacrifice in the short run. For a hunter, for example, the cost of ensuring a perpetual ability to harvest seals (or bears or antelope) may be to take fewer of them this year than that hunter would have otherwise chosen to do. But this tradeoff is only worthwhile if the species is successfully protected and the hunter is able to continue to hunt in the reasonable future. If other actors do not successfully restrict their behavior (either because they have not agreed to do so or because they do not live up to their agreements), the hunter has given up access to resources for no eventual gain. Actors are not likely to restrict their behavior unless they can be reasonably certain they will gain in the long run from their sacrifice.

An essential role of international institutions is to increase the likelihood that states will live up to their commitments to protect the environment. An institution can do so by increasing transparency; in other words, by making it easier for others to know when actors are, or are not, living up to their obligations. Reporting requirements, for example, make it easier to determine when states are not doing what they have agreed to do. Increasingly intrusive types of monitoring (such as mandating observers on fishing vessels) have recently been created within existing institutions to overcome the potential unreliability of self-reporting. The European agreements on acid rain include a monitoring process that is able to evaluate the accuracy of emissions data reported by states. Institutions can also increase the likelihood of implementation by establishing penalties for those who do not follow the rules set by the institution. Though strong enforcement mechanisms are rarely found in international environmental institutions, the Convention on International Trade in Endangered Species of Wild Fauna and Flora has called for the cessation of all species trade with some states with poor records at upholding the requirements of the agreement.[5]

Similarly, if the information underlying the cooperative effort – how many members of a given species exist, how (and how quickly) restrictions on hunting or harvesting will impact the regeneration of the species, what other factors are implicated in the decline of the species – is uncertain, even restricting harvesting may not have the promised payoff. So even in protecting renewable resources, which from the perspective of incentive structures is easier to address than many other global environmental problems, the uncertainty increases the difficulty of doing so. For pollution issues uncertainty may cause even greater problems: it may not be clear what the cause of a polluted ecosystem is, and since those actors causing pollution will frequently not directly benefit from preventing it, they will resist action as long as the cause can be questioned. For problems like ozone depletion or climate change, where the long residence time of the chemicals deemed to cause environmental damage requires that action be taken long before effects are clearly manifest, uncertainty is magnified and cooperative action more difficult.

International institutions can work to decrease uncertainty. Most environmental agreements begin by creating scientific assessment bodies as a part of the institutional structure of the agreement. These scientific committees study the resource in question, determining the level and cause of environmental harm. Associated requirements that states examine and report on their own behavior and environmental conditions generate further information to use in evaluating a given problem. The recent trend towards creating general framework conventions without substantive obligations for states reflects situations in which policymakers argue that there is insufficient evidence of environmental damage or its human causes to justify costly action. In many issues, such as ozone depletion and acid rain, the scientific processes in these institutions informed states that environmental damage was more extensive than they realized and states were willing to change their behavior once they realized the severity of the environmental problems.

International environmental institutions vary in their effectiveness at addressing the problems on which they focus. The following chapters describe the creation and operation of the major global environmental institutions, discussing their decision making processes, their interactions with other institutions, and the effects they have had. The multiplicity of existing environmental institutions provides the opportunity to consider them comparatively, and increases the likelihood that new institutions created can take account of the lessons learned from the operations of existing ones. This volume attempts to provide information for those who wish to do so.

Notes

1 Millennium Ecosystem Assessment, *Living Beyond Our Means: Natural Assets and Human Well-Being*, Statement from the Board, available at http://www.millenniumassessment.org/en/products.aspx, 5.
2 Sebastian Oberthür and Thomas Gehring, "Reforming International Environmental Governance: An Institutional Perspective on Proposals for a WEO," in Frank Biermann and Steffen Bauer, eds., *A World Environment Organization* (Aldershot: Ashgate, 2005), 206.
3 See, for example, Harriet Bulkeley and Michele Betsill, *Cities and Climate Change: Urban Sustainability and Global Environmental Governance* (London and New York: Routledge, 2003).
4 David Vogel, "Representing Diffuse Interests in Environmental Policymaking," in R. Kent Weaver and Bert A. Rockman, eds., *Do Institutions Matter? Govlernment Capabilities in the United States and Abroad* (Washington, D.C.: The Brookings Institution, 1993), 237–71.
5 Peter H. Sand, "Whither CITES? The Evolution of a Treaty Regime in the Borderland of Trade and Environment," *European Journal of International Law* 8(1) (1997), 29–58.

2 United Nations environmental machinery

This chapter examines the institutions within the United Nations that take responsibility for environmental governance. The United Nations Environment Programme (UNEP) is the institution most directly responsible for coordinating the response to environmental concerns within the UN, and has played an important role in negotiating and overseeing environmental agreements. Many other existing UN institutions play some role, as well, especially in research, to address specific environmental problems. The United Nations has also called for and coordinated major global conferences on environmental issues that have in turn spawned new institutional structures to address these issues. In addition, UN commissions – such as the World Commission on Environment and Development (WCED) and the Commission on Sustainable Development (CSD) – and other programs, such as the Millennium Development Goals, have served to focus world attention on environmental issues.

UN overview

In order to examine the environmental machinery of the United Nations it helps to begin with a basic understanding of how the organization as a whole works. The core of the United Nations is composed of six principle organs: the Secretariat, General Assembly, Security Council, Economic and Social Council (ECOSOC), the International Court of Justice, and the Trusteeship Council, the latter of which is currently inoperative and may be phased out under proposed UN reforms. The United Nations has a number of component parts whose focus is environment, almost all of them under the rubric either of the General Assembly (where resolutions are passed to set up the institutional structures described in this chapter or to approve their work product) or of ECOSOC. Decisions by the General Assembly do not, on their own, bind states, but they reflect and often influence international opinion. When the General Assembly votes to approve the work of subsidiary institutions, states gain no new obligations. In this way the United Nations machinery pertaining to the environment is weak from the perspective of compelling action from states.

Much of the actual action undertaken by the United Nations is conducted through programs and funds of the organization. These entities of the United Nations officially report to the General Assembly but have their primary working relationship with ECOSOC. UNEP is the program most directly involved with environmental issues within the United Nations. Other programs, most prominently the United Nations Development Programme (UNDP), sometimes work with UNEP on environmental issues with implications for development.

The UN also makes use of commissions, which report directly to ECOSOC. The CSD is the primary organization of this type addressing environmental issues. Regional commissions are also in this administrative position; the United Nations Economic Commission for Europe (UNECE) is engaged in environmentally relevant work, primarily related to air pollution, energy, and municipal planning. The United Nations Forum on Forests is another UN body affiliated with ECOSOC that undertakes environmentally relevant action.

UN specialized agencies function largely as independent organizations but work under the broad umbrella of the United Nations and coordinate with each other and with the United Nations under ECOSOC. Though not required to, they often submit reports to the General Assembly. Of these, several have contributed in important ways to environmental protection. The United Nations Food and Agriculture Organization (FAO) is concerned with food safety, including the role of pesticides, which has led to its involvement in international governance of hazardous chemicals (see Chapter 6). Its concern with international food supply has led it to play a strong role in the study, if not the regulation, of international fisheries (see Chapter 4). The United Nations Educational, Scientific and Cultural Organization (UNESCO) oversees agreements protecting the common heritage of humankind. The World Health Organization (WHO) has played an important role in examining the health consequences of environmental issues. The World Meteorological Organization (WMO) conducts research relating to climate change and ozone depletion.

Also of central importance in the development of institutions that oversee international environmental issues are several large international conferences organized by the United Nations to develop principles and institutions for environmental governance. The most influential of these have been the United Nations Conference on the Human Environment (UNCHE), held in 1972 in Stockholm, and the United Nations Conference on Environment and Development (UNCED), held in 1992 in Rio de Janeiro, as well as the follow-up conferences related to each of these. These were created by the General Assembly, but have been more directly overseen and negotiated by UNEP and the CSD since these entities were created.

United Nations Environment Programme

UNEP is the closest thing there is to an overarching global institution for the environment. The organization is intended both to coordinate the environmental aspects of United Nations operations and to catalyze further environmental action. UNEP has played active roles in environmental monitoring and scientific research on environmental issues; has worked to build the capacity of states, non-state actors, and other international institutions to negotiate and implement international environmental agreements; and has coordinated and supported the negotiation of international environmental agreements. In addition to playing a coordinating function in global environmental governance generally, it has undertaken specific programs to address international environmental issues. Notable among these is its Regional Seas Programme.

UNEP was founded by Resolution 2997 of the General Assembly of the United Nations in 1972. It was created as a program of the United Nations, reporting to ECOSOC. The General Assembly was acting on a recommendation from the UNCHE in Stockholm that year (see p. 22–25) that advocated the creation of a secretariat, governing council, and environment fund, all of which would work for the "protection and improvement of the human environment."[1] UNEP was intended to play a catalytic role, coordinating the environmental activities of other UN agencies.

From the beginning there were arguments about what kind of body within the UN should be created to address environmental issues. Opinions differed about the whether it should be a UN agency or a (weaker, in UN governance) program, how independent it should be, and how it would be funded. UN secretary-general U Thant had expressed an interest in creating an agency that would act as a "switchboard" to bring together existing capacities within the UN system, rather than creating a strong and purely independent agency.[2] Thant's view did, however, involve an organization that could "police and enforce its decisions."[3]

Some, primarily small European states, preferred an entirely independent agency within the UN, with strong enforcement powers. One idea that was floated before the Stockholm Conference was that the Trusteeship Council, having carried out its intended function, should be transformed into an Environment Council. Related proposals would have created an organization separate from, but on equal footing with, ECOSOC.[4]

At the other extreme, there were those who argued that the task of addressing the environment could be conducted within existing UN organizations (such as UNDP), or that different environmental issues could be divided up to be addressed by organizations such as the WMO, FAO, WHO, or the International Maritime Organization (IMO) simply by modifying their mandates. Developing countries were also wary of the creation of a global environmental institution within the United Nations, expressing a preference for regionally based approaches focusing on specific environmental problems or locations.[5]

Some of the strongest states in the system – the United States, the United Kingdom, and France – also strongly opposed the creation of a strong and independent agency. They preferred the creation of a program, and argued that its funding should be voluntary.[6] The compromise position was close to that advocated by the powerful states: to create UNEP as a program funded through voluntary donations. From the beginning the role of this new institution was downplayed: the General Assembly resolution creating UNEP notes that "responsibility for action to protect and enhance the environment rests primarily with government and, in the first instance, can be exercised more effectively at the national and regional levels."[7]

UNEP's main office is in Nairobi, Kenya, making it the first major United Nations organization to be headquartered in a developing country. The decision to locate the organization in the developing world was deliberate but somewhat contentious. Many supported the idea of widening the reach of the United Nations, especially because of the important connection between environment and development and the need to persuade developing countries that a UN focus on the environment could benefit them.[8] Some negotiators from developed states, however, expressed concern that if the primary role of UNEP was to be coordination among existing UN institutions, then situating it near those institutions would be wise.[9]

The organization also has regional offices focusing on Europe, Africa, North America, Asia and the Pacific, Latin America and the Caribbean, and West Asia, as well as offices in Vienna and Paris. Other

UNEP employees serve in the secretariats for international agreements throughout the world. Approximately 60 percent of the staff work in Nairobi.

The choice of Nairobi for UNEP headquarters was applauded for its inclusion of the developing world in UN governance, but it has caused a number of operational difficulties. Because of its distance from most international meetings and secretariats, travel (by UNEP officials to negotiations or by international environmental diplomats to UNEP headquarters) can be costly and time consuming. A report to the General Assembly by the UN secretary-general in 1997 concluded that UNEP personnel spend too much time traveling.[10] The infrastructure available in Nairobi has also at points been unreliable and costly,[11] and attracting qualified staff has been made more difficult by concern about security and personal safety.[12]

Governance

UNEP is run by a 58-member Governing Council, with each member representing a state. States serve four-year terms, staggered so half are elected every two years. Election to the Governing Council is intended to ensure regional representation, with 16 members from Africa, 14 from Western Europe "and other" (including Oceania and North America), 13 from Asia, 10 from Latin America, and 6 from Eastern Europe. There have been frequent recent proposals from the European Union to make the Governing Council a universal participation organization, but this move is opposed by the United States as well as by Russia, Japan, and some G-77 members.[13]

The Governing Council meets in regular session every two years, though it has recently begun to meet in what are called "special sessions" in conjunction with the Global Ministerial Environmental Forum. This forum was created in 1998 at the urging of a UN-appointed Task Force on the Environment and Human Settlement, to review emerging policy issues with respect to the environment.[14]

The Governing Council meetings tend to have a specific focus and the delegates pass policy measures relating to UNEP's activities. The 23rd Governing Council Meeting, in 2005, for example, considered how to implement the UN Millennium Development Goals, discussed later in this chapter (see p. 36). It made 11 policy decisions on issues such as the adoption of a water and sanitation policy for UNEP, agreement to address the issue of gender equality in its programs, and the creation of a policy statement on chemicals management. The Governing Council also formally adopted the Bali Strategic Plan on

Technology Support and Capacity Building, though a specific process for financing it had not yet been created.

Similarly, the 19th Governing Council meeting (in 1999) adopted the Nairobi Declaration on the Role and Mandate of UNEP, which clarified the focus of the organization as analysis and assessment, development of international law, advancing the implementation of international norms and policies, coordination of UN environmental activities, and expanding awareness of environmental issues. The 21st Governing Council meeting (in 2003) created an Open-Ended Intergovernmental Group of Ministers or Their Representatives to assess and address UNEP's weaknesses.

The organization is headed by an executive director, the most visible representative of the organization. UNEP's executive directors have been highly visible and bring attention to the organization. The most influential of these was Mostafa Tolba of Egypt, who served between 1976 and 1992. He became the public face of the organization and his energy is widely credited with making possible the organization's successes, especially pertaining to the Rio Conference. There is some concern, however, that the importance of the role of executive director masks – or perhaps even helps to create – other organizational weaknesses.[15]

Financing UNEP

UNEP has faced financial difficulties from the start. One of the main implications of being a "program" within the United Nations, rather than a specialized agency, is that it is primarily reliant on voluntary donations, rather than required contributions, for its funding. The voluntary nature of the funding means that the organization must spend time and effort courting donations. There is always a degree of uncertainty about how much funding will materialize; in the mid-1990s

---

Box 2.1 UNEP executive directors

Maurice Strong (Canada)	1973–1975
Mostafa Tolba (Egypt)	1976–1992
Elizabeth Dowdswell (Canada)	1992–1998
Klaus Toepfer (Germany)	1998–2006
Achim Steiner (Germany)	2006–

when more than $100 million promised by donor states was not delivered the organization faced shortfalls and had to decrease its budget.[16]

The organization's operational budget has grown dramatically, from $20 million in its first year to $120 million in 2003. A small portion of the funding comes from the regular UN budget (in 2003 3.9 percent of its financial resources came from the regular UN budget),[17] but most comes from voluntary contributions from states and other actors to the Environment Fund. More than 170 states have contributed to this fund since UNEP's founding, with the most significant contributions coming from the United States, Japan, the United Kingdom, and Germany, followed by the Nordic countries, Russia, and the Netherlands.[18] Which states, and how many, contribute in a given year, varies considerably. For example 73 states gave money to this fund in 1998 but only 56 contributed in 2000.[19] UNEP works with other organizations for most of its activities; these other organizations provide funding and personnel for these shared projects.

Much of the organization's funding is placed in trust funds to address particular environmental issues, and UNEP even asks for targeted donations for specific issues. An extreme example of this approach came in 1998 during the negotiation of the Stockholm Convention on Persistent Organic Pollutants (discussed further in Chapter 6), in which the UNEP office overseeing the negotiation sent a letter to governments, industry leaders, and non-governmental organizations to ask for donations to allow it to continue the negotiations.[20]

The Governing Council became concerned in 2003 that funding had not increased commensurately with the program's needs, and began an effort to increase donations. This effort included creating a "voluntary indicative scale of contributions" as of 2003, in which the organization suggests to states what their contributions should be.

In addition to concerns about insufficient funding, UNEP is also criticized for the way its funding is spent. An Internal Oversight review found that the organization spent excessively on advisors and consultants.[21]

These financial shortfalls have caused problems. They have meant not only that the organization cannot conduct the activities it believes it should, but also (as the 1997 external assessment of the program noted) that managers and staff have had to focus on how best to cut programs, leaving them "less time to do environmental work."[22] Some go so far as to suggest that UNEP's lack of a reliable financial base is the primary reason for its lack of influence internationally.[23]

Monitoring and scientific research

UNEP's founding resolution indicates that one of the primary roles of its Governing Council is "to keep under review the world environmental situation in order to ensure that emerging environmental problems of wide international significance should receive appropriate and adequate consideration by Governments."[24] To that end, one of UNEP's principal activities is the coordination of monitoring and assessment of environmental conditions. It does this review through a number of programs, most of which fall structurally under the organization's Division of Early Warning and Assessment (DEWA). This division coordinates information gathering on issues relating to water, ecosystems, climate change, toxic substances, land degradation, and other issues in an effort to identify environmental problems and provide information about environmental conditions to policymakers.

The first monitoring program to be created was the Earthwatch program. Its role is to coordinate and catalyze the creation of environmental information across all UN organizations, to inform national and international decisionmaking on environmental issues.[25] This program began with three loosely connected components: an International Referral System (INFOTERRA), a Global Environmental Monitoring System (GEMS), and an International Register of Potentially Toxic Chemicals (IRPTC).

INFOTERRA's focus is coordination and exchange of information collected by others. In particular it coordinates a system of nationally designated "focal points" for environmental information, each of which responds to queries, provides guidance on where to find data, and creates information leaflets. UNEP's role is to oversee this process and provide technical assistance to help make national offices run smoothly.

The role of GEMS is to collect its own information, via surveys and other data gathering from states, to elucidate global and regional environmental trends. It is in this area that the lack of UNEP resources has had the most serious effect. The WMO was supposed to take the lead at getting GEMS up and running by setting up more than 100 monitoring stations; in the first five years of operation only 12 were set up.[26] More recently, however, it has managed to gather a large array of data. Though initially focused on a number of environmental indicators, the GEMS program now focuses primarily on fresh-water quality and availability. It has more than 1400 water quality monitoring stations that gather data on 100 different parameters. It makes this information widely available.[27]

IRPTC, based in Geneva because of the proximity to sources of information, began in 1976. Its role was to create a data clearinghouse for information about potentially toxic chemicals. This mechanism has become central in the toxics treaties, especially the Rotterdam Convention on the Prior Informed Consent Procedure for Certain Hazardous Chemicals and Pesticides in International Trade (discussed further in Chapter 6).

UNEP's monitoring activities now also include a Global Resource Information Database (GRID), a network of regional data collection centers, as well as some regionally specific projects to collect environmental information. UNEP also promotes the Global Reporting Initiative, which encourages companies to voluntarily report environmental information; this process involves a set of guidelines for corporate reporting on issues of sustainability. In addition, the organization has produced a Global Environmental Outlook (GEO) Yearbook, beginning in 1997 and now produced bi-annually. These volumes give overviews of environmental trends internationally and are widely available. UNEP also has worked with other UN organizations such as FAO, WMO, and WHO to conduct monitoring on air and water quality.

One of the major difficulties found across UNEP's efforts to coordinate data gathering and analysis has been incompatibilities in methods and processes. Initially after the creation of UNEP there was enthusiasm by governments at all levels "for monitoring virtually everything," but most of these efforts at monitoring did not bear fruit. Some were too vague in their purposes, other entities did not have the background or training to undertake serious monitoring efforts, and data, once collected, were often not usefully aggregated (or even comparable).[28] Even now, data collected for other purposes by individual states or researchers are often either not comparable or not representative. It is in this area that UNEP's coordination is most sorely needed but occasionally lacking. And ironically, one of the criticisms of the organization is that it does not sufficiently monitor its own programs to determine their impact or even their progress.

Regional Seas Programme

From the beginning one important negotiating focus of UNEP has been on protecting oceans; to this end, it runs a program on regional seas that oversees agreements to protect shared ocean resources by states surrounding largely enclosed seas. The problem of ocean pollution was prominent at the Stockholm Conference, at the behest of Maurice Strong.[29] The negotiations before Stockholm launched the idea of focusing on individual seas one at a time, rather than working primarily on global initiatives. The Regional Seas Programme under UNEP began in 1974 and is headquartered in Geneva.

Currently there are 140 states involved in programs to protect 13 regional seas. Six of these arrangements are directly overseen by UNEP. An additional seven programs are under the Regional Seas Programme but managed by independent secretariats. There are other regions that have set up programs completely apart from the UNEP process that still participate in the overall global coordinating process on regional seas

Box 2.2 Regional Seas agreements

Administered by UNEP

- Caribbean Region
- East Asian Seas
- Eastern African Region
- Mediterranean Region
- North-West Pacific Region
- West and Central Africa Region

UNEP-affiliated

- Black Sea Region
- North-East Pacific Region
- Red Sea and Gulf of Aden
- ROPME Sea Area
- South Asian Seas
- South-East Pacific Region
- South Pacific Region

Independent

- Arctic Region
- Antarctic Region
- Baltic Sea
- Caspian Sea
- North-East Atlantic Region

Source: http://www.unep.org/regionalseas/Programmes/default.asp.

(that includes international meetings for Regional Seas Programmes) run by UNEP. There are another five programs in this category.

The centerpiece of a given Regional Seas Programme is its action plan, in which states surrounding a sea agree on the basic process for studying and protecting the affected sea. The next step is (most frequently) the creation of an international agreement on the general protection of the area that functions in conjunction with protocols that contain the specific measures states need to take in order to protect the sea. The protocols attempt to address the wide variety of sources of pollution, including land-based pollution. The general approach that was developed in the earlier Regional Seas agreements has been used in subsequent ones, avoiding the need to begin negotiations from scratch. Also central to the entire process is monitoring, undertaken primarily by the surrounding states themselves, and information exchange.

The first, and highest profile, effort in the Regional Seas Programme was the Mediterranean Action Plan (MAP), agreed to in 1975.[30] The MAP called for joint monitoring and research of ocean conditions, a program to integrate issues of development with the need for environmental protection, and a set of legally binding agreements limiting polluting activities by states. All the states in the region (except Albania, which has since joined) met the following year to negotiate the Barcelona Convention for the Protection of the Mediterranean Sea Against Pollution and two protocols, one to prohibit dumping of hazardous substances, the other on addressing emergencies that result from unintentional discharges into the sea. Four additional protocols were negotiated in the following years, on conservation, pollution from land-based sources, hazardous wastes, and offshore exploration and exploitation.[31] States ratifying the convention must simultaneously adopt at least one of the protocols (and all parties to the protocols must also be parties to the convention).[32] The entire convention and protocol structure was renegotiated in 1995 to try to streamline it and incorporate principles of sustainable development,[33] while keeping essentially the same substantive obligations. Although it is under the UNEP Regional Seas Programme, the MAP and associated agreements have their own secretariat, with UNEP personnel, located in Athens.

The Mediterranean is both deep and small, relatively enclosed geographically but with a densely populated coastline. These characteristics, along with specific activities (such as irrigation) by surrounding states, led to a high degree of pollution. The efforts by UNEP to gather a set of scientists and begin the process of research to better understand the condition of the sea was central to the process of cooperation to protect it. The idea was that international cooperation would deepen as the problems were better understood. At least initially, this process worked: new protocols were negotiated to address problems that were more fully understood. And there have clearly been positive impacts from these agreements: states in the region have built sewage treatment plants, established marine protected areas, and taken steps to decrease the dumping of waste into the sea. But lack of funding from UNEP has hampered cooperation, and monitoring has been weak. While it is likely that the condition of the sea has at least not worsened – itself an accomplishment in an area with a growing population and increasing industrial activity – it is not clear that it has improved as much as the negotiated agreements intended.

The Regional Seas Programme overall was, at least initially, considered to be one of UNEP's greatest successes. The organization itself refers to the program as "one of UNEP's most significant achievements in the past 30 years."[34] It required coordination among many UN organizations and thus represented precisely the kind of organizational and catalytic role UNEP was designed to take on.[35] The individual programs have indeed achieved some degree of success in terms of widespread participation and awareness.

Politically, the level of cooperation within the individual agreements has been impressive. Many of the regional seas surround states that have hostile relationships with each other (Israel, Libya, and Egypt together in the Mediterranean agreements; the United States and Cuba together in the Caribbean Region agreements) but nevertheless work together in this context. In most agreements most of the relevant states are members. Many of these agreements also involve states with radically different levels of development and they have been able to agree on basic principles of environmental protection.

But the Regional Seas Programme has also run into both institutional and environmental difficulties. As has come to be common within UNEP, financing has been a perennial problem. The funding for the individual agreements as well as for the overall program is voluntary. The promised funding has been uneven, with some states shouldering most of the responsibility and promised funding coming in late. The lateness of promised funding left the MAP almost broke at points in the 1980s.[36] Similarly, the trust fund for the Kuwait Region program had a $2 million shortfall in promised funding in early 1981.[3]

Monitoring, the central element of coordination, has also been problematic. An early evaluation of the Regional Seas Programme found that many national monitoring and research capacities do not meet the scientific standards UNEP requires. Many of the facilities provided by states are inadequate, and data reports are late and incomplete. States do not submit information they are required to, or fail to do so in a timely manner. Different UN agencies have not fully supported the program and have not made use of regional seas-generated data, preferring to use other sources of data.[38]

More importantly, it is difficult to point to solid evidence of improvement in the environmental condition of many of the seas in the program. In some cases this lack of evidence may be due to missing data, but in other cases it appears that environmental conditions have not necessarily improved. A 1990 study commissioned by UNEP commented that, other than in the Mediterranean, none of the programs "has had much success in combating pollution."[39] It is important to consider the counterfactual, however: even in places where the environmental conditions may not have improved, it is possible that they have deteriorated less quickly than they would have without the programs. This result does not match the optimism with which the program began, but may accurately reflect the useful but not dramatic work that UNEP has been able to do in this area.

Ultimately, the problems faced by the Regional Seas Programmes are similar to those experienced by other global environmental institutions: the difficulty of trading short-term sacrifice for long-term gain, especially when the longer-term advantages depend on continued cooperation by all relevant states. And to be fair, the problems addressed in these plans are difficult, and they often involve collaboration among states with widely differing levels of development and sometimes contentious political relationships. Nevertheless, it is hard to regard the Regional Seas Programmes as the significant achievement that UNEP believes them to be.

Overseeing international agreements

One of the other central roles of UNEP has been its role in the process of negotiating international environmental agreements, calling for and coordinating international negotiations on a range of issues. This role of UNEP is discussed in this volume in the context of the specific agreements it has played a role in negotiating. Once the agreements are operational, however, UNEP also takes responsibility for overseeing their daily operations, providing secretariat functions for a number of international environmental agreements.

These secretariats are located around the globe: in Geneva, Switzerland, the Convention on International Trade in Endangered Species of Wild Fauna and Flora (CITES), the Basel Convention on the Transboundary Movement of Hazardous Wastes and their Disposal, and the Stockholm Convention on Persistent Organic Pollutants (POPs); in Montreal, Canada, the Montreal Protocol Multilateral Fund and the Convention on Biological Diversity. UNEP also oversees the Convention on Migratory Species in Bonn, Germany, and the Vienna Convention on the Protection of the Ozone Layer and its Montreal Protocol, in Nairobi, Kenya.

It is not always clear what it means to have UNEP as the secretariat for an agreement: in practical terms, the people working in a given office spend all their time working for the treaty organization they are connected to, rather than working for UNEP in any broader sense. Nevertheless, this connection both means that UNEP bears some funding responsibility for the secretariat offices and, ideally, allows communication across issues and treaty organizations since ultimately they are all coordinated by UNEP.

UNEP's difficulties and successes

Criticisms of UNEP abound. Its role is a bit haphazard. It is not the only source of assessment and monitoring; it is only one source of many for funding, coordination, and secretariat services; and – though this is not unique to UNEP – some of the negotiations it has overseen have produced weak measures.

Some of these difficulties are structural. UNEP was created with a small staff and budget compared to most UN agencies.[40] The vast number and scope of international environmental agreements, some of which are discussed in the rest of this volume, make UNEP's coordinating role particularly difficult. Each of these agreements has its own conference of the parties, which acts as the primary decisionmaking body. Though UNEP provides secretariat services for some (which thus gives it more central involvement than it would otherwise have in these issues), they each operate independently.

In other ways, UNEP has been a victim of its own success. Since the early 1970s the number and variety of environmental issues addressed on the international level have grown dramatically, due at least in part to UNEP's role in gathering and disseminating information about environmental problems, raising awareness, and galvanizing action. But the result is a set of environmental institutions that are too numerous and varied for UNEP to be able to control. As David Downie and Marc Levy point out, this degree of success has increased the need for UNEP to be able to coordinate activities.[41] As will be seen in the following chapters, various issue areas have multiple distinct agreements and organizations governing state activities, and the level of coordination is not what it could be. Other UN-related processes in recent decades, such as the World Commission on Environment and Development in 1987 and UNCED in 1992, have called for a strengthening of UNEP's role.

An external review of UNEP in 1997 noted that the goal of coordination, the primary role of UNEP, can be problematic. The review pointed out that UNEP has "neither the right of budgetary veto nor the financial resources to insist on or induce coordination."[42] The lack of finances and staff makes it difficult for UNEP to play the catalytic or coordinating role it was intended to, since it has no leverage to persuade other institutions within the UN to go along with its wishes.

The successes of the organization should not be overlooked, however. Its role in gathering and disseminating environmental data has been important, and it truly has acted as a catalyst for the negotiation of important international environmental agreements. It is essential to remember that there is only so much that structure can accomplish if the political will to implement strong international environmental management is absent. Many of the shortcomings attributed to UNEP should be more accurately ascribed to the unwillingness of states to undertake stronger environmental action.

United Nations environment conferences

One of the major ways that the United Nations has worked towards the development of international institutions for the protection of the global environment has been by holding major international conferences to discuss emerging environmental issues. These conferences themselves create no new institutional structures or binding law, though they often result in resolutions and action plans that lead to the eventual creation of institutional structures to oversee them. They also provide a timing peg around which new international agreements may be negotiated so that they can be signed at the conferences themselves, or provide the impetus for future negotiation of international agreements. There is widely differing opinion on the usefulness of these conferences, with some scholars arguing that they are essential to the international governance of the environment and others suggesting that they deflect energy and attention from other important efforts.

The major conferences on environmental issues began in Stockholm in 1972; later dates for conferences were chosen to occur in ten-year intervals from this first conference. But these were not the first or only efforts of the United Nations to address environmental issues through global conferences. As early as 1949 ECOSOC convened the United Nations Scientific Conference on Conservation and Utilization of Natural Resources. This conference was attended by representatives of 49 states and eight international organizations. Its function was more the exchange of information between experts and those in government responsible for managing resources than the creation of any international consensus.[43]

Other UN-sponsored conferences with environmental implications include the Symposium on Patterns of Resource Use, Environment and Development Strategies, sponsored by UNEP and UNCTAD, and held in Cocoyoc, Mexico, in October 1974. The Cocoyoc Declaration from the conference emphasized the need to improve the economic and social system for the poorest states without relying on market mechanisms. Environmentally it focused on the implications of unequal levels of North–South development as a cause of environmental degradation and pointed to poverty as a cause of environmentally destructive behavior.[44] A set of population conferences, most notably the International Conference on Population and Development, held in Cairo in 1994, also addressed aspects of environmental protection. The plan of action from the conference contains a section on the relationship between population and environment, acknowledging that "meeting the basic human needs of growing populations is dependent on a healthy environment."[45] A 1995 World Summit on Social Development in Copenhagen focused on human needs, including the importance of protecting "the integrity and sustainable use of our environment."[46]

United Nations Conference on the Human Environment

The first UN conference entirely focused on environmental issues was the UNCHE, which was held in Stockholm, Sweden, 5–16 June 1972. Sweden first suggested to ECOSOC in 1968 the idea of having a UN conference to focus on human interactions with the environment. ECOSOC passed resolution 1346 supporting the idea. General Assembly Resolution 2398 in 1969 decided to convene a conference in 1972 and mandated a set of reports from the UN secretary-general to focus the scope of the conference. The secretary-general suggested that the conference focus on "stimulating and providing guidelines for action by national governments and international organizations" facing environmental issues.

Maurice Strong, the head of the Canadian International Development Agency, was appointed secretary-general of the conference.[47] He commissioned Barbara Ward and René Dubois to write a document that would provide the intellectual framework for the conference. Their work, *Only One Earth*, argued in favor of an international responsibility for studying the relationships between humans and the natural environment, and called for a shared "loyalty to the earth" and policy, coordinated internationally, to address global environmental issues.[48] More than 80 individual states submitted national reports on their environments as well as reports on particular environmental problems. The process of gathering and submitting this information gave some states the first overview of the conditions of their domestic environments.

The General Assembly created a committee composed of representatives from 27 states to advise the secretary-general on the preparation of the conference. This committee held four meetings between 1970 and 1972. These meetings discussed the issues to be examined in the conference and drafted the declaration and action plan. Among other issues, these meetings addressed the concerns of developing countries that protection of the environment would interfere with their ability to develop and their interest in defending their sovereign rights over natural resources.

The concerns of developing countries were most directly addressed in a meeting by 27 experts convened in the village of Founex in Switzerland in 1971. This meeting produced the *Founex Report on Development and Environment* and elaborated the interests of developing countries with respect to environment and development. This report helped to broaden the agenda of the conference to bring in issues of poverty in addition to issues of industrialization.[49] It also set the stage for later conferences to focus more directly on the link between environment and development.

States from most parts of the world – 113 in all – sent representatives to the Stockholm Conference. The one notable exception was Soviet bloc states, most of which boycotted the conference in protest at the voting status of East Germany in the conference. Though these states participated in most of the preparatory meetings, a UN General Assembly decision in 1971 at the behest of states from the West (most notably the United States) declared that participation in the conference would only be open to states that were members of the United Nations or its specialized agencies, which excluded East Germany.[50] Maurice Strong, however, communicated consistently during the conference with Soviet representatives, and brought their perspectives into the debates at the conference despite their absence from the meetings.[51]

Non-governmental organizations (NGOs) were invited as well, to a UN-sanctioned Forum for NGOs that was held outside the official negotiations. Though NGOs voiced concerns about their separation from the governmental negotiating process, the Stockholm Conference is credited with beginning the trend of recognizing the importance of NGOs and creating access for them at official conferences.

The official products of the conference consisted of the Declaration of the United Nations Conference on the Human Environment (generally referred to as the Stockholm Declaration) and an Action Plan for the Human Environment. The conference also passed several resolutions. The most important of these was the Resolution on Institutional and Financial Arrangements, which recommended the creation of several pieces of UN environmental machinery to oversee a continuing process within the United Nations of addressing environmental issues. Other resolutions from the conference recommended the creation of a second conference on the human environment (to be coordinated by the new UN environmental processes set up), called for the creation of a World Environment Day, and condemned nuclear weapons tests.

As a direct response to these resolutions, the General Assembly created UNEP. Other international agreements reached in the 1970s had their roots in the Stockholm Conference, most notably the Convention on Long-Range Transboundary Air Pollution, the Convention Concerning the Protection of World Cultural and Natural Heritage, the Convention on International Trade in Endangered Species, and a number of the international maritime pollution agreements.

The conference is credited with bringing international attention to environmental issues, which previously had been addressed in uncoordinated and mostly local efforts. In particular it clarified important North–South conflicts over how to consider the relationship between environment and development. It also helped to codify international legal principles that had been developing in international law but had not been elaborated in a specifically environmental context. And it prompted states to undertake action domestically on environmental issues.

Ten years after the Stockholm Conference, UNEP held a special Governing Council session in Nairobi to evaluate the impacts of the conference. This session, open to all UN members, is sometimes referred to as Stockholm+10. It was attended by representatives of 134 states. Reports commissioned for the meeting indicated that implementation of Stockholm goals was mixed, noting in particular the difficulty of people in developing countries in meeting their basic needs and the increase in various forms of environmental degradation.[52] The declaration from this session, referred to as the Nairobi Declaration, reaffirmed support for the Stockholm Declaration and the Action Plan for the Human Environment, and called for the strengthening of UNEP. Most importantly, however, it expressed "serious concern about the present state of the environment worldwide" and called for an intensification of efforts to improve it.[53]

United Nations Conference on Environment and Development

After UNEP's creation, the organization took on the role of coordinating high-profile international conferences for the United Nations. The most prominent of these was UNCED (also called the Earth Summit), held from 3–14 June 1992 in Rio de Janeiro. The timing of the conference was chosen to be the twentieth anniversary of the Stockholm Conference that had led to UNEP's founding. The focus of the Rio Conference was the relationship between environment and development, motivated in part by the 1987 publication of *Our Common Future*, the report of the World Commission on Environment and Development. The secretary-general of the conference was Maurice Strong, former UNEP executive director (and secretary-general of the Stockholm Conference).

The idea of a second major United Nations conference on environmental issues was first brought up in the UN General Assembly in 1986. A resolution in December 1989 officially called for a conference to "elaborate strategies and measures to halt and reverse the effects of environmental degradation" in the context of "sustainable and environmentally sound development in all countries."[54]

The negotiation process was contentious. The UN held four preparatory committee meetings between March 1990 and April 1992, and much remained undecided at the final meeting. The negotiations revealed the depth of the North–South divide on issues of environment and development. Developing countries were concerned that international environmental regulations would impact their ability to develop. They wanted acknowledgment that most of the damage to the global environment had been done by the developed countries, and assurance that they would not be prevented from developing using the same technology their predecessors had. They pushed for new development assistance, as well as technology transfer, and influence in determining how it would be allocated, no linking of trade to environmental behavior in developing states, and the idea that developed states must act first on environmental protection.

Developed states, on the other hand, wanted acknowledgment of the role of population growth in environmental degradation, and an equal allocation of responsibility for addressing environmental problems. Some, led by the United States, argued against creating new aid obligations, suggesting that using resources more efficiently and bringing in the resources of industry would be sufficient.[55] There were disagreements among developed states as well. The United States played a largely limiting role, trying to prevent the creation of specific new obligations. The Nordic countries generally supported the concerns of developing states, and Japan and the European Union fell somewhere in the middle.

The conference was considered at that point to be the largest gathering of world leaders anywhere. Representatives (often heads of state) of 178 states attended, along with representatives from agencies of the United Nations and other international organizations. The conference featured a parallel "Global Forum" for NGOs. Approximately 1500 NGOs were accredited to the conference, and another 800 sent individuals to the conference. The forum allowed NGOs to exchange information, plan strategies, and build alliances. While some were pleased with the opportunity to meet with so many activists from around the world, others were unhappy that this event was kept separate from the official meeting.

Two international agreements, the Convention on Biological Diversity and the Framework Convention on Climate Change, were negotiated separately from the UNCED preparation process but specifically timed so that they could be signed in Rio. Efforts were made to negotiate a global treaty on forests as well, but states could not reach agreement; the result was a Non-Legally Binding Authoritative Statement of Principles for a Global Consensus on the Management, Conservation, and Sustainable Development of All Types of Forests.

The conference produced two other non-binding statements. The Rio Declaration on Environment and Development elaborated 27 principles that states should use in integrating environment and development. These include a reiteration of the right of states to sovereignty over their natural resources, support of the precautionary principle and the polluter pays principle, and broad principles pertaining to participation in decisionmaking on issues relating to environment and development. The second statement, Agenda 21, is a much longer document, intended to serve as an action plan for the implementation of the principles and goals of the conference. In each of its 40 chapters it suggests ways to prioritize the issues discussed and estimates the costs of addressing them.

Box 2.3 Highlights of Agenda 21

Central elements include:

- Protection of the atmosphere (chapter 9)
- Integrated approach to the planning and management of land resources (chapter 10)
- Combating deforestation (chapter 11)
- Combating fragile ecosystems
  - Desertification and drought (chapter 12)
  - Sustainable mountain development (chapter 13)
- Promoting sustainable agriculture and rural development (chapter 14)
- Conservation of biological diversity (chapter 15)
- Environmentally sound management of biotechnology (chapter 16)
- Protection of oceans and related ecosystems (chapter 17)
- Protection of freshwater resources (chapter 18)
- Environmentally sound management of toxic chemicals, hazardous and radioactive wastes (chapters 19–21)

Reactions to Rio were mixed. UNCED is credited with bringing new attention internationally to issues of environment and development. Though efforts to negotiate a forest convention failed (and have continually failed since Rio), negotiating two binding conventions on difficult issues in the context of an international conference is acknowledged as an impressive accomplishment. The conference gave an international voice to thousands of NGOs and gave these organizations new avenues for cooperation. It also created a number of new institutions. These included institutions created within the climate change and biodiversity conventions, the Business Council on Sustainable Development (which later added "World" to the beginning of its name), and the CSD (see pp. 32–35), created after the conference to oversee implementation of its decisions.

UNCED also receives much criticism. The profound disagreement between developed and developing states led to weak language in the Rio Declaration and Agenda 21 that satisfied neither bloc. Even those weakened commitments (such as a reaffirmation by developed states of the goal of providing 0.7 percent of their gross national product (GNP) in development assistance) have gone largely unfulfilled. And though the involvement of NGOs was extensive, those from the developed world were much more prominent than those from developing countries, and critics decried the northern dominance within the NGO process.

Most fundamentally, Rio is criticized as the pinnacle of what Steven Bernstein calls "the compromise of liberal environmentalism."[56] The declarations and agreements at UNCED largely reflect the dominance of the liberal international economic order, in pointing towards a compatibility of economic growth and environmental protection in the context of a market economy. Those who believe that true environmental protection requires a fundamental change from business-as-usual decry the extent to which the Rio Conference fully institutionalized the shift from seeing industry and wealth as the cause of environmental degradation to viewing them as the solution to environmental problems.[57] Whatever one believes about this relationship, the conference at Rio helped to cement an international policymaking process in which industry and economic growth are central to the way environmental protection is negotiated.

Two follow-up meetings have been held as well; the first one, five years after Rio (often called the Earth Summit+5), was a special session of the General Assembly to evaluate the implementation of UNCED's obligations and goals, held in New York in June 1997. Though the two binding agreements had entered into force by this point, this session indicated that progress on many of the Rio goals was sorely lacking. Negotiators had also hoped to be able to complete a forest treaty in time for this special session but were not able to. Preparations for this meeting involved the presentation of reports on state action and specific environmental problems, many of them emphasizing the distance between Agenda 21's goals and its implementation. A General Assembly resolution reaffirmed the commitment of states to the implementation of Agenda 21.[58]

World Summit on Sustainable Development

UNEP also coordinated the World Summit on Sustainable Development (WSSD) as a follow-up ten years after UNCED. It took place between 26 August and 4 September 2002, in Johannesburg, South Africa. It was attended by representatives of 191 states (including 104 heads of state). As has become the norm, there was also a parallel NGO forum with more than 40,000 participants,[59] more than 21,000 accredited to the conference itself. The World Business Council on Sustainable Development held a business forum during the conference, showcasing environmental actions.

The preparations for the conference were much less focused than those for preceding UN environment conferences. The General Assembly resolution establishing the meeting called for a summit "to reinvigorate the global commitment to sustainable development,"[60] but did not provide specific guidance on the agenda, though it listed a set of issues for consideration that were both broad and vague. The CSD was responsible for organizing the preparation, but moved slowly during the preparatory meetings, with little resolved until shortly before the actual conference.

In the negotiations before the conference there were disagreements on whether to seek new obligations. Most agreed that the main short-comings on issues of sustainable development were that existing agreements and goals from the 1992 Rio Conference had not been sufficiently implemented. Even then, much discussion took place before the meeting about whether to seek specific commitments for implementation and funding. The General Assembly resolution creating the summit had called for "specific time bound measures to be taken and institutional and financial requirements,"[61] but the United States and others strongly resisted specific new commitments.

The summit produced a weak Johannesburg Declaration on Sustainable Development that adds little to the declaration from Rio. The conference also produced a Plan of Implementation of the WSSD. Even the modest goals in this document were controversial and few issues had been resolved before the conference began.

The conference focused thematically on water and sanitation, energy, health, agriculture, and biodiversity. On water the Plan of Implementation identifies the goal of reducing the number of people without access to sanitation by 50 percent by 2015. Individual states also pledged more than a billion dollars in investments and loans for projects on water and sanitation. On energy, states made vague commitments to phase out energy subsidies "where appropriate" and to increase energy efficiency, use of renewable energy, and access to modern energy services. Health results included the commitment that by 2020 chemicals should be used and produced in ways that avoid damage to the environment and to human health; states also agreed in principle to cooperate to reduce air pollution and to improve the access by developing states to substitutes for ozone-depleting substances. Discussions on agriculture included the agreement by the Global Environment Facility (GEF) (discussed further in Chapter 7) to consider including funding for the Convention to Combat Desertification (CCD) in its funding areas. The Plan of Implementation noted vague commitments to protect biodiversity: to reduce biodiversity loss by 2010, to reverse trends in degradation of natural resources, to restore fisheries and to create marine protected areas.[62] Many of these points reflected commitments already made in the context of the UN Millennium Development Goals (discussed on p. 30).

The WSSD made an effort to integrate private industry into the governance of environmental issues. One approach is what came to be known as "Type II agreements" – a set of public–private partnerships for sustainable development, involving national governments, civil society and business actors. The UN notes 220 partnerships (involving a commitment of $235 million) reached before the summit and an additional 60 announced during the event.[63] These ranged from a gas exploration project in the Philippines to an agreement among Brazil, the GEF, the World Bank, and the World Wide Fund for Nature (WWF) to create a regional protected area in the Amazon. Many were concerned, however, that these types of initiatives had no clear guidelines or oversight, channeled pressure for action away from official government commitments, and had no clearly stated rationale.[64]

The United States was singled out for disapproval at the meeting. Not only did U.S. President George W. Bush decline to attend, but the United States was the primary opponent of strong and specific obligations for states from the conference. The negotiators from the United States weakened or blocked most proposals.[65]

Most observers were not impressed with the Johannesburg Summit. James Gustave Speth called it "a huge missed opportunity."[66] The vice-president of Palau pointed to the "failure of key nations to recommit to the goals of the Rio Earth Summit."[67] The executive director of Oxfam Community Aid referred to the outcomes of the conference as "a number of major defeats."[68] The weaknesses of the conference certainly reflect the lack of international pressure for strong action. An anonymous UN officer suggested that the popular mood was not focused on deep environmental commitments: "If we had negotiated Rio at Johannesburg we would have gotten half of what we got ten years ago."[69] The conference has nevertheless been praised for fully integrating economic issues, environmental issues, and social issues on an equal footing,[70] and those whose primary concerns were development were happier with the outcome of the conference than those whose focus was environmental action.

UN commissions

World Commission on Environment and Development

As the tenth anniversary of the Stockholm Conference in 1982 neared, UNEP prepared to examine environmental approaches looking towards the year 2000. It recommended the creation of an independent commission made up of distinguished individuals to raise awareness of and frame these issues. Prompted by the pessimistic assessment ten years after the Stockholm Conference, the United Nations General Assembly accepted this recommendation and called for the creation of a commission to address the intersection of issues of environment and development.[71] Its mandate was to suggest long-term strategies for sustainable development, propose mechanisms for bringing developing countries into international environmental cooperation and for increasing environmental cooperation between developed and developing states, and to examine ways to foster effective international environmental action. Gro Harlem Brundtland, the former (and future) prime minister of Norway, was appointed by the UN secretary-general to chair the commission, with Mansour Khalid, the former minister of foreign affairs of Sudan, as vice-chair. These two appointed the 21 remaining members, all serving as individuals rather than as representatives of their states. Established in 1983, the commission (often referred to as the Brundtland Commission) met from 1984 to 1986, held public meetings in regions across the globe, and consulted with individuals, scientists, NGOs, and representatives of industry. The commission also appointed a set of special advisors on particular issues.

The primary output of this process was the report *Our Common Future*,[72] published in 1987. This volume gave an overview of the difficulties facing the common and intersecting desires for economic development and environmental protection. It identified as specific challenges the issues of population, food security, the protection of species and ecosystems, energy, industry, and urban issues. It also proposed specific legal principles and institutional structures extending existing principles. Most prominent of these are the idea of intergenerational equity, the necessity for states to conduct environmental assessments and to notify affected individuals before undertaking activities that might impact the environment, the need to limit risk and accept liability, and the idea that states share "common but differentiated responsibilities" in protecting the environment.[73] Though it did not coin the term, the WCED is responsible for popularizing the concept of sustainable development, and defining it in its most often used formulation: development that meets "the needs of the present without compromising the ability of future generations to meet their own needs."[74]

Commission on Sustainable Development

Agenda 21 at the Earth Summit called for the creation of a Commission on Sustainable Development to ensure that the decisions from the conference were fully implemented. The 47th Session of the UN General Assembly in December 1992 created the organization and its composition, terms of reference, and guidelines.[75] The organization is charged with ensuring the effectiveness of UNCED by monitoring and reporting on implementation of the agreements from the conference, and with facilitating dialogue among all the groups identified in Agenda 21 as important non-governmental actors. After WSSD the CSD also took on responsibility for monitoring the execution of the Johannesburg Plan of Implementation.[76]

At the same time the CSD was created, the UN undertook a major structural reform to give it oversight, creating the Division for Sustainable Development to serve as the secretariat for CSD and related activities. The CSD reports to ECOSOC in the UN hierarchy, which means that CSD decisions must be approved by ECOSOC before they can be presented to the General Assembly for action. Fifty-three states are elected as members of the CSD by ECOSOC, with regional representation so that 13 African states, 11 Asian states, 10 Latin American and Caribbean states, 6 Eastern European states, and 13 Western European and North American states serve at any point in time. Each member serves a three-year term, staggered so that one-third of the seats are elected annually. Members of international organizations, NGOs, and other states may attend meetings as observers.

The organization focuses its work with yearly themes. Initially the CSD attempted to review all of the elements of Agenda 21, but after the Rio+5 special session in 1997 the General Assembly adopted a new, more focused, work plan for the CSD. After WSSD in 2002 these work-cycles were extended to two years. These themes are intended to cover the most central elements of Agenda 21 and the other Rio commitments. The CSD meets annually in plenary session, but designates ad hoc working groups on the year's themes, and those on cross-sectoral issues, to work intersessionally.

The CSD asks for the submission of national reports to fulfill its monitoring role. This gathering of information has been controversial,

Box 2.4 CSD themes

1994   Health; human settlements; fresh water; toxic chemicals and hazardous wastes

1995   Land; desertification; forests; biodiversity

1996   Atmosphere; oceans and seas

1997   Review of implementation of Agenda 21

1998   Consumer protection and sustainable consumption; fresh water; industry and sustainable development

1999   Sustainable tourism; oceans and seas; small island developing states; consumption and production patterns

2000   Agriculture; finance; land management; trade

2001   Energy for sustainable development; atmosphere; transport; information for decisionmaking and participation; international cooperation for an enabling environment

2002   Preparation for WSSD

2003   Follow-up from WSSD

2004/05 Water; sanitation; human settlements

2006/07 Energy for sustainable development; industrial development; air pollution/atmosphere; climate change

2008/09 Agriculture; rural development; land; drought; desertification; Africa

2010/11 Transport; chemicals; waste management; mining; a ten-year framework of programs on sustainable consumption and production

2012/13 Forests; biodiversity; biotechnology; tourism; mountains

2014/15 Oceans and seas; marine resources; small island developing states; disaster management and vulnerability

2016/17 Appraisal of Agenda 21, the Program of Further Implementation of Agenda 21, and the Johannesburg Plan of Implementation

Note: themes from 2010 onward are subject to change if the CSD so decides

Source: http://www.un.org/esa/sustdev/csd/csd.htm.

with developing states insistent that reporting should be voluntary and that comparison should not be made across states. As a result, there are guidelines for reporting but no requirements, and comparison across reports made with differing frequency and formats is difficult.[77] Though the process of reporting may be useful at the national level, it is not clear that much useful information has emerged for the CSD or others from the reporting process. The CSD also asks for information from other UN programs and organs on their incorporation of Agenda 21 recommendations. Inter-agency coordination in the preparation for WSSD was poor.

An important task for the CSD has been providing policy guidance for actions to follow up on UNCED. To that end it served as the preparatory committee for coordinating the Rio+5 special session of the General Assembly and for WSSD. It has provided such policy guidance in other areas as well, most importantly relating to forest governance and assessing fresh water.

It is difficult to determine what the influence of this institution has been. It is not charged with creating any new obligations for states and has no legal authority to compel states to act. Its primary impact is in the generation of information, the creation of norms, and the development of capacity. One set of scholars described it as "long on dialogue and speech-making but short on stimulating action."[78] The importance of its dialogue should not be entirely dismissed, however: it plays an important role in bringing non-state actors into the otherwise largely intergovernmental focus within the United Nations, and increases access by these actors in UN discussions and negotiations.[79] After the Rio+5 session the General Assembly mandated even more dialogue with representatives of major groups, and the CSD integrated "multi-stakeholder dialogue segments" into each annual meeting. Even so, the representation of the "major groups" identified at Rio has been uneven, and discussion from these dialogues rarely makes it into the decisions by diplomats meant to represent them.[80] The resolutions put forth by the CSD are weak and non-specific.

Some argue that the CSD has increased concern about sustainable development internationally, though of course such an impact is difficult to measure. It has perhaps succeeded in helping governments to make links across the many issues it considers under its mandate, and it has given focus to NGO activities locally, nationally, and internationally.[81] But on the whole it has not had a major impact on placing concern about sustainable development on the agenda of states or international organizations not already interested in discussing it. Its weaknesses suggest that it was created as a way to avoid, rather than institutionalize, action.

Other UN programs

Additional UN efforts have helped to create new information and bring attention to environmental issues. An early program, for example, focused on gathering scientific data, was the Man and Biosphere Program, run through UNESCO. It began in 1970 as an effort to bring together natural and social science to focus attention on the ability of people to live harmoniously within their environment. It works through the coordination of national offices, and encourages states to develop protected biosphere reserves.[82] This program was influential in achieving support for the World Heritage Convention (discussed further in Chapter 3).

UNEP has also worked with NGOs at raising awareness of environmental problems among states, through a number of programs. One influential one was an initiative called the World Conservation Strategy (WCS), created by UNEP, along with the World Conservation Union (IUCN) and WWF. Beginning in 1980, this effort sought to bring development and conservation together in local and national strategies. Thirty-five states along with international NGOs and UN agencies (the FAO and UNESCO joined UNEP) worked initially to negotiate a document that reflected a common set of goals for conservation across developed and developing states. The major negotiating difficulties involved achieving agreement between those whose primary concern was conservation and those who were most interested in issues of development. The final document used the concept of sustainable development as a goal, and encouraged states to create their own national conservation strategies. It called for states to "maintain essential ecological processes and life-support systems; preserve genetic diversity; and ensure sustainable utilization of species and ecosystems."[83] The final version of the WCS was signed by the heads of UNEP, the IUCN, and WWF to signal the broad support it received.

IUCN also drafted a World Charter for Nature in the late 1970s, building on an idea that was originally proposed at the 1949 Scientific Conference on Conservation and Utilization of Natural Resources. After much negotiation (and some weakening of the language) the UN General Assembly adopted the charter in October of 1982,[84] albeit with 18 abstentions and over the opposition of the United States. The charter largely reflected the principles already elaborated in the Stockholm Conference. It called for the need for conservation and economic development to take place simultaneously and reaffirmed the principle that states have sovereignty over their own resources along with a duty not to exploit their resources in a way that causes harm to other states.

Millennium Development Goals

The most influential recent initiative comes from the United Nations broadly. The UN in 2000 adopted a set of aspirations called the Millennium Development Goals. These non-binding goals refer to eight accomplishments to aim for by 2015. These include reducing by 50 percent the proportion of people who have an income of less than $1 per day, suffer from hunger, and do not have access to safe drinking water or sanitation, as well as working to promote gender equality, reduce child mortality, and improve maternal health. One goal specifies the need to "ensure environmental sustainability."[85]

Along with these goals, the UN created a process for evaluating progress towards meeting them. The first report, issued in 2005, suggested with respect to environmental sustainability that achieving the goals will depend on focusing on the needs of the world's poor to an extent that has not previously happened.[86] Though the goals themselves are not binding obligations, they have garnered a fair amount of attention, and have replaced the concept of sustainable development as the coordinating focus across UN agencies. One of the outcomes of the WSSD was to endorse these goals. It remains to be seen what they will accomplish, but they have at least focused attention on the issues and led to regular data gathering to evaluate progress.

Box 2.5 Millennium Development Goals

1   Eradicate extreme poverty and hunger
2   Achieve universal primary education
3   Promote gender equality and empower women
4   Reduce child mortality
5   Improve maternal health
6   Combat HIV/AIDS, malaria, and other diseases
7   Ensure environmental sustainability
8   Develop a global partnership for development

Conclusions

The United Nations environmental machinery has grown dramatically in the last several decades. It now consists of a program, a commission, and a large number of activities and goals within the organization. UNEP itself is a multifaceted institution with a hand in running many of the treaty organizations discussed in the following chapters, most of these under separate organizational structures. The number and extent of specifically UN-based institutional structures to focus on the environment is both a strength and a weakness of the system. On the positive side, the continuing integration of environmental concerns into increasing numbers of UN organs and agencies is an accurate reflection of the pervasiveness of environmental problems and their central connection to issues such as development and human rights. The international conferences on environmental issues created by the United Nations have played an important role in raising environmental awareness and have led to the negotiation of large numbers of international environmental agreements.

On the other hand, the organic growth of these structures leads to duplication of effort and confusion about mandate. The simultaneous existence of both UNEP and the CSD, for instance, has led to confusion about their relationship.[87] Multiple sources for the collection of data mean that effort is duplicated and sometimes information collected for one purpose is not available or not appropriate for other uses. And since funding for most environmental issues is both scarce and voluntary, many of the UN initiatives have run into funding problems that have only increased as there have been more UN-based activities competing for the same sources of funding.

Ultimately the activities within the UN environmental machinery should be seen as the background that enables or supports much of the other institutional activity to address international environmental issues described in the rest of this volume. These UN processes have clearly been instrumental in raising the level of attention paid to environmental issues internationally, but specific action taken to address environmental problems within international institutions happens more prominently at the level of treaty institutions, discussed by issue area in the following chapters.

Notes

1 Stockholm, "Resolution on Institutional and Financial Arrangements," 1972, available at http://www.unep.org/Documents.Multilingual/Default. Print.asp?DocumentID = 97&ArticleID = 1493.

2 Mark F. Imber, *Environment, Security and UN Reform* (New York: St. Martin's Press, 1994), 68.

3 Andrew W. Cordier and Max Harrelson, *Public Papers of the Secretaries-General of the United Nations, vol. 3: U Thant, 1968–71* (New York: Columbia University Press, 1977), 350.

4 Brian Johnson, "The United Nations' Institutional Reponse to Stockholm: A Case Study in the International Politics of Institutional Change," *International Organization* 26(2) (Spring 1972), 272–73.

5 Gordon J. MacDonald, "International Institutions for Environmental Management," *International Organization* 26(2) (Spring 1972), 372–400.

6 Henrik Selin and Björn-Ola Linnér, "The Quest for Global Sustainability: International Efforts on Linking Environment and Development," Working Paper No. 5, Cambridge, Mass.: *Science, Environment, and Development Group*, Center for International Development, Harvard University, January 2005, 33.

7 General Assembly Resolution 2997, "Institutional and Financial Arrangements for International Environmental Cooperation," 15 December 1972.

8 John McCormick, *Reclaiming Paradise: The Global Environmental Movement* (Bloomington: Indiana University Press, 1989), 106.

9 Michael Hardy, "The United Nations Environment Program," *Natural Resources Journal* 13 (April 1973), 235–55; McCormick, *Reclaiming Paradise*, 106.

10 Report of the Office of Internal Oversight Services on the Review of the United Nations Environment Programme and the Administrative Practices of its Secretariat, including the United Nations Office at Nairobi, Document A/51/810.

11 David L. Downie and Marc A. Levy, "The UN Environment Programme at a Turning Point: Options for Change," in Pamela S. Chasek, ed., *The Global Environment in the Twenty-First Century: Prospects for International Cooperation* (Tokyo, New York, and Paris: United Nations University Press, 2000), 361.

12 McCormick, *Reclaiming Paradise*, 111.

13 IISD, *Earth Negotiations Bulletin* 16(47) (28 February 2005) GC-23, 10.

14 UN General Assembly Resolution 53/242, 10 August 1999.

15 Downie and Levy, "The UN Environment Programme at a Turning Point;" in Imber, *Environment, Security, and UN Reform*, 77.

16 UNEP, "The Environment Fund Budgets: Revised Proposals for 1996–97 and proposals for 1998–99," UNEP/GC. 19/22; 17 January–19 February 1997.

17 UNEP, Regular Budget n.d., available at http://www.unep.org/rmu/en/Financing_regularbudget.htm.

18 UNEP, "Contributions to UNEP's Environment Fund – by Country: 1973–2004," Environment Fund (2005), available at http://www.unep.org/rmu/en/Table_donors1973to2004.htm.

19 Jodie Hierlmeier, "UNEP Retrospect and Prospect – Options for Reforming the Global Environmental Governance Regime," *Georgetown International Environmental Law Review* 14 (Summer 2002), 786.

20 Downie and Levy, "The UN Environment Programme at a Turning Point," 360–61.

21 *Report of the Office of Internal Oversight Services on the Review of the United Nations Environment Programme*, 3.
22 *Report of the Office of Internal Oversight Services on the Review of the United Nations Environment Programme*.
23 Hierlmeier, "UN Retrospect and Prospect," 786.
24 General Assembly Resolution 2997, Article 1(d).
25 UNEP, "About Earthwatch," available at http://earthwatch.unep.net/about/index.php.
26 McCormick, *Reclaiming Paradise*, 107.
27 Branislav Gosovic, *The Quest for World Environmental Cooperation: the Case of the UN Global Environment Monitoring System* (London: Routledge, 1992); see also http://www.gemstat.org/.
28 J.R. Sandbrook, "The UK's Overseas Environmental Policy," in the Programme Organizing Committee of the Conservation and Development Programme for the UK, *The Conservation and Development Programme for the UK* (London: Kogan Page), 392.
29 Don Hinrichsen, *Our Common Seas: Coasts in Crisis* (London: Earthscan Publications, in conjunction with UNEP, 1990), 23–24.
30 For the most extensive discussion of this agreement, see Peter M. Haas, S*aving the Mediterranean: The Politics of International Environmental Cooperation* (New York: Columbia University Press, 1989).
31 An additional two are replacements for earlier protocols on specially protected areas and emergencies.
32 Barcelona Convention, Article 23.
33 Henrik Selin and Stacy VanDeveer, "Hazardous Substances and the Helsinki and Barcelona Conventions: Origins, Results, and Future Challenges," paper presented at the policy forum Management of Toxic Substances in the Marine Environment: Analysis of the Mediterranean and the Baltic, Javea, Spain, 6–8 October 2002.
34 UNEP, Regional Seas Programme, "Who We Are & What We Do," available at http://www.unep.org/regionalseas/About/default.asp.
35 McCormick, *Reclaiming Paradise*, 114–15.
36 McCormick, *Reclaiming Paradise*, 116.
37 Peter Hulm, "The Regional Seas Program: What Fate for UNEP's Crown Jewels?," *Ambio* 12(1) (February 1983), 2–13.
38 McCormick, *Reclaiming Paradise*, 116.
39 Hinrichsen, *Our Common Seas*.
40 Downie and Levy, "The UN Environment Programme at a Turning Point," 356.
41 Downie and Levy, "The UN Environment Programme at a Turning Point," 358.
42 *Report of the Office of Internal Oversight Services on the Review of the United Nations Environment Programme*, 10.
43 "Homes for Forest Workers," Unasylva 4(1) (1950), available at http://www.fao.org/documents/show_cdr.asp?url_file = /docrep/x5354e/x5354e02.htm.
44 Mostafa Tolba, with Iwona Rummel-Bulska, *Global Environmental Diplomacy: Negotiating Environmental Agreements for the World, 1973–1992* (Cambridge, Mass.: MIT Press, 1998).
45 Program of Action of the UN ICPD, Section C (3.24).

46   Copenhagen Declaration on Social Development, Paragraph 25(b).
47   He replaced Jean Moussard, a Swiss biologist originally chosen in 1969 to head the process.
48   Barbara Ward and René Dubos, *Only One Earth: The Care and Maintenance of a Small Planet* (New York: Norton, 1972).
49   Founex Report on Development and Environment, 1971, available at http://www.southcentre.org/publications/conundrum/conundrum-04.htm.
50   Wade Rowland, *The Plot to Save the World: The Life and Times of the Stockholm Conference on the Human Environment* (Toronto: Clarke, Irwin & Company Ltd., 1973).
51   Selin and Linnér, "The Quest for Global Sustainability."
52   UNEP, *The World Environment 1972–1982* (Nairobi: UNEP, 1982); *The Environment in 1982: Retrospect and Prospect* (Nairobi: UNEP, 1982).
53   Nairobi Declaration.
54   UNGA Resolution 44/228, 22 December 1989.
55   Andrew Jordan, "Financing the UNCED Agenda: The Controversy Over Additionality," *Environment* 36(3) (1994), 12–20, 31–36.
56   Steven Bernstein, *The Compromise of Liberal Environmentalism* (New York: Columbia University Press, 2001).
57   See, for example, Bernstein, *The Compromise of Liberal Environmentalism*; Neil Middleton, Phil O'Keefe, and Sam Moyo, *Tears of the Crocodile: From Rio to Reality in the Developing World* (London: Pluto Press, 1993).
58   UN General Assembly Resolution 19/2, 19 September 1997.
59   Pablo Gutman, "What Did WSSD Accomplish? An NGO Perspective," *Environment* 45(2) (March 2003), 22.
60   UN General Assembly Resolution 55/199, 22 December 1989.
61   UN General Assembly Resolution 55/199, Paragraph 15.
62   UNEP, "Johannesburg Summit 2002: Highlights of Commitments and Implementation Initiatives," available at http://www.un.org/events/wssd/pressreleases/highlightsofsummit.pdf.
63   United Nations, *Key Outcomes of the Summit* (New York: United Nations, 2002).
64   Liliiana B. Andonova and Marc A. Levy, "Franchising Global Governance: Making Sense of the Johannesburg Type II Partnerships," *Yearbook of International Co-operation on Environment and Development* (2003/04), 19–31.
65   Gutman, "What did WSSD Accomplish?," 24.
66   James Gustave Speth, "Perpsectives on the Johannesburg Summit," *Environment* 45(1) (January/February 2003), 25.
67   Jonas Hagen, "Don't Leave Us Alone to Pay the Price," *UN Chronicle* No. 4 (2002).
68   Quoted in Ronald Baily, "Wilting Greens," *Reason* (December 2002), 18–19.
69   Quoted in Gutman, "What did WSSD Accomplish?," 22.
70   Speth, "Perspectives on the Johannesburg Summit," 28.
71   UN General Assembly Resolution 38/161, 19 December 1983.
72   World Commission on Environment and Development (WCED), *Our Common Future* (Oxford: Oxford University Press, 1987).
73   WCED, *Our Common Future*, Annex I, 348–51.
74   WCED, *Our Common Future*, 8.
75   UN General Assembly Resolution 47/191, 29 January 1993.

76 Division for Sustainable Development, "Commission on Sustainable Development," available at http://www.un.org/esa/sustdev/csd/csd.htm.

77 Pamela Chasek, "The UN Comission on Sustainable Development: The First Five Years," in Pamela Chasek, ed., The Global Environment in the 21st Century: Prospects for International Cooperation (Tokyo: UNU Press, 2000), 378–98.

78 James Gustave Speth and Peter M. Haas, *Global Environmental Governance*: *The Challenge of Sustainability* (Washington, D.C.: Island Press, 2006).

79 Lynn M. Wagner, "A Commission Will Lead Them? The UN Commission on Sustainable Development and UNCED Follow-Up," in Angela Churie Kallhauge, Gunner Sjöstedt, and Elisabeth Corell, eds., *Global Challenges*: *Furthering the Multilateral Process for Sustainable Development* (London: Greenleaf Press, 2005).

80 Chasek, "The UN Commission on Sustainable Development," 387.

81 Chasek, "The UN Commission on Sustainable Development," 386–87.

82 UNESCO, "The MAB Program," available at http://www.unesco.org/mab/; Michel Batisse, "Developing and Focusing the Biosphere Reserve Concept," *Nature and Resources* 22 (1986),1–10.

83 George Greene, "Caring for the Earth," *Environment* 36(7) (September 1994), 25–28.

84 United Nations General Assembly Resolution 37/7, 28 October1982.

85 United Nations, "Millennium Development Goals," available at http://www.un.org/millenniumgoals/index.html.

86 United Nations, *Millennium Development Goals Report* (New York: United Nations, 2005).

87 Joy Hyvarinen and Duncan Brack, *Global Environmental Institutions*: *Analysis and Options for Change* (London: The Royal Institute of International Affairs, 2000).

3 Species and conservation

The conservation of species makes sense as a focus for international institutions. Animal and plant species are increasingly at risk from human activity. The World Conservation Union characterizes 23 percent of mammal species, 33 percent of amphibian species, and 12 percent of bird species as threatened with extinction.[1] Species that are under threat due to use by individuals from multiple states cannot be adequately protected by any one state alone. In addition, the incentive structure for species management should be conducive to efforts at conservation: most species harvested for use have the ability to reproduce if sufficient numbers remain. Successful management can thereby ensure the future of harvesting by simply making sure that enough of a population remains to perpetuate itself. In other words, those who make use of a given species benefit in the long run by its conservation, because they will be able to continue to harvest the species indefinitely if international institutions can successfully conserve species. Even under these simple incentive structures international cooperation for species protection has proved exceedingly difficult, however.

In international efforts to protect endangered species and conserve natural resources, cooperation has focused primarily on species that exist internationally or that migrate across jurisdictions. Early species protection agreements focused on the concept of using a species sustainably (though that terminology would not initially have been used); the first types of agreements protecting endangered species were centered around ways to ensure that a sufficient breeding population would be left in the wild so that harvesting the species could continue indefinitely.

The idea of the protection of species and the conservation of natural resources has grown more complicated, in a number of ways, since the early agreements. The first source of complexity is the idea that there may be some cases in which human use of species may not always be justified. Some species are particularly intelligent, show signs of suffering, or play an especially important role in their ecosystems, and some argue that these species should not be hunted under any circumstances. At the extreme there are those who suggest that the relationship of humans to their environment needs to change even more dramatically and that it is never justified for people to kill other species for their own use.[2]

The second source of complexity is the evolution from a focus on a given organism to a focus on the ecosystem in which that organism operates. This evolution began as a consideration of how to best protect resources. The Convention on Wetlands of International Importance Especially as Waterfowl Habitat (1971) protects migratory birds, in part, by ensuring that the places to which they migrate will be conserved. Though the initial focus of negotiation efforts in this agreement were to protect specific species, it was acknowledged that without protecting the habitats on which they depend other efforts at species conservation would fail.

The evolution of conservation away from a focus on individual species also reflects a genuine recalculation of what is important from a conservation perspective, towards the idea that the ecosystem and the diversity of species (rather than the perpetuation of any one species) are of the greatest environmental value. Though these approaches are different they are in some ways compatible; protecting an ecosystem may be the best way to ensure the survival of a given species within it.

This chapter first examines the early species conservation agreements that began the process of multilateral cooperation to protect species so that they would be available for continued human use over time. It then discusses the major agreements to protect endangered species from international trade (the Convention on International Trade in Endangered Species) and to protect those that migrate internationally (the Convention on Migratory Species), as well as discussing some other important agreements to protect wetlands and natural heritage. The chapter then examines the move from focusing on individual species to protection of ecosystems and biodiversity (through the Convention on Biological Diversity (CBD) and its Biosafety Protocol). It concludes with a consideration of some of the conservation institutions that have been created by governments, international organizations, and NGOs, and examining the nascent but generally minor links across species and conservation institutions.

Early species conservation agreements

Early species conservation agreements focused on individual species and were negotiated among a small number of parties. These agreements made efforts to ensure that species were not overhunted so that hunting could continue over time. There were informal agreements between Russia and the United States as early as 1893. The Convention for the Preservation and Protection of Fur Seals (1911), among the United States, Great Britain, Russia, and Japan, prevented seal catching beyond three miles from land, and imposed other conservation measures to prevent seal populations from declining. States negotiated similar agreements to protect migratory birds, including a 1936 agreement between the United States and Mexico, and the 1950 International Convention for the Protection of Birds, primarily among European states.

A number of agreements to protect whales emerged in the first half of the twentieth century as well. The Geneva Convention for the Regulation of Whaling (1931) was negotiated under the auspices of the League of Nations to limit high seas whaling of depleted whale species and prohibit the harvesting of whale calves. Some of the most important whaling states, notably Japan, Germany, and the Soviet Union, did not sign this agreement, so there was a limit to how much it could accomplish. Another effort at restricting whale catches multilaterally was made in 1937 with the International Agreement for the Regulation of Whaling. This agreement designated a whaling season and set catch size limits, but it did not set limits on the number of whales that could be caught, and had little effect at protecting whales.[3] After World War II (and the interruption of whaling it caused) the main whaling states were able to pass the International Convention for the Regulation of Whaling (1946), which remains the governing agreement for the protection of whale species today (and is discussed further in Chapter 4).

There were several attempts early in the twentieth century to create general agreements on wildlife protection, but they did not succeed. The first was the London Convention Designed to Ensure the Conservation of Various Species of Wild Animals in Africa Which are Useful to Man or Inoffensive (1900), which was an agreement among colonial powers. A second, similar, agreement came in 1933: the London Convention Relative to the Preservation of Fauna and Flora in their Natural State. Both these agreements listed protected species in annexes, limited hunting of species considered to be threatened, and provided for licenses to export certain wildlife products. Though the

1900 convention did not enter into force, the 1933 agreement did (in 1936), but it lacked a broader institutional structure and thus the ability to make and oversee decisions to expand protection. It was therefore also unable to adapt to the end of colonialism and the changes in wildlife management this dramatic political change necessitated.[4]

A regionally focused general agreement was the Washington Convention on Nature Protection and Wildlife Preservation in the Western Hemisphere (1940), which contained an annex of species that parties were required to protect, and controlled trade in protected species by requiring certificates authorizing export or import. Parties were required to create national parks and other wildlife conservation areas, including those where wildlife could not be hunted. This agreement was never fully implemented, at least in part due to the lack of secretariat or other institutional mechanisms to govern the treaty.[5]

The Convention on International Trade in Endangered Species of Wild Fauna and Flora

One of the first truly global species conservation agreements still in effect is the Convention on International Trade in Endangered Species of Wild Fauna and Flora (CITES), signed in 1973. Pressure to create the agreement began in the 1960s when species trade increased dramatically and the (then) International Union for the Conservation of Nature (IUCN) began to ask its member states to restrict such trade. The IUCN General Assembly called in 1963 for the creation of a treaty to regulate trade in rare and threatened wildlife and the skins thereof. It drafted an initial proposal for a convention, which circulated in the late 1960s, but negotiations stalled over disagreements between importing and exporting countries. In particular, developing countries, led by Kenya, wanted to be able to determine their own lists of species that could be traded, rather than relying on one collective list. The Action Plan agreed to at the Stockholm Conference in 1972 included a resolution recommending that a conference be convened to negotiate "a convention on export, import and transit of certain species of wild animals and plants."[6] Following Stockholm the United States convened a negotiating conference in Washington in February and March of 1973, with a U.S. draft that attempted to include both the IUCN and Kenyan approaches.[7]

This agreement focuses on protecting endangered species through limiting trade, since it is often demand in one part of the world that impacts conservation status in another part of the world. If trade in the most endangered species could be prohibited, the species might be

Box 3.1 Selected international agreements protecting species and nature

- The Convention for the Preservation and Protection of Fur Seals (1911; no longer in force)
- The London Convention Relative to the Preservation of Fauna and Flora in their Natural State (1933)
- Washington Convention on Nature Protection and Wildlife Preservation in the Western Hemisphere (1940)
- International Convention for the Protection of Birds (1950)
- International Convention for the Protection of New Varieties of Plants (1961; revised 1978)
- African Convention for the Conservation of Nature and Natural Resources (1968)
- European Convention for the Protection of Animals During International Transport (1968)
- BENELUX Convention Concerning Hunting and the Protection of Birds (1970)
- Convention on Wetlands of International Importance Especially as Waterfowl Habitat (1971)
- Convention for the Conservation of Antarctic Seals (1972)
- Convention for the Protection of the World Cultural and Natural Heritage (1972)
- Convention on International Trade in Endangered Species of Wild Fauna and Flora (CITES) (1973)
- Agreement on the Conservation of Polar Bears (1973)
- Convention on the Conservation of Migratory Species of Wild Animals (1979)
- Convention on the Conservation of European Wildlife and Natural Habitats (1979)
- Convention on the Conservation of Antarctic Marine Living Resources (1980)
- World Charter for Nature (1982)
- Convention on Biological Diversity (CBD) (1992)

better able to be protected, because the incentive for killing or capturing these species would be diminished. Regulating trade is also easier, from an international relations perspective, than trying to influence what states do within their own borders. CITES requires almost no domestic obligations, only a commitment to follow the trade restrictions in question.

Each party to the treaty must designate a national management authority and a scientific authority responsible for determining whether conditions for trade have been met and issuing permits that allow trade to take place. States are also prohibited from trading in protected species with states that are not party to the convention unless they meet all the requirements of the convention with respect to trade.[8]

The agreement operates by listing species on three appendices to the treaty. Appendix I consists of species that are the most seriously endangered. Commercial trade in these species is prohibited and trade for other purposes can only take place if it can be shown not to be harmful to the species' survival. Species listed in Appendix I can only cross borders when issued with both an export permit from the country from which the specimen originates and an import permit from the country for which it is bound, each indicating that it was not taken in contravention of any conservation regulations and that the trade in this specimen will not harm the overall survival of the species. More than 800 species are listed in Appendix I.[9]

Species are listed in Appendix II if they would be likely to become endangered if trade is not controlled. In other words, the whole purpose of Appendix II is to avoid having to engage in the level of restriction in Appendix I. For Appendix II species, trade is tightly regulated. In order to trade in these species, or their parts, exporters must have an export certificate from the state indicating that trade will not harm the survival of the species, that the specimen was not obtained illegally under domestic law, and that shipment of living specimens will not harm them. The designated scientific authority in each state must examine the export permits granted generally, to limit them for the purposes of protection of the species in its range. Anyone who wants to import an Appendix II species must show a valid export permit. This appendix lists by far the bulk of the species regulated by CITES, approximately 32,500.[10]

A third appendix allows states to list species within their jurisdiction that are protected domestically. If a species is listed in Appendix III, trade from the state that has listed it requires an export permit granted with the state's management authority is assurance that it was not taken in contravention of any domestic conservation regulations. In other words, this appendix serves primarily as international recognition of domestically protected species and allows states to seek international assistance in regulating trade in species they have protected but others may not have. There are nearly 300 species listed in Appendix III.[11]

Institutionally, the convention creates a Conference of the Parties (COP) that meets biennially to make decisions. While individual states may list species within their borders in Appendix III, species can only be listed in the other two appendices with the approval of the conference of the parties. A proposal that a species be listed in Appendix I or II requires approval by two-thirds of the parties and after that becomes binding. Once a proposal is passed, any state has 90 days in which to decide whether to lodge a reservation indicating that it will not be bound by the provision. (If any state enters a reservation the other states have an additional 60 days during which they can decide to do so as well.) After the reservation period has expired, all states that have not made reservations are bound by the provision and no new states may enter reservations to the listing of that species. States may also remove reservations later.[12]

UNEP was chosen to serve as the secretariat for CITES, and the COP set up additional institutional structures. UNEP provided initial funding for the treaty operations, but a UNEP Governing Council decision in 1978 to phase out UNEP financing for CITES necessitated the creation of a CITES trust fund, with contributions from member states following the UN scale of assessment.[13] CITES also runs a number of subsidiary bodies to allow the institution to function in between COP meetings. These include a Standing Committee, and committees on animals, plants, identification manuals, and nomenclature. Unlike many wildlife conservation agreements (or broader environmental institutions), CITES does not have a scientific committee, though there were, ultimately unsuccessful, efforts in the late 1980s to create one.[14] Instead, issues of the status of species are addressed by the relevant national scientific authorities (as created under CITES Article IX).

As with most international environmental agreements, information on compliance comes mostly through self-reporting; states are obligated to generate annual reports with export and import data (as well as submit biennial reports on other measures they have taken to protect species under the agreement). These mandated reports, however, are often late or missing, and many of the ones that are submitted do not contain necessary information. The percentage of states reporting in a given year has ranged from a high of 80 percent in 1987 to a low of 30 percent three years later. The secretariat began to address this problem directly in the early 1990s and sent letters informing parties that failure to report would be considered a "major implementation problem" under the treaty. Reporting did increase following this effort, but is still nowhere near complete, and many reports are still missing information.[15]

One of the reasons for the importance of reporting in this process in particular is that the information in the reports can be used as an additional way to check how well the overall system is functioning. Numbers of species exported to a country should match number of imported species, and if they do not it is indicative of a problem of enforcement somewhere in the process. But because of late and incomplete reports it has been difficult to make use of this kind of analysis. The CITES secretariat does publish an Infractions Report at each COP, listing those states that have breached trade rules. Other ways the organization helps to increase the level of enforcement is through training officials in member states who will be charged with implementing CITES rules.

CITES provides few direct consequences for non-compliance, but the Standing Committee, which reviews allegations of non-compliance, has in some cases recommended that CITES member states take action (by restricting trade in species generally) against those states seen to be persistently flouting CITES rules. States that have been subject to this provision include the United Arab Emirates (1985–90, during which time the state withdrew from CITES; when it returned the ban was lifted), Thailand (1991–92), and Italy (1992–93). This mechanism has also been used to encourage states engaging in wildlife trade to become CITES members; both El Salvador (1986–87) and Equatorial Guinea (1988–92) joined the agreement after being targeted by member state trade restrictions.[16] The United States has also used domestic legislation to impose unilateral trade restrictions on states that the CITES Standing Committee identified as operating outside CITES rules, including Singapore in 1986 and China and Taiwan in 1994.[17]

The best-known efforts under CITES are those to protect the African elephant, which is hunted for its ivory, for which there is high demand in a number of countries in Asia. This species was listed in Appendix II in 1977 but population levels declined precipitously. In 1989 the COP voted to move the species to Appendix I, amid much controversy. Many of the African states that opposed the Appendix I listing entered reservations, hoping to continue to sell ivory. But Japan, the largest importer of ivory, yielded to U.S. and NGO pressure to support the Appendix I listing. Once it was listed in Appendix I the populations of elephants in some African countries stabilized and grew, so much so that in some areas the elephant populations were too large, in the assessments of those managing them, to coexist with human populations. In other states, however, the elephant population numbers remained low. Some of the states where elephants had been well protected argued in favor of "downlisting" the species to Appendix II to allow managed trade. These states argued that limited trade would allow them to earn money (including by selling off stockpiles of confiscated ivory) that could support their successful conservation programs financially. Zimbabwe threatened to leave the agreement and trade outside the system if CITES would not allow for renewed trade in elephant parts.[18]

The tenth COP meeting in Zimbabwe in 1997 agreed to allow a partial downlisting; Botswana, Namibia, and Zimbabwe would be allowed to sell ivory internationally in a tightly managed program. Sales could only be to specified countries, which initially meant Japan. Trade would happen in conjunction with a monitoring system that would monitor both trade in elephant species and elephant killing overall. Results have been mixed. Trade has been tightly controlled. One collective sale was allowed in 1999 shortly after the partial down-listing, and another sale in 2002. Namibia was allowed to sell some worked ivory but not raw ivory in 2004. Conservation groups point to an increase in poaching in Zimbabwe since the ban was lifted and also in Kenya and the Central African Republic, where trade is not allowed.[19] Despite the controversy, a study by the African Elephant Specialist Group of the IUCN indicates that the population of African elephants increased by approximately 4.5 percent annually between 1990 and 2002, much of it likely attributable to CITES regulations. The study concluded, however, that populations in southern Africa were in better shape than those in West and Central Africa.[20]

In assessing CITES, one controversial element is the ability of states to enter reservations to the listing of species in CITES appendices. Those who do are not bound by the regulation in question. This approach is part of an effort to allow changes to protection status in a timely manner. Amendments to the appendices become binding on all parties without having to go through a lengthy ratification process that would normally be required for changes to international obligations; this process allows the agreement to be modified quickly. But states – which have the ultimate decision over whether to join or remain in the agreement as a whole – would not agree to such a system if they did not retain the ability to opt out of decisions they found to be particularly objectionable. Most treaties that allow for changed obligations in this manner include some kind of reservation (also called objection) procedure. States may only enter reservations during the specified time period, and are encouraged to remove them over time.

For the most part, the reservations process in CITES has not played a major role in undermining the objectives of the agreement, but there certainly are some instances in which it has prevented or delayed species protection efforts. One example is the efforts to regulate trade in the saltwater crocodile, which is killed to make leather products out of its hide. When CITES listed this species in Appendix I in 1979, France, Germany, Italy, Japan, and Switzerland, which at that point accounted for 80 percent of the trade in such leather, all lodged reservations.[21] In this case, however, the system worked as intended. With time and external pressure, most these states have removed their reservations. Certainly, in some instances, states that are important markets or sources for endangered species maintain reservations – Japan has reservations for many listed sea turtle species – but for the most part the reservations process has not caused major problems for the protection of endangered species under CITES.

Overall, CITES has had mixed success in its efforts to protect species through trade restrictions. It faces an inherently difficult task, involving thousands of protected species (many of which look remarkably like unprotected species) at multiple points of export, with border inspections conducted by those untrained in taxonomy and with too many inspections to carry out, and many opportunities to transport species across borders undetected. Those who intend to smuggle protected species can often do so without being caught. Major problems have come in developing states that simply lack the capacity to maintain control over their borders.

While its focus is both plants and animals, the animal protection has gained more attention, and verifying the identity of plant products can be especially difficult. The agreement has thus had a greater degree of success restricting trade in endangered animal species than in plants.[22] It is also important to note that the nature of CITES regulations means that even when wildlife is protected from international trade there is no guarantee that it will be safe within states, which are not bound by CITES to create any domestic protection of regulated species.

An additional problem with the implementation of CITES comes from the difficulty in managing Appendix II species. This appendix should be the centerpiece of CITES protections, and species listed in it should be able to be adequately protected by international efforts to manage trade. But the parties have been unable to make meaningful estimates of the potential of the impact of trade on these species because so little information is known on their abundance and population trends. In the face of uncertainty about what level of trade is acceptable, members of the agreement have tended to err on the side of allowing more trade rather than less. In this situation, species can be harmed by trade that is perfectly legal under the treaty but results from insufficient information to set realistic management goals.

To some extent, given the difficulties the CITES structure faces, its successes are all the more notable. Trade in Appendix I-listed species has generally declined, and the popularity of truly endangered species used in luxury goods (ivory in piano keys, fur coats from wild cats) has waned in favor of substitute products. In some cases, domestic ranching operations provide the raw materials (such as crocodile hides) that would previously have been harvested from endangered animals.[23] Institutional efforts to protect endangered species by controlling trade face an uphill battle, but have managed to accomplish some level of protection in some instances.

The Convention on the Conservation of Migratory Species

CITES focuses on species that are moved internationally by human trade, but many species migrate internationally of their own accord, and require a different form of international protection. The Convention on the Conservation of Migratory Species (1979) (CMS, or Bonn Convention) was also negotiated in the wake of the Stockholm Conference call for greater protection of endangered species. Recommendation 32 from the conference urged states, while enacting international species conservation agreements, to give special attention to "those which migrate from one country to another." West Germany drafted an initial proposal for such an agreement in 1974, working with IUCN, and negotiations followed.[24] Seventy-seven states met for two weeks in Bonn in June 1979 for the final conclusion of the agreement. Difficulties arose over how to define migratory species. A major source of contention as well was whether the agreement would include marine animals, something that was opposed by the United States, the Soviet Union, and others. Similar proposals would have excluded Antarctic species. The final version does include aquatic species, and includes "the entire population or any geographically separate part of any species or lower taxon of wild animals, a significant proportion of whose members cyclically and predictably cross jurisdictional boundaries."[25]

The CMS takes a hybrid approach to the protection of endangered species. Like most preceding agreements to protect specific species, it begins with lists of species, in appendices, that must be protected by member states. The first appendix lists species considered to be critically endangered; member states must "provide immediate protection for" these species, as well as taking steps to conserve and restore their habitats, and refrain from taking any action that will impede their migration. There are more than 100 species listed in Appendix I.[26] The second appendix lists species with an "unfavorable conservation status" that therefore require international protection. States have fewer specific obligations with respect to these species, but should cooperate to protect them. Nearly 200 species are listed in Appendix II.[27]

The focus of this agreement, like CITES, is species that move from one place to another, only in the case of the CMS it is species that themselves migrate from one geographic location to another. The innovation of this agreement is that a primary way to protect species is for "range states" – those states through which a given species migrates and that exploit that species – to negotiate specific agreements to protect that species. Additionally, states that are not party to the broader convention but that are range states for a protected species can – and should – be included in these agreements. There have thus far been six binding agreements negotiated under this process: to protect bats in Europe (EUROBATS), cetaceans in the Baltic and North Sea (ASCOBANS), cetaceans in the Black Sea, Mediterranean Sea, and contiguous areas (ACCOBAMS), African-Eurasian migratory water birds (AEWA), Wadden seals, and albatrosses and petrels (ACAP). Each of these agreements creates its own governance structure, usually involving regular meetings, funding, and research and reporting.

There are also a large number of agreements in various stages of negotiation. These would protect Sahelo-Saharan antelopes, the Houbara bustard, sand grouse, Central Asian flyway, raptors, sturgeons, the whale shark, marine turtles, small cetaceans and sirenians in West and Central Africa, small cetaceans and dugongs in Southeast Asia, cetaceans in the Pacific Island region, the monk seal, the Mongolian gazelle, the gorilla, and African bats.[28] The negotiation of agreements and other forms of specific species protection has increased in recent years.

In addition to legally binding agreements, states may also negotiate memoranda of understanding (MoUs). These informal agreements acknowledge the threatened status of the specific species to which they apply and constitute a non-binding agreement to attempt to protect them. These types of agreements are largely intended to address short-term coordination and scientific research needs. Seven of these MoUs have thus far been negotiated, protecting the Siberian crane, the slender-billed curlew, marine turtles in Africa, marine turtles in the Indian ocean, the great bustard, the Bukhara deer, the aquatic warbler, the West African elephant, and the Saiga antelope. The shorter time it takes to negotiate these agreements (including the avoidance of a ratification period), along with the higher extent of participation by range states (as compared to the formal agreements under the CMS),[29] suggests potential advantages to the use of MoUs for species protection under the CMS.

Institutionally, the Bonn Convention creates a COP that meets approximately every three years to review implementation and make specific conservation recommendations. Decisions, including those to add or remove species from the appendices, require a two-thirds majority vote. After a successful vote to amend the appendices, all states are bound by the decision except those that make a reservation within 90 days after the decision.[30] A Standing Committee fulfills necessary governance functions between the COP meetings. The first COP created a Scientific Council to coordinate research and recommend conservation measures and species to add to the two appendices.[31] UNEP provides secretariat services, with the secretariat located in Bonn.

The effectiveness of this agreement has been limited, in part, by lack of participation. There are 93 member states, but some important ones (from the perspective of species protection) are missing: the United States, Canada, China, Russia, and Brazil are not a part of the agreement. The United States, Russia, and China have agreed to participate in specific agreements (all three are members of the Agreement on the Conservation of Albatrosses and Petrels, for instance) and MoUs, as have 21 other states not bound by the convention itself. Some regions, especially Asia, are underrepresented in the membership of the CMS and in the negotiation of specific agreements.

The functioning of the agreement has been seriously hampered by financial difficulties. A number of parties are in arrears in their contributions, and the COP has periodically reduced the amount of the budget requested by the secretariat in order to decrease the amount required as dues to the organization. Of particular concern is the expanding institutional structure that results from the many agreements under the CMS, each of which has its own secretariat and meetings, and therefore requires additional funding.

It is also difficult to determine what impact the specific agreements negotiated under the convention have had, largely because so little is known about the populations of these species to begin with. There also are threats to these species that are not directly attributable to human activity (though in some cases they may be indirectly attributable). For example, in the Wadden Sea, which contains up to 40 percent of the world's population of seals, seal deaths have come largely from a distemper virus.[32] In addition, the existing agreements were concluded in the 1990s and later (and spent their first few years working out operational matters), which means they have not yet had much time to operate. The fact that some of the most significant agreements and MoUs have been recently concluded, however, suggests that the organization may be beginning to take a more active role in species conservation than it did for its first decade of operation.

Other early species conservation agreements

There are other relevant species and nature conservation processes created by international agreement in the 1970s. While these agreements do not have strong institutional processes, they have widespread participation by states and have probably had some impact on nature conservation.

The Ramsar Convention

The Convention on Wetlands of International Importance Especially as Waterfowl Habitat (known as the Ramsar Convention) is sometimes considered the first treaty to involve the protection of ecosystems. Its negotiation brought together two different interests: protecting birds and preserving wetlands. The International Committee for Bird Protection, the International Waterfowl Research Bureau, and the IUCN (see pp. 62–63) proposed a treaty on this topic. Negotiations towards an agreement began in 1963, and the treaty was opened for signature in 1971.[33]

States party to the agreement must designate at least one wetland within their territory that they agree to safeguard from human encroachment; they can make changes to the boundaries of or remove a listed wetland as long as they replace it with a new one.[34]

Institutional structure is weak, however. The original agreement did not provide for a funding mechanism and there is no provision for making changes to the treaty. Decisions in the agreement are made by a Conference of Contracting Parties, made up of representatives from all contracting states. It meets every three years and is in charge of overseeing the implementation of the agreement generally.[35] A Standing Committee meets annually to conduct business between the meetings of the Conference of Contracting Parties. The governing process also includes a Scientific and Technical Review Panel. IUCN serves as the secretariat.

Individual decisions have improved governance. In 1990 the convention made the list of protected sites public. It also adopted a monitoring procedure, designed to assist parties in evaluating their protected sites (rather than punishing them for inadequate protection).

Ramsar has reasonably widespread participation, with 148 member states (including most of those with important wetlands). These states have collectively protected 1526 sites comprising 130 million hectares of wetlands.[36]

The problem of wetlands destruction (generally associated with development) has not been ameliorated by Ramsar, though wetlands are certainly better protected than they were in the early 1970s, with beneficial impacts for migratory waterfowl. The most important development for the protection of wetlands has been the change in the general perception of wetlands. Where once they were seen as problematic swamps in areas that could otherwise be developed, they are now understood as beneficial ecosystems that provide useful ecological services. That change is likely more important than the specific protection of sites under Ramsar, but to the extent that the agreement has helped create that change it has had a diffuse impact nevertheless.

The World Heritage Convention

The Convention Concerning the Protection of the World Cultural and Natural Heritage (generally referred to as the World Heritage Convention, or WHC) protects far more than wildlife. It takes as its purview the protection of sites of particular cultural or natural importance. States party to the agreement may propose sites within their boundaries that they deem worthy of international recognition. The World Heritage Committee, comprising 21 member states elected for six-year terms, decides whether a site may be placed on the list. States commit to the protection of sites on the list, and have access to a modest amount of funding in pursuit of this goal. One hundred and eighty states in the world, including all the most prominent ones, are members of the agreement.[37]

The World Heritage Committee also maintains the list of "World Heritage Sites in Danger," identifying those protected sites that are threatened by factors such as war, pollution, urbanization, and tourism. National parks and wildlife preserves in the Democratic Republic of Congo, for example, were placed on the list in 1994 because of the toll of years of war. The Río Plátano Biosphere Reserve in Honduras is also listed on the "sites in danger" list (since 1996) to reflect "commercial and agricultural intrusion" into the area. There has been controversy over whether a site could be inscribed on the "sites in danger" list without the acquiescence of the state in which it was located. This issue came up when some NGOs proposed designating the Florida Everglades in the United States as endangered, over U.S.

Box 3.2 Examples of Natural World Heritage Sites (and date first protected)

- Galápagos Islands (Ecuador), 1978
- Virunga National Park (Democratic Republic of the Congo), 1979
- Tikal National Park (Guatemala), 1979
- Everglades National Park (United States), 1979
- Great Barrier Reef (Australia), 1981
- Serengeti National Park (Tanzania), 1981
- Río Plátano Biosphere Reserve (Honduras), 1982
- Rocky Mountain Parks (Canada), 1984
- Yosemite National Park (United States), 1984
- Hawaii Volcanoes National Park (United States), 1987
- Lake Baikal (Russia), 1996
- Mount Kenya National Park/Natural Forest (Kenya), 1997
- New Zealand Sub-Antarctic Islands, 1998
- Pantanal Conservation Area (Brazil), 2000

opposition. The World Heritage Committee concluded, however, that sites could only be given that designation with the approval of the state. Sites on this list – currently 34 out of 812 sites protected by the process generally – have access to additional funding.[38]

One of the major difficulties faced by the efforts to protect world heritage is the inherently contradictory nature of the agreement. It aims to protect the world's most important natural sites by publicizing them, and states agree to list their sites primarily for the recognition, and resulting tourism, that accrues from being designated as a World Heritage Site. Income from tourism almost certainly helps contribute to the protection of listed sites, but the tourism itself inevitably decreases the ecological health of these locations, sometimes dramatically. It is a contradiction the WHC cannot address, because it is at the core of the agreement's operations.

The Convention on Biological Diversity

The negotiation of the United Nations Convention on Biological Diversity (CBD), signed at United Nations Conference on Environment and Development in 1992, represented a shift in conservation strategy from the previous approaches reflected in most of the organizations described thus far in this chapter. Instead of a focus on individual species, the CBD focuses on the whole of biodiversity conservation, the idea that it is the diversity of species and genetic material that must be protected, rather than specific species or locations.

Even before the negotiation of the CBD there had been some steps in this direction in international institutions. One such move came in the negotiation of the Convention for the Conservation of Antarctic Marine Living Resources (CCAMLR) in 1980. CCAMLR is in many ways a traditional resource management agreement in that its goal is to ensure that the marine resources of the Antarctic are used sustainably so that they can continue to be harvested indefinitely. But the approach it takes, at least theoretically, is one of ecosystem management rather than a focus on individual species of concern. The idea is to take the entire ecosystem into consideration when setting catch limits for species in the area. The impact that a decrease in the population of one species has on its predator or prey species, for example, should be considered when setting catch limits. In practice this approach has been hard to implement, and CCAMLR has often functioned in ways sometimes indistinguishable from a traditional fisheries management organization. But it was important in introducing the concept of taking broader ecosystemic effects into consideration in global environmental governance.

The negotiations towards the CBD were initiated by the IUCN, beginning in 1988. The UNEP Governing Council then called, in 1989, for a convention that would address the conservation of ecosystems and genetic material as well as species. From the beginning the goal was to create an "umbrella" agreement that would bring together existing international protections of species.[39] Negotiations exposed contradictory objectives between developed and developing states. Developing states prioritized protection of their rights to the benefits from biodiversity within their territory, and wanted protection from multinational corporations or pressures from industrialized states. They were also concerned about the cost of new international obligations and wanted access to technology and funding. Developed states, on the other hand, wanted to increase their level of access to the world's genetic material, much of which is located in developing states.[40] Some also argued that biodiversity should be seen as the "common heritage of [hu]mankind," though this principle had been advocated inconsistently by developed states, who avoided such principles when their agricultural industries preferred proprietary access to genetic material to develop it commercially. Along these lines, the United States and some others were concerned with the protection of intellectual property rights for pharmaceutical and biotechnological developments that come from biodiversity resources.

Because many of the areas with the greatest biodiversity are physically located in the jurisdiction of developing states, acquiescence to their sovereignty and aid concerns was necessary to achieve agreement. And since any funding and technology transfer would need to come from the wealthier states, some of their concerns needed to be met in order for them to agree to a convention. UNEP executive Mostafa Tolba personally helped broker the compromises among these positions that allowed the negotiations to be completed in time for the agreement to be signed in 1992 at the United Nations Conference on Environment and Development. The CBD entered into force in December 1993. Currently 188 states are parties to the agreement.[41] The United States, however, is not among them; it signed the agreement in 1993 but has not ratified it.

The resulting agreement outlines three basic objectives: conservation of biodiversity, the sustainable use of biological resources, and a "fair and equitable sharing" of the benefits of using genetic resources. It reiterates an increasingly prevalent principle of customary law that states have "the sovereign right to exploit their own resources pursuant to their own environmental policies," along with "the responsibility to ensure that activities within their jurisdiction or control do not cause damage to the environment of other states."[42]

The agreement is a framework convention that outlines a set of general principles that states commit themselves to, but contains little in the way of specific obligations. Parties are required to develop national biodiversity conservation strategies, to identify and monitor biodiversity, to establish protected areas and protect important biodiversity resources, and to develop a set of related, and vague, goals for protection. There are specific obligations for states to report to the COP on measures taken to implement the treaty and on the effectiveness of these measures.[43]

The treaty sets up an institutional structure as well. The organization is headquartered in Montreal, Canada, with UNEP fulfilling the secretariat role. The COP is the major decisionmaking body. It normally meets every two years, though it met in special session for the negotiation of the protocol. Most substantive decisions require a two-thirds majority vote, though every effort is made to gain consensus. The exceptions are that financial rules and any modification to the rules of procedure require consensus, and that procedural decisions require only a simple majority.[44]

The treaty creates a Subsidiary Body on Scientific, Technical, and Technological Advice (SBSTTA), which assesses biodiversity and the activities undertaken to protect it. It holds regular meetings and reports to the COP. Additional working groups can be created as needed, and at this point include working groups on indigenous knowledge, access to genetic resources and benefit sharing, review of implementation, and protected areas. These working groups are established by the COP.

The CBD designated the GEF (see Chapter 7) as its interim funding mechanism. In initial negotiations most developing states (except those in Latin America) resisted using the GEF as the funding mechanism for the agreement, fearing that developed states exerted too much control in the institution. Part of the agreement Tolba brokered included designating the GEF role as interim and pressuring the institution for reform to address the developing country concerns. In addition, the COP is responsible for determining the extent of contributions to the GEF for CBD funding. The GEF was made the permanent funding mechanism for the agreement in 1994, and a memorandum of understanding created between the two institutions. This agreement calls for a greater degree of CBD oversight of the GEF than would otherwise have transpired, including a periodic review of the GEF's effectiveness as the financial mechanism for the agreement.[45]

The CBD has ambitious goals but, as a framework convention, has little in the way of specific obligations or ways to ascertain its impact on biodiversity conservation. The underlying lack of knowledge about the vast array of species that make up the world's biodiversity is perhaps the major impediment to successful conservation.[46] If we cannot even describe most of the world's species, much less ascertain their health and ecosystemic role, it can be nearly impossible to determine if the convention is serving to protect them.

The Biosafety Protocol

The convention allowed for – in fact, the negotiations assumed – the creation of protocols that would provide more specific implementation obligations. The first of these, the Cartagena Protocol on Biosafety was signed in 2000 and entered into force in September 2003. Negotiations took place beginning in 1996 at the behest of developing states concerned about their ability to control the entry across their borders of genetically modified organisms (GMOs) that could harm natural biodiversity, supported by European states who generally favored tight controls on trade in GMOs. But the non-European agricultural exporting countries (including the United States, despite its lack of membership in the CBD) opposed restrictions on trade and held up agreement on the protocol.

The focus of this agreement is avoidance of possible harms from genetic modification of organisms. The protocol requires that states intending to export living modified organisms (LMOs; a subset of genetically modified organisms that are "capable of transferring or replicating genetic material")[47] assess the possible risks of this export and obtain informed consent from those states to which they are sending these products.

This process of seeking consent from importing states is called "advanced informed agreement" (AIA) under the protocol; while it is almost indistinguishable from the process of "prior informed consent" (PIC) under treaties relating to trade in toxic and hazardous substances (see Chapter 6), the negotiators of the Biosafety Protocol chose a new term, perhaps in an effort to avoid the connotation that LMOs were hazardous.[48]

Institutionally the most important aspect of the Biosafety Protocol is the creation of a Biosafety Clearing House through which information on potential risks of LMOs can be transmitted among parties. The clearing House is established under Article 20(1) of the protocol, to "assist governments and other users to fulfill their information-sharing obligations under the Biosafety Protocol." It exists in electronic form, accessible on the Internet, and provides information on national policies of member states, contact information for "national focal points" and "competent national authorities," as well as specific details of which states have, under advanced informed agreement, refused to allow the import of which specific LMOs.[49] This mechanism has not been operational for a sufficient amount of time to judge its effectiveness.

The Biosafety Protocol helps to augment the ability and authority of developing states to exercise sovereign control over what comes across their borders; as such, it is much more akin to the institutional processes to protect against transboundary hazards (as discussed in Chapter 6) than it is a direct protection of biodiversity. Both the convention and the protocol likely have at least a diffuse beneficial impact on conservation of species, ecosystems, and genetic material, though at this point their benefits come largely through research, increased awareness, and the development of the general principle that protecting biodiversity is a broader task than simply conserving individual species.

Quasi-governmental conservation institutions

In the area of species and nature conservation, much of the institutional activity to monitor, evaluate, and research the status of species or the behavior of actors takes place outside of intergovernmental institutions, in organizations that have some governmental involvement and some involvement of non-governmental actors. In many cases these organizations were the progenitors of the intergovernmental institutions described above.

The World Conservation Union

The World Conservation Union began in 1948 as the International Union for the Protection of Nature. It was created out of a meeting called in France by UNESCO along with the government of France and the Swiss League for the Protection of Nature. In 1956 the organization changed its name to the International Union for the Conservation of Nature and Natural Resources (IUCN). While keeping the same acronym (and officially the full version of the name), it changed the name it uses more generally again in 1990 to the World Conservation Union.

It is a hybrid organization, with membership of 82 states, 111 government agencies, at least 800 NGOs, and approximately 10,000 individual scientists.[50] It serves a variety of functions in the process of international conservation of species and ecosystems. Its complex membership means that it sometimes acts as an intergovernmental organization and sometimes as a non-governmental organization, though it is really a combination of both; more than anything its role is as a scientific (and legal) advisory institution.

Originally the organization chose Brussels for its headquarters, but it moved to Gland, Switzerland, in 1961. Every four years the organization holds a World Conservation Congress, where decisions are made on the work program of the organization. This meeting of the full membership also elects a 32-member council, which meets once or twice a year to conduct IUCN business, including setting priorities for the organization. The organization also maintains six standing commissions of experts that work on the implementation of IUCN priorities and give advice beyond the organization.

The Species Survival Commission (SSC), originally named the Survival Service Commission, is one of the six task forces of the IUCN. It was established in 1949 as a volunteer network of members around the world that work in more than 120 smaller task forces pertaining to specific species or habitats. Since 1966 the SSC has compiled the Red List of Threatened Species, generally acknowledged to be the most complete list of the status of the world's threatened plants and animals.[51] The list categorizes more than 75,000 species as extinct,

extinct in the wild, critically endangered, endangered, vulnerable, near threatened, or least of concern (those that are not considered to be threatened), and also indicates where there is insufficient information to make a conclusion about status ("data deficient") or where a species has not been evaluated. The organization uses five carefully elaborated criteria in making the determination of species status, which include population size and trajectory, geographic range and extent of geographic fragmentation, and population viability analysis. Some criticize this process, however, as being insufficiently transparent and overly politicized.[52] Others suggest that while the lists themselves are not problematic, they are used by others for purposes for which they are not intended and are not well suited, such as for setting priorities in allocating limited resources for conservation. These lists tend to overrepresent some types of species (large mammals) and underrepresent others (insects and fungi). And it is argued that level of extinction threat should not be the primary focus of conservation plans.[53]

One of the most important roles of the IUCN has been in working on the negotiation of international conservation agreements; doing so was one if its charter objectives. The IUCN Commission on Environmental Law is the main actor on behalf of the organization in this area. It played a central role in the drafting of the Ramsar Convention, the WHC, CITES, Part XII of the United Nations Convention on the Law of the Sea (on the high seas, including conservation), the CMS, and the CBD.[54]

It has other official roles with respect to international conservation agreements. For instance, the World Heritage Committee under the WHC is required to "cooperate with IUCN."[55] The IUCN cooperates closely with CITES and has observer status at CITES meetings. The organization also participates in the role of "expert advisor" to a number of the treaties on the Antarctic Treaty System and as a principal scientific advisor to the COP under the CBD.[56] Its most institutionalized role is in the Ramsar Convention, where the IUCN performs secretariat functions.[57]

The IUCN also works with the WWF (itself an offshoot organization, founded by IUCN members but entirely non-governmental) in the organization TRAFFIC, which monitors trade in endangered species. This organization was founded in 1976 to "ensure that trade in wild plants and animals is not a threat to the conservation of nature." It was designed from the beginning to help collect information useful for the implementation of CITES, though its purview has since expanded and it issues reports on species trade more broadly.[58]

The World Conservation Monitoring Centre

The World Conservation Monitoring Centre (WCMC) was founded by the IUCN in 1979 to "support international programs for conservation and sustainable development through the provision of reliable scientific data."[59] A restructuring in 1988 added the WWF and UNEP as partners, and in 2000 the WCMC was subsumed entirely under UNEP.[60] It currently maintains a number of databases relevant to protection of endangered species, including the Species Database (with information on conservation status of species) and the CITES Trade Database (with information on trade from annual reports of CITES members). It also manages species databases for the EU Wildlife Trade Regulation and the Convention on Migratory Species, and helps with assessment of implementation for the CBD. Collectively these institutions serve as information sources outside of the specific treaty institutions described earlier in this chapter. As such, they expand the sources of knowledge available and are able to provide information in a way that is less directly tied to the regulatory process.

Cross-institution linkages

There is a fairly high degree of overlap across some of the institutions designed to protect specific endangered species. CITES and the CMS regulate a number of the same species (and both include whale species also regulated under the International Convention for the Regulation of Whaling). The protected areas and ecosystems protected by Ramsar and the WHC contribute to the conservation of biodiversity (and, in the case of the WHC, are sometimes listed for their contribution to that goal). Any agreement that results in greater space left aside for conservation will likely have a positive result for the individual species that live there. The same advisory institutions (the WCMC, TRAFFIC, and the IUCN) provide data to the range of species and conservation agreements.

There is some cooperation among secretariats of the overlapping agreements. In the late 1990s the CMS secretariat and those of the CBD and Ramsar negotiated memoranda of cooperation,[61] and CITES and the CBD have also negotiated a memorandum of understanding that involves joint studies.[62] Occasionally the CBD, CITES, the CMS, Ramsar, and the WHC appear as five points on a circle in an icon that the individual organizations use on their websites, indicating that the organizations are at least aware of the interconnectedness of their mandates.

Recently the multiple conservation organizations have included in their activities a shared focus on a commitment from the 2002 WSSD to achieve "by 2010 a significant reduction of the current rate of loss of biological diversity."[63] This concept came originally from the Conference of the Parties to the CBD.[64] The CBD has addressed this goal through encouraging states to set national and regional targets. The SBSTTA has held a number of meetings to create indicators for achieving this goal, and held a meeting in 2003 on this goal. Both the CMS and CITES have invoked the 2010 date as an organizing principle for their activities, with the CMS evincing a strong commitment to the project as of its eighth COP in 2005.

The UNEP connection across these institutions helps the coordination of goals. The UNEP executive director mentioned the 2010 target in speeches before COPs for both CITES and the CMS. Ultimately, then, the coordination that happens across institutions focused on different aspects of species and biodiversity conservation happens because of actors involved in more than one organization. Sometimes it is individual scientists or representatives of governments who attend COP meetings for more than one conservation institution, and in other cases it is the fact that UNEP plays the secretariat role for the most important of the conservation institutions. The level of actual coordination is low, however.

Conclusions

Institutions attempting to protect endangered species or conserve ecosystems or biodiversity face myriad difficulties. The underlying uncertainty about the health of species populations and the functioning of ecosystems means that it is hard to ascertain how threatened a species is or how well it is being protected. Many opportunities exist for non-state actors to circumvent existing treaties: border agents with little conservation experience protecting lengthy borders cannot hope to prevent CITES-protected species from being traded internationally by poachers sufficiently motivated by profit. Species migrating internationally can be harmed in numerous ways across multiple states and oceans by individual actors with different motivations for harming them. That the CMS, and especially CITES, has had some successes in protecting some species is a testament to the potential for international institutions to use research to demonstrate the vulnerability and importance of species, and to persuade people to protect them.

The move towards concern about biodiversity more generally reflects a clearer understanding of the importance of protecting a broader range of species and, most importantly, the ecosystems in which they exist. This approach only increases the complexity of the issue of concern. The CBD is sufficiently vague that its effects initially are likely to be diffuse, involving increased understanding and awareness of the problem of biodiversity but little direct inducement to protect ecosystems from human encroachment.

The issue area is thus marked by multiple institutions all facing difficult tasks and with different approaches to conservation. It may be that overlapping institutions provide conflicting advice and divide time and resources, increasing the difficulty of conservation. Or it may be that individual species or ecosystems stand a greater chance of successful protection because they are protected in different ways under different institutional structures. Or both.

Notes

1 IUCN Species Survival Commission, *Red List of Threatened Species* (Washington, D.C.: Island Press, 2004).
2 Peter Singer, *Animal Liberation* (New York: Avon Books, 1990).
3 Daniel Francis, *A History of World Whaling* (Ontario: Viking, 1990), 208–10.
4 Peter H. Sand, "Whither CITES? The Evolution of a Treaty Regime in the Borderland of Trade and Environment," *European Journal of International Law* 8(1) (1997), 32–33.
5 Kathleen Rogers and James Moore, "Revitalizing the Convention on Nature Protection and Wild Life Preservation in the Western Hemisphere: Might Awakening a Visionary but 'Sleeping' Treaty Be the Key to Preserving Biodiversity and Threatened Natural Areas in the Americas?," *Harvard International Law Journal* 36(2) (Spring 1995), 467.
6 United Nations Conference on the Human Environment, Action Plan for the Human Environment, Recommendation 99(3) (1972).
7 Sand, "Whither CITES," 6.
8 CITES, Articles X, XI.
9 Pamela S. Chasek, David L. Downie, and Janet Welsh Brown, *Global Environmental Politics*, 4th edn. (Boulder: Westview Press),152.
10 Chasek, Downie, and Brown, *Global Environmental Politics*, 152.
11 Chasek, Downie, and Brown, *Global Environmental Politics*, 152.
12 CITES, Article XV.
13 CITES Conference Resolution 2.1, 30 March 1979.
14 D.S. Favrie, *International Trade in Endangered Species: A Guide to CITES* (Dordrecht: Martinus Nijhoff, 1989).
15 Edith Brown Weiss, "The Five International Treaties: A Living History," in Edith Brown Weiss and Harold Jacobson, eds., *Engaging Countries: Strengthening Compliance with International Environmental Accords* (Cambridge, Mass.: MIT Press, 1998), 112.
16 Sands, "Whither CITES," 10.

17 Elizabeth R. DeSombre, *Domestic Sources of International Environmental Policy: Industry, Environmentalists, and U.S. Power* (Cambridge, Mass.: MIT Press, 2000), 173–78.
18 Chasek, Downie, and Brown, *Global Environmental Politics*, 153–55.
19 Barry Kent MacKay, "Legal Elephant Ivory Sales Encourage Poaching," *Toronto Star* (8 August 1999).
20 IUCN African Elephant Specialist Group, *African Elephant Status Report 2002* (Gland: IUCN, 2002).
21 Sands, "Whither CITES," 12.
22 W.C. Burns, "CITES and the Regulation of International Trade in Endangered Species of Flora: A Critical Appraisal," *Dickinson Journal of International Law* 8(2) (1990), 203–33.
23 Sand, "Whither CITES," 54.
24 Richard Caddell, "International Law and the Protection of Migratory Wildlife: An Appraisal of Twenty-Five Years of the Bonn Convention," *Colorado Journal of International Law and Policy* 16 (Winter 2005), 113–56.
25 CMS Secretariat, "25 Years of Journeys: A Special Report to Mark the Silver Anniversary of the Bonn Convention on Migratory Species (1979–2004)," available at http://www.cms.int/news/PRESS/nwPR{2004/25}th_Anniversary/25th_A_CMS_mainpage.htm.
26 CMS Appendix I, as most recently amended in 2002; available at http://www.cms.int/documents/appendix/cms_app1.htm.
27 CMS Appendix II, as most recently amended in 2002; available at http://www.cms.int/documents/appendix/cms_app2.htm.
28 IISD, "8th Conference of the Parties to the Convention on the Conservation of Migratory Species of Wild Animals – Summary and Analysis," *Earth Negotiations Bulletin*, 18(27) (28 November 2005).
29 Clare Shine, "Selected Agreements Concluded Pursuant to the Convention on the Conservation of Migratory Species of Wild Animals," in Dinah Shelton, ed., *Commitment and Compliance: The Role of Non-Binding Norms in the International Legal System* (Oxford: Oxford University Press, 2000), 221–22.
30 CMS, Articles VII and XI.
31 IISD, "Summary of the Sixth Conference of the Parties to the Convention on Migratory Species and Related Meetings: 4–16 November 1999," *Earth Negotiations Bulletin* 18(11) (19 November 1999), 2.
32 CMS Secretariat, "Wadden Seals," available at http://www.cms.int/species/wadden_seals/sea_bkrd.htm
33 John Lanchberry, "Ramsar Convention," in Andrew S. Goudie, ed., *Encyclopedia of Global Change, vol. 2* (Oxford: Oxford University Press, 2002), 289–90.
34 Convention on Wetlands of International Importance Especially as Waterfowl Habitat (hereafter Ramsar Convention), Article 2.
35 Ramsar Convention, Article 6.
36 Ramsar Secretariat, "About the Convention on Wetlands" (2005), available at http://www.ramsar.org/index_about_ramsar.htm.
37 World Heritage Convention Secretariat, "States Parties," available at http://whc.unesco.org/en/statesparties/.
38 World Heritage Convention Secretariat, "World Heritage in Danger," available at http://whc.unesco.org/pg.cfm?cid = 158.

39 Fiona McConnell, *The Biodiversity Convention: A Negotiating History* (London: Kluwer Law International, 1996), 5.
40 Marian A.L. Miller, *The Third World in Global Environmental Politics* (Boulder: Lynne Rienner Publishers, 1995), 118–21.
41 CBD Secretariat, "Parties to the Convention on Biological Diversity," available at http://www.biodiv.org/world/parties.asp.
42 CBD, Articles 1 and 3.
43 CBD, Articles, 6, 7, 8, and 26.
44 CBD Secretariat, "Rules of Procedure for Meetings of the Conference of the Parties to the Convention on Biological Diversity," available at http://www.biodiv.org/convention/rules.shtml.
45 CBD Decision III/8 1994.
46 Peter H. Raven and Jeffrey A. McNeely, "Biological Extinction: Its Scope and Meaning for Us," in Lakshman D. Guruswamy and Jeffrey A. McNeely, eds., *Protection of Global Biodiversity: Converging Strategies* (Durahm, N.C.: Duke University Press, 1998), 15.
47 Cartagena Protocol on Biosafety, Articles 3(g) and (h).
48 Eric Schoonejans, "Advanced Informed Agreement Procedures," in Christoph Bail, Robert Falkner, and Helen Marquard, eds., *The Cartegena Protocol on Biosafety* (London: Earthscan, 2002), 299–320.
49 CBD Secretariat, "Biosafety Clearing House: Welcome to the Central Portal," available at http://bch.biodiv.org/default.aspx.
50 IUCN, "IUCN Overview," available at http://www.iucn.org/en/about.
51 Peter-John Meynell, "Use of IUCN Red Listing Process as a Basis for Assessing Biodiversity Threats and Impacts in Environmental Impact Assessment," *Impact Assessment and Project Appraisal* 23(1) (2005), 65–72.
52 N. Mrosovsky, "Commentary: IUCN's Credibility Critically Endangered," *Nature* 389 (2 October 1997), 436.
53 Hugh P. Possingham, Sandy J. Andelman, Mark A Burgman, Rodrigo A. Medellín, Larry L. Master, and David A. Keith, "Limits to the Use of Threatened Species Lists," *Trends in Ecology & Evolution* 17(11) (2002), 503–7.
54 Nicholas A. Robinson, "IUCN as Catalyst for a Law of the Biosphere: Acting Globally and Locally," *Environmental Law* 35 (2005), 249–310.
55 WHC, Article 13(7).
56 Robinson, "IUCN as Catalyst for a Law of the Biosphere," 303.
57 Ramsar Convention (1971), Article 8.
58 TRAFFIC, "About TRAFFIC," available at http://www.traffic.org/about/.
59 Robin A. Pellew, "The World Conservation Monitoring Center (WCMC): What It Is and What It Does," *Environmental Conservation* 17(2) (1990), 179–80.
60 UNEP, "Vision & Mission: UNEP–WCMC's Strategic Plan 2003/2004," www.unep-wcmc.org/aboutWCMC/ strategic_report/WCMC_Strat_Plan.pdf.
61 Shine, "Selected Agreements Concluded Pursuant to the Convention on the Conservation of Migratory Species of Wild Animals," 201.
62 Rosie Clooney, "CITES and the CBD: Tensions and Synergies," *Review of European Community and International Environmental Law* 10 (3) (November 2001), 260.
63 Johannesburg Plan of Implementation, Section IV (44).
64 CBD Decision VI/6, 2002.

4 Ocean commons

Global governance by maritime institutions has taken two different tacks over the past century, as represented by the institutions examined in this chapter. One approach began with a focus on the legal issues pertaining to international shipping. For centuries, or perhaps even millennia, shipping has been the main way that goods have been transported internationally. Even now, 95 percent of all international trade as measured by weight and two-thirds as measured by volume is transported on the ocean by ships.[1] Since the high seas do not belong to any sovereign state, rules about conduct on the open ocean can only be implemented by international agreement. Initial efforts to govern ocean spaces involved issues of liability and salvage rights at sea, followed by rules on assistance to ships on the high seas. These evolved over time into agreements to increase the level of safety on ships, with an increasing concern (especially in the wake of the Titanic disaster) for those who work or travel on them. The International Maritime Organization (IMO) is the international institution that addresses these issues.

The second approach involved attention to the resources of the ocean. Beginning in the 1970s, with an increase in global concern about environmental damage, the focus shifted to the prevention and mitigation of ocean pollution. In addition to, and intersecting with, existing regulatory institutions under the IMO are those created by the 1982 United Nations Convention on the Law of the Sea (UNCLOS) and occasioned by the international legal changes stemming from it. Fisheries are another important ocean resource. Collective action to protect fisheries began in earnest by the mid-20th century, with another wave of fisheries organizations created in the 1980s. These institutions are numerous and narrowly focused, and, though they have had difficulty preventing global overfishing, they have evolved to address emerging governance issues.

International Maritime Organization

The current institution with the most direct responsibility for ocean governance is the IMO, which represents the culmination of a series of efforts to govern maritime activities, specifically related to shipping. Its earliest precursor was the Comité Maritime International, created in 1897 in Belgium with participation by seven other maritime states. It addressed legal issues related to merchant shipping, via 19 conferences held between 1897 and 1937.[2] It was involved in drafting a number of international agreements with respect to safety and salvage at sea, including the first version of the Convention for the Safety of Life at Sea (SOLAS, 1914), which has been modified and updated periodically since then and remains in force. This organization still exists but as an international NGO.[3]

During World War I the Allied Maritime Transport Council, which operated between 1917 and 1919, was created to help with the logistics of transporting U.S. troops across the Atlantic Ocean and ensuring the continuation of trade and necessary military uses of shipping during the war. Also important shortly thereafter in maritime governance was the League of Nations' Organization for Communications and Transit, which operated between 1921 and 1946. This organization was created partly to fulfill the mandates of the Treaty of Versailles that required Germany to adhere to any conventions "regarding the international regime of transit, waterways, ports or railways" approved by the League of Nations.[4] Important effects of this organization included the recognition of the right of landlocked states to have merchant fleets and the elaboration of the principle that ships should be treated equally in maritime ports, regardless of flag. It also began the process of regularizing the measurement of ship tonnage.

Another institution with responsibility for coordinating shipping was created by the Allies during World War II. In the summer of 1944 eight allied states (Belgium, Canada, Greece, the Netherlands, Norway, Poland, the United Kingdom, and the United States, along with unofficial representation from Denmark and the French Committee of National Liberation) discussed the coordination of shipping during the ending stages of the war and thereafter. These discussions led to the creation of the United Maritime Authority as the war was concluded, which operated in 1945 and 1946.[5] This organization attempted to manage the transition between wartime and peacetime shipping operations.

The United Maritime Authority was designed to end six months after the official suspension of hostilities in the war. Before it ceased operating it recommended that the new United Nations organization establish an interim consultative council to take up its duties. The first of these successor organizations, the United Maritime Consultative Council, operated briefly, beginning in March of 1946. The Economic and Social Council of the United Nations created another interim organization to fill this role, the Temporary Transport and Communications Commission, later that year. This commission began by examining existing international institutions pertaining to maritime issues, and concluded that there were none that could meet the needs of international coordination. It recommended to ECOSOC that a permanent commission be established, and the United Nations pursued conversations with the United Maritime Consultative Council, which supported (and had already contemplated) the creation of such an organization and recommended to its member states that such an organization be created through the United Nations.[6]

Negotiations to create this permanent organization, the Intergovernmental Maritime Consultative Organization, took place in 1948. Several initial disagreements in the drafting negotiations involved the scope of the new organization: whether shipping issues should be addressed by UN commissions or in a separate UN organization, and whether the mandate would be to address narrow technical issues pertaining to shipping or would include broader commercial issues as well. The eventual agreement created a broad and independent organization that can address any shipping issues referred to it by the United Nations or its specialized agencies. The organization only came into being, however, with the entry into force of its founding convention, which took another decade. The cooperative environment at the end of the war had subsided as business returned to normal, and states, and the shipping interests within them, were less willing to trust an international institution. Some states feared that the organization was too broad and others thought it was not sufficiently protective of the interests of the shipping industry; still others feared it would not focus on protecting those who worked on ships.[7] Nevertheless, by 1958 a sufficient number of states had ratified the agreement that it could enter into force.

The organization is headquartered in London, the central location for international shipping regulation. All states that are members of the United Nations may join, and others may apply to become members, which they can do with the approval of two-thirds of existing member states.[8] It is funded by assessed contributions from member states, based on the UN scale of assessments, with additional technical cooperation funding through additional (voluntary) donations. The size and structure of the IMO secretariat have not changed dramatically during the course of its existence, while the number of tasks it has taken on and the number of member states in the organization have increased dramatically.

The founding convention has been modified several times. The first modification came in 1977 when Article 2 of the original convention, which stated that "the functions of the Organization shall be consultative and advisory," was simply deleted,[9] indicating the view of the member states that the organization was (and should be) doing more than simply advising. The name of the organization was changed in 1982 (to the International Maritime Organization, or IMO) as a further reflection of this change in focus.

The primary decisionmaking body of the organization is the assembly, which meets every other year and includes all member states. The council undertakes the business of the organization when the assembly is not in session. It consists of 32 member states and meets at least twice a year. Other bodies within the organization include the Maritime Safety Committee (MSC), the Maritime Environment Protection Committee (MEPC) (and its subcommittees), a Legal Committee, and a Technical Cooperation Committee (TCC),[10] all as established in the convention that created the organization. Other committees (such as the Facilitation Committee) and subcommittees are created by the assembly as needed.

One of the main difficulties in IMO governance was a change in the practice of ship registration. Ships are registered in states and until the 20th century states would only register ships owned by their citizens. For regulatory purposes these ships are considered to belong to the state in which they register, and must follow all relevant domestic and international rules adopted by those states. Some states, as early as the 1920s, began to allow ship registration by non-nationals. Panama, Honduras, and Liberia were the first to register ships belonging to people from other countries, and lured ship registrations in part by promising that registered ships would not be held to strict regulatory standards. Shortly after World War II the growth in ship registration in open registry states (also known as "flags of convenience") increased dramatically.[11]

The phenomenon of open registration caused some initial controversy over governance of the IMO that has continued periodically, since representation in the organization and some of its committees was determined in part based on ship registration. For example, the composition of the MSC originally was to be 14 states with eight of those positions designated for representatives of the eight largest ship-owning nations.[12] By the time the agreement entered into force the growth in open registry shipping meant that Liberia and Panama were among the eight largest registries (at third and eighth respectively). These states attempted to claim their place on the MSC. Their bid was opposed by the traditional maritime states, however, and neither was elected to the commission. This dispute was eventually decided by the International Court of Justice the following year, in favor of Liberia and Panama.[13] Perhaps as a result, the MSC was expanded first to 16 members by the 1965 amendments (which entered into force in 1968) and then to the entire IMO membership by the 1974 amendments (which entered into force in 1978).[14]

The IMO undertakes two sorts of regulatory activities. First, acting through its committees and assembly, it issues codes (sometimes called guidelines) and recommendations to its members. Second, it sponsors intergovernmental conferences leading to negotiation of binding multilateral conventions on maritime matters, the implementation of which it then oversees.

The most important of the IMO recommendations are issued as codes, such as the Code of Practice for the safe unloading and loading of bulk carriers[15] or the International Safety Management Code (or ISM Code; officially called the Guidelines on Management for the Safe Operation of Ships and for Pollution Prevention).[16] While not legally binding, these codes represent IMO wisdom on how best to conduct operations. Most states implement these codes and other recommendations nationally. Often these codes provide specific guidelines on how to implement conventions, and sometimes the treaties themselves refer the responsibility for providing such guidelines to the IMO.

Sometimes, however, a code is created by amending an existing convention, as is the case for the International Ship and Port Facility Security (ISPS) Code, which was created as an amendment to the SOLAS Convention, in 2002. In these cases the codes are indeed legally binding on states that have ratified the relevant amendments. Other codes may be made legally binding by the assembly after they have been in operation for a while, as happened with the ISM Code in 1998.

The IMO also issues recommendations pertaining to matters that have not yet been negotiated internationally. These sometimes serve as forerunners to the negotiation of legally binding instruments or modifications of existing agreements. For example, the Recommendation on Basic Principles to be Observed in Keeping a National Watch came about because of studies performed in the wake of ship collisions. These recommendations were later incorporated into the International

Convention on Standards of Training, Certification, and Watchkeeping for Seafarers (STCW, 1978).

The primary regulatory activity undertaken by the IMO comes through the negotiation of international conventions, though technically these are simply intergovernmental negotiations that are convened by the IMO, rather than IMO regulations per se. The IMO then also serves at the secretariat for agreements negotiated in this way. The IMO currently oversees more than 50 international agreements and protocols pertaining to ships, plus additional amendments. While some of them, such as SOLAS, were pre-existing agreements that have been periodically updated under the auspices of the IMO, most have been negotiated since the organization came into being. Because these conventions are negotiated individually, each requires a separate process of ratification by states; not all IMO member states are bound by all IMO agreements.

Most IMO agreements have a double ratification threshold, in which a certain number of states accounting for a certain percentage of registered shipping tonnage must ratify an agreement for it to enter into force. For example, the International Convention for the Prevention of Pollution from Ships (MARPOL, 1973) required ratification by a minimum of 15 states that collectively accounted for at least 50 percent of the gross tonnage of the world's registered merchant shipping fleet.[17] That threshold was not met within the first several years after negotiation, so a protocol that modified the original agreement was created to assuage the concerns of potential member states by separating obligations for oil discharges from those relating to hazardous chemicals and adopting different requirements for new tankers versus those already in service. The convention and protocol eventually entered into force as MARPOL 73/78.

Even though members need not accept IMO-negotiated agreements, the organization has a high degree of participation in its conventions, including by the major shipping states. The states party to MARPOL now represent nearly 98 percent of the world's registered tonnage. The same is true for the STCW and the International Convention on Load Lines (1966). Other agreements that have entered into force represent a lower percentage of registered tonnage among member states, such as the International Convention for Safe Containers (1972), whose members account for 62 percent of registered shipping. Some, such as the International Convention on Liability and Compensation for Damage in Connection with the Carriage of Hazardous and Noxious Substances by Sea (1996), have not met the minimum threshold to enter into force.[18]

The IMO classifies its agreements into three categories: safety, marine pollution, and liability and compensation, though some do not fit into this categorization. The organization's initial focus was safety, updating the SOLAS Convention, which is considered to be the centerpiece of modern efforts on maritime safety. The original version of the convention was created in 1914 in the wake of the Titanic disaster; it was renegotiated in 1929 and 1948, and by the IMO in 1960. After the 1960 version proved difficult to amend in a timely manner, a substantially revised SOLAS agreement was negotiated under IMO auspices in 1974. It is the 1974 agreement that is the current operational version; it has been amended more than 35 times since then.[19]

The IMO also oversaw the negotiation of the STCW Convention in 1978, which standardized training and qualification requirements across states and allowed those who hired seafarers to be able to determine what training they needed to have undergone.[20] A similar agreement was negotiated in 1995 for personnel on fishing vessels.

The regulation of marine pollution has become one of the most important aspects of IMO governance. The organization itself sees the MARPOL as one of its most important accomplishments.[21] This agreement, which now mandates equipment standards that oil tankers must adopt in order to prevent operational discharge of oil, has fundamentally changed the way ships are built and has dramatically decreased the extent of oil pollution.[22] Later amendments added provisions requiring that double hulls be installed on newly built tankers as well as the eventual retrofit of older tankers,[23] in an effort to decrease the likelihood of accidental oil spills. The agreement also mandates that specified chemicals only be discharged at designated reception facilities, and forbids discharge under any conditions of these substances within 12 miles of land.[24] MARPOL has optional annexes that attempt to minimize pollution by sewage, garbage, and harmful packaged substances. A new annex, which entered into force in May 2005, limits air pollution (sulfur dioxide, nitrogen oxides, and ozone-depleting substances) from ships.[25]

Additional IMO agreements address aspects of oil pollution. Among these are provisions for coastal states to take emergency action "to prevent, mitigate, or eliminate danger to [their] coastline" when faced with the dangers of an oil spill nearby and the requirement that states create emergency response plans for use in case of oil spills.[26] Later agreements included the same measures for noxious and hazardous substances other than oil.[27]

The IMO oversees conventions that address other pollution issues as well. Most important among these is the Convention on the Prevention of Marine Pollution by Dumping of Wastes and Other Matter (1972), referred to as the London Dumping Convention or more recently simply the London Convention. Prior to this agreement it was common for states to dispose of municipal and industrial waste by dumping or incinerating it at sea. The London Convention prevents states from intentionally disposing at sea a set of wastes listed on a "blacklist" in the agreement and requires them to gain permits before disposing of other types of waste intentionally.[28] Amendments concern incineration of waste at sea and prohibit the dumping of low-level radioactive waste. A protocol negotiated in 1996 would replace the entire convention with an agreement that takes a more precautionary approach, requiring that all dumping be banned unless it can be demonstrated to cause no harm. This protocol has not yet entered into force. The IMO did not convene the negotiation of the original London Convention but was made the secretariat for it; in that role it was in charge of the negotiation of the 1996 protocol. The agreement has reasonably widespread membership but lacks important participation from coastal developing states, and the obligations for states to report on their dumping activities are often unmet. Nevertheless, the level of acceptance of the practice of dumping wastes into the ocean has decreased dramatically under this regime. More recently, the IMO has turned to the operational pollution created by anti-fouling systems[29] and ballast water.[30]

Efforts to address both safety and pollution have led to a focus as well on compensation for those who are victims of unsafe ships or oil spills, and on allocating responsibility for problems that arise. The IMO oversees a number of agreements that assess liability from different angles: some limit the extent of liability that ship owners may face; others create mandatory levels of compensation for victims of accidents or pollution.

Finally, several IMO agreements do not fit into any of these categories. The most important of these is the International Convention on Tonnage Measurement of Ships (1969), which standardized the way that the size of ships was measured around the world. This standard measurement now forms the basis for most of the world's information about, and regulations pertaining to, ships.

Criticisms of the IMO abound. There is concern over the mixed level of implementation of IMO conventions, even when states have legally adopted them. Though it is up to individual states to decide whether to adopt IMO-run agreements, the organization has not done much to persuade states to take on obligations. More importantly, once states have committed to following IMO rules the organization

Box 4.1 IMO conventions

Maritime safety

- International Convention for the Safety of Life at Sea (SOLAS), 1974
- International Convention on Load Lines (LL), 1966
- Special Trade Passenger Ships Agreement (STP), 1971
- Protocol on Space Requirements for Special Trade Passenger Ships, 1973
- Convention on the International Regulations for Preventing Collisions at Sea (COLREG), 1972
- International Convention for Safe Containers (CSC), 1972
- Convention on the International Maritime Satellite Organization (INMARSAT), 1976
- The Torremolinos International Convention for the Safety of Fishing Vessels (SFV), 1977
- International Convention on Standards of Training, Certification and Watchkeeping for Seafarers (STCW), 1978
- International Convention on Standards of Training, Certification and Watchkeeping for Fishing Vessel Personnel (STCW–F), 1995
- International Convention on Maritime Search and Rescue (SAR), 1979

Marine pollution

- International Convention for the Prevention of Pollution from Ships (1973), as modified by the Protocol of 1978 relating thereto (MARPOL 73/78)
- International Convention Relating to Intervention on the High Seas in Cases of Oil Pollution Casualties (INTERVENTION), 1969
- Convention on the Prevention of Marine Pollution by Dumping of Wastes and Other Matter (LDC), 1972
- International Convention on Oil Pollution Preparedness, Response and Cooperation (OPRC), 1990
- Protocol on Preparedness, Response and Cooperation to Pollution Incidents by Hazardous and Noxious Substances, 2000 (HNS Protocol)

- International Convention on the Control of Harmful Anti-Fouling Systems on Ships (AFS), 2001
- International Convention for the Control and Management of Ships' Ballast Water and Sediments, 2004

Liability and compensation

- International Convention on Civil Liability for Oil Pollution Damage (CLC), 1969
- International Convention on the Establishment of an International Fund for Compensation for Oil Pollution Damage (FUND), 1971
- Convention Relating to Civil Liability in the Field of Maritime Carriage of Nuclear Material (NUCLEAR), 1971
- Athens Convention Relating to the Carriage of Passengers and their Luggage by Sea (PAL), 1974
- Convention on Limitation of Liability for Maritime Claims (LLMC), 1976
- International Convention on Liability and Compensation for Damage in Connection with the Carriage of Hazardous and Noxious Substances by Sea (HNS), 1996
- International Convention on Civil Liability for Bunker Oil Pollution Damage, 2001

Other

- Convention on Facilitation of International Maritime Traffic (FAL), 1965
- International Convention on Tonnage Measurement of Ships (TONNAGE), 1969
- Convention for the Suppression of Unlawful Acts Against the Safety of Maritime Navigation (SUA), 1988
- International Convention on Salvage (SALVAGE), 1989

Source: IMO, "List of Conventions," available at http://www.imo.org/home.asp.

does not do as much as some advocate to ensure that they are following the rules they have accepted.[31] The organization is also less transparent than many other international environmental institutions, in terms of its control over access to information about its conventions and the behavior of member states.

Governance difficulties in the IMO come from the distribution of various types of power and influence across member states. The traditional European and North American maritime states (who are, not coincidentally, the most powerful states in the international system generally) have less influence in the IMO than originally envisioned, because of the growth in flag-of-convenience ship registration, most of which takes place in developing states. A tension thus exists in the system between states generally powerful internationally that do not have as much structural influence and those states that are centrally important in determining international ship standards but do not otherwise have much international influence.

The most important impediments to strong governance on shipping issues, however, are domestic. Shipping is of central importance to most economies, and cheap shipping (without a high degree of external regulation) is of interest to the most powerful constituencies within these states. International trade depends on the availability of cheap shipping, which in turn depends on an international regulatory system that does not demand too many costly standards for ships. Because of the role of shipping in the economies of states, they are loath to do too much to antagonize these constituencies, leading to less regulation and oversight than governments initially call for.

Nevertheless, there is much that the IMO has done well. An external review of the organization conducted in 2001 pointed to successes in passing increasingly strict regulations in the wake of major accidents, in the ability of the organization to adapt to an increasing international focus on environmental issues, and in a decreasing amount of oil pollution from tankers due to both accidents and other causes.[32]

The fact that one institution addresses different types of issues pertaining to ships is a major advantage of the IMO framework. These seemingly disparate issues are in fact linked. Agreements to provide for increased safety on ships decrease the likelihood that ships will cause environmental disasters. Design features to prevent pollution may have related impacts for the people who work on ships. The issues of compensation and liability are in direct response to problems with safety and pollution that other IMO agreements address. Because the IMO is one forum in which many of these issues can be addressed simultaneously, the interconnections can be accounted for. The IMO has served as a central mechanism for regulatory efforts pertaining to marine pollution and other regulations, and has played this coordinating role reasonably successfully.

The United Nations Convention on the Law of the Sea

The United Nations Convention on the Law of the Sea was negotiated in the Third United Nations Conference on the Law of the Sea (UNCLOS III; the treaty is often simply referred to as UNCLOS). Discussions began in the General Assembly's Committee on Peaceful Uses of the Seabed in the late 1960s, after Arvid Pardo of Malta brought up the issue of access to deep-seabed resources. Increasing pressure came from the United Nations General Assembly more broadly for a universal law of the sea in the wake of the 1972 Stockholm Conference, and negotiations began in 1973. The completed draft emerged, finally, in 1982. As the title suggests, it was not the first effort to create an overarching governance structure for the oceans, even under the United Nations. The First and Second United Nations Conferences on the Law of the Sea were convened in 1958 and 1960. The first of these produced four international agreements addressing territorial seas, the high seas, fishing on the high seas, and the continental shelf, though the environmental provisions in these were weak or non-existent. The second conference attempted but failed to delineate the extent of the territorial sea.

The goal of UNCLOS was to create one legal instrument in which all peacetime ocean regulations could be consolidated, to prevent contradictions among or gaps between existing international laws pertaining to the oceans. The scope of the 1982 agreement is large: its 320 articles and nine annexes attempt to cover all aspects of ocean regulation. Rather than provide specific substantive obligations, the agreement primarily creates a framework for governance, indicating which entities have authority over which areas. It is most widely known for its role in creating the jurisdictional area of the Exclusive Economic Zone (EEZ), an area extending 200 nautical miles out from a state's coastline in which the state may control access to resources. This process put more than 35 percent of ocean spaces under some form of national jurisdiction.[33] It also redefined the legal nature of the continental shelf and the territorial sea. States were given complete sovereign control over the resources of the natural waters extending 12 miles out (the previously accepted distance was three miles) from their coasts while still allowing a right of innocent passage by ships in such territorial waters,[34] and over the "sea-bed and subsoil" that constitute "the natural prolongation of [their] land territory to the outer edge of the continental margin," which can be delineated at 200 miles from shore or further if the continental margin can be shown to extend that far. If states choose to exploit resources of the continental shelf beyond 200 miles from their coasts they must, after five years of exploitation, pay a small but increasing percentage of their revenue to an international fund (under the International Seabed Authority, see p. 81, see below) that will redistribute the wealth to other parties to the convention, taking special consideration of the needs of developing states.[35]

The obligations that UNCLOS creates within specific ocean issues are normative and often vague, and generally require that states participate in existing institutional structures for governance. On ocean pollution, for example, UNCLOS mandates that states reduce and control pollution. States must take any necessary measures to "prevent, reduce and control pollution of the marine environment from any source" and must ensure that "activities under their jurisdiction or control are so conducted as not to cause damage by pollution to other states." States must generally monitor the risks and effects of pollution, and publish available data from this monitoring process. Coastal and port states are given new authority to enforce rules against polluting vessels.[36]

UNCLOS does, however, create a number of new institutional structures. Among these are the International Seabed Authority (ISA) and the International Tribunal for the Law of the Sea (ITLOS). The ISA was created to oversee any extraction of minerals from the deep seabed. This aspect of the law of the sea negotiation was among the most controversial and divisive. Developed countries favored a first-come, first-served principle of access to these resources. As the only seabed-mining entities with the technology to be able to conduct such mining operations in the near future, they wanted acceptance of their rights to do so commercially. Developing countries preferred a "common heritage" approach in which mineral exploitation would only be conducted through an international organization, in hopes such an arrangement would ensure that they would benefit from these resources.[37] The resulting arrangement represents a creative compromise between these two positions. The deep seabed is considered to be "common heritage" and UNCLOS creates a complicated set of procedures for making use of these resources, governed by the ISA.

The right of an UNCLOS party to explore or exploit the resources of an area in the deep seabed requires a contract from the ISA. A member state of UNCLOS (or a company sponsored by a member state) proposes two areas to explore. One of these is awarded to the company or state and the other is reserved for the ISA either to exploit on its own through its commercial entity, the Enterprise, or to be designated for mining by a developing country. Any entity conducting mining operations under this system must pay royalties to the ISA, which will "distribute the receipts equitably, taking into account the interests and needs of developing countries."[38]

The ISA itself is headquartered in Kingston, Jamaica. It held its first meeting in 1994 and became fully operational in 1996. It includes an assembly (made up of all members of the ISA, each of whom has one vote) and a council of 36 members elected for four-year terms. Members are elected within five different categories, to ensure that large consumers, large investors, land-based producers, and developing states (including those with special interests such as large populations or landlocked status) are represented. The council has the authority to decide issues of seabed exploration by supermajority (two-thirds or three-quarters) or consensus, depending on the specific issue.[39] The ISA also operates a Legal and Technical Commission and Finance Committee.

Also under the ISA is the Enterprise, the UNCLOS-created entity that is designed to undertake the actual exploitation of deep-seabed minerals. This is one of the most controversial elements of the agreement. As of 2006 the Enterprise had not yet been constituted and was not operating, with the ISA secretariat filling its operational functions until seabed mining begins.[40]

These provisions on the institutional oversight of mining and the extent to which they are designed to redistribute wealth internationally were the primary reasons given for the refusal of the United States to ratify the agreement. The controversy over these provisions led to the negotiation of an additional agreement, the Agreement Relating to the Implementation of Part XI of the United Nations Convention on the Law of the Sea of 10 December 1982 (1994). This agreement modifies a number of the procedures to be followed by the Authority set up under UNCLOS. It ensures U.S. representation in the council, and modifies several aspects of voting and representation to increase the influence of the United States in decisionmaking in the ISA and the council. It also removes these bodies from choosing among mining applicants deemed to be qualified, instead allocating access by a first-come, first-served process. An UNCLOS requirement that companies engaged in mining be obligated to transfer technology to developing states and to the Enterprise was deemed by the Agreement to "not apply," in favor of a general duty of cooperation to ease the acquisition of such technology, and the parties are not required, as they would have been under

UNCLOS, to fund the activities of the Enterprise.[41] The Agreement entered into force in July 1996. The United States has signed, but as of 2006 had not ratified, this agreement.

The initial work of the ISA focused on organizational matters, including drafting a set of regulations for mineral exploration. In 1997 it began considering the first proposals from states for mineral exploration. The first contracts for 15-year exploration were signed in 2001. Seven entities were granted the first contracts: the governments of India and the Republic of Korea; a state-owned enterprise of the Russian Federation; research and development companies from China, Japan, and France; and a consortium of firms from Bulgaria, the Czech Republic, Poland, the Russian Federation, Slovakia, and Cuba.[42] Very little exploration has actually taken place, however, and thus far no mining of the approved sites. Mineral extraction has not yet become as economically viable as it was predicted to become when UNCLOS was under negotiation.

UNCLOS specifies that states are to settle disputes peacefully and offers them a choice of dispute settlement instruments. The most important of these are ITLOS, along with an arbitral tribunal, and a special technical arbitral tribunal. States are also allowed to make use of the International Court of Justice for the obligation they accept when joining UNCLOS to settle disputes by peaceful means. UNCLOS member states elect the 21 independent individuals who compose ITLOS. The tribunal began operations in 1996, headquartered in Hamburg, Germany, and as of early 2006 had decided 13 cases.[43]

In addition, UNCLOS reinforces existing institutions and the rules they have created. It refers in multiple locations to the necessity of joining existing organizations. It also refers to the necessity of establishing agreements and standards internationally to control such things as pollution from ships. UNCLOS designates a number of functions to the relevant "competent international organization,"[44] which most commentators interpret to be the IMO in the contexts in which it operates.[45] UNCLOS also makes repeated reference to "generally accepted international rules,"[46] which are generally interpreted as IMO rules. For instance, UNCLOS indicates that foreign ships exercising the right of innocent passage through another state's territorial sea must comply with "generally accepted international regulations relating to the prevention of collisions at sea,"[47] a reference to the only existing set of regulations under IMO's Convention on the International Regulations for Preventing Collisions at Sea (COLREG, 1972).

Moreover, the IMO is functionally given additional jurisdiction in some contexts, to approve rules that states themselves propose. Articles 41 and 53, for example, indicate that states designating sea lanes and similar measures can only do so with approval from "the competent international organization," interpreted as the IMO; the agreement doesn't mention what procedure the IMO should use for this approval process, thus giving a wide degree of autonomy to the institution. These provisions in UNCLOS have the effect of expanding IMO jurisdiction to states that have not ratified individual IMO conventions (but have ratified UNCLOS), since these obligations are accepted in UNCLOS as the relevant governing regulations for using the oceans.[48]

It took a long time for UNCLOS to gain a sufficient number of ratifications to become operational; it entered into force in November 1994, 12 years after its negotiation was complete and more than 20 years after negotiations began. Some important states, such as the United States, remain outside the agreement. Many of the provisions of UNCLOS, however, are viewed as evolving into customary law through their active use by states, and thus are considered to be binding on all states, regardless of ratification status. These include provisions pertaining to EEZs, territorial sea, rights to innocent passage, prevention of pollution, and others. Many states that are not UNCLOS members nevertheless follow most of its provisions.

Fisheries institutions

Institutional arrangements to conserve fisheries were among the earliest efforts to protect natural resources internationally. The Convention on North Sea Overfishing, for example, was negotiated in 1882 to harmonize domestic fishing regulations. Others, such as the Agreement for the Establishment of the Asia-Pacific Fishery Commission (1948) and the International Convention for the Northwest Atlantic Fisheries (1949), followed in the mid-20th century. This early focus is understandable: open ocean fisheries cannot be conserved except by international cooperation, since no one actually has jurisdiction over the oceans. Fisheries therefore represent the perfect instance of an open access resource that underpins Hardin's notion of the "tragedy of the commons."[49] These resources create their own incentive for management: if enough fish of a given species remain in the ocean, they will reproduce and thereby create new fish, and they do so on a reasonably short timeframe for natural resources. If fishers can successfully cooperate to ensure that sufficient numbers remain, they will be able to continue fishing indefinitely. Yet even with this incentive structure it has been difficult to manage international fisheries successfully.

Initially the resources of the sea seemed sufficiently inexhaustible that no one considered the need for international governance. That very abundance, however, led to a focus on how to harvest them more efficiently and in greater number. Technological advances made possible the use of factory ships that could stay out for more than a year and process their catches on board. At the same time the increasing availability of refrigeration, coupled with newly efficient forms of travel, meant that catches could be frozen and transported, relatively cheaply, over long distances. Ocean fish thus became a staple food for people in the interior of countries. The decreasing cost and increasing speed of transport also meant that fresh fish could be shipped long distances. Technology was also used in the service of finding and catching fish: first radar and then sonar were used to locate large schools of fish. Global positioning system (GPS) technology aided ships in navigation to fishing grounds. All of these contributed, along with the increasing use of driftnets and longline fishing techniques, to the alarming decline in the abundance of commercially harvested fish stocks.

Fishery institutions, often referred to as regional fishery management organizations (RFMOs), generally regulate fishing by concentrating on a region, a species, or some combination of the two. Most important are the institutions that set fishing policy for their member states, with decisions that restrict fishing seasons, locations, equipment, and species and amount of fish that can be caught. Most of these organizations share a number of similarities in their regulatory processes. Commissions are empowered to make annual regulatory decisions that change rules for states each year without the requirement that states ratify the new rules. In general these fishery commissions have scientific committees that conduct or gather research and make recommendations to the decisionmaking body about what a sustainable level of catch would be. This scientific process is separate from the actual political decisionmaking, however, and commissions frequently set catch limits higher than those suggested by their scientific bodies. Most – though not all – commissions are empowered to make their decisions by supermajority voting rather than by unanimity. For this reason, most also have an objections process, by which states can choose to opt out of a given regulation if they do so within a specified time period.

These processes combine to allow for rapid changes in regulations that can take account of new scientific information and the potential impacts of previous regulatory decisions. But they also allow for political factors (such as the interests states have in supporting their domestic fishers) to trump scientific ones in the setting of quotas, and allow for some member states to occasionally operate outside the regulatory system.

There are important differences across commissions, as well. One major difference is whether a commission sets a collective global quota or divides its quotas by state. A global quota, used in many of the earliest commissions like those regulating whales and Pacific tuna, often has the unintended consequence of causing a "race" among states to catch the regulated species, creating an incentive for overcapitalization of fishing vessels (to enable more successful catching). This investment can then make it difficult for fishers to exit the fishery even when fishing is not economically productive, because they must repay the loans they took out to get equipment so they could compete for fish.[50]

The only geographically global fishery commission regulates the catching of whales – mammals rather than fish, but regulated as a fishery – worldwide. The International Whaling Commission (IWC) was formed in 1946 to ensure the sustainable harvesting of whales to enable "the orderly development of the whaling industry."[51] For decades quotas were set higher than the whale population estimates justified, whaling states periodically used a legal "objections" procedure to opt out of regulations they did not wish to implement, a global quota created an incentive for overcapitalization as individual vessels attempted to catch a greater percentage of the quota, and the Soviet Union engaged in systematic state-sponsored non-compliance. Whale stocks were decimated. The commission voted to impose a moratorium on commercial whaling beginning in 1986. This moratorium, still in place, remains controversial. Some whale stocks have recovered and Japan, Iceland, and Norway (the latter of which lodged an objection to the original moratorium and so is allowed to conduct commercial whaling under the agreement) have attempted for years to garner enough votes to lift the moratorium. Other states argue that stocks have not recovered sufficiently or that whale hunting should not be allowed for ethical reasons.

Some commissions focus on a species or a set of related species in a specific geographic range. The most prevalent are regional organizations for the management of tuna and tuna-like species (such as swordfish and billfish). The Inter-American Tropical Tuna Commission (IATTC), created in 1959, addresses tuna management in the eastern Pacific Ocean. It implemented catch quotas until the 1980s, when much of its regulatory area was brought within state-controlled EEZs after the signing of UNCLOS. Since then it has continued to conduct research and has worked on policies to decrease bycatch of dolphins. The International Commission for the Conservation of Atlantic Tunas (ICCAT) has regulated the catches of tuna (most prominently bluefin tuna) and tuna-like species in the Atlantic since 1969. Quotas have regularly been set higher than scientists advised, and stocks have generally been declining. Two more recent geographically based tuna commissions are the Indian Ocean Tuna Commission (IOTC), established in 1993, and the Commission for the Conservation of Southern Bluefin Tuna (CCSBT), established in 1994.

There are several organizations to manage salmon as well. This species is subject to regulatory challenges, because salmon exist for part of their lifecycle in rivers within state jurisdiction, in which the fish are born and return to spawn. The fish therefore have a connection to an individual country. Yet adult salmon travel to the open ocean, where they may be caught without regard to their country of origin. In addition to bilateral salmon commissions, not discussed here, the North Atlantic Salmon Conservation Organization (NASCO) and the North Pacific Anadramous Fish Commission (NPAFC) address management of salmon that migrate outside of the EEZs in the geographic areas they regulate. One of the major problems these commissions face, however, is that they are only empowered to set catch limits on the open ocean and can do little to mandate conservation and habitat protection in the locations where the salmon reproduce and mature.[52] While this limitation is not surprising, given sovereignty concerns, it does limit the potential effectiveness of institutions protecting anadramous fish.

Other RFMOs are organized by geographic region and focus on the myriad fish species within a given region. The Northeast Atlantic Fisheries Commission (NEAFC), the General Fisheries Commission for the Mediterranean (GFCM), the West and Central Pacific Fisheries Commission (WCPFC), the International Baltic Sea Fisheries Commission (IBSFC), and the Northwest Atlantic Fisheries Organization (NAFO) manage the range of relevant fish stocks in their respective regions.

One such regional commission, the Commission for the Conservation of Antarctic Marine Living Resources (CCAMLR), regulates fishing in Antarctic waters. When created in 1982, the initial primary concern was potential overharvesting of krill, a species near the bottom of the food chain. Demersal fish species were also severely depleted. The collapse of the Soviet Union decreased the extent of krill harvesting and other fishing in the region, and allowed stocks to recover somewhat. Currently the main species of concern is Patagonian toothfish, which, in addition to being harvested by member states, is subject to illegal harvesting and fishing by ships registered in non-member states that are thereby not bound by the agreement. The most important regulatory aspect of CCAMLR is its intention to create regulations based on an "ecosystem approach," setting catch limits while taking into consideration the overall functioning and interaction of the ecosystem.[53] In practice, however, the regulatory process does not look dramatically different than in other fishery commissions.

In addition to these management organizations, there is an even greater number of fisheries organizations that provide scientific research and management advice to member states but do not actually determine fishing regulations. These include such organizations as the Regional Fisheries Advisory Committee for the Southwest Atlantic and the South Pacific Forum Fisheries Agency, among many others.[54]

Yet another group of international fisheries institutions conducts scientific research and provides information internationally but does not give advice about how to manage specific fisheries. Several of these institutions operate under the UN FAO. The Advisory Committee on Fishery Research (ACFR), established in 1961, is a small group of experts constituted under the FAO to advise its director-general on all aspects of fisheries.[55] The Coordinating Working Party on Fisheries Statistics works with fisheries data gathered across fisheries organizations, disseminates this information and gives advice on the coordination of data gathering.[56] Other organizations operate outside of the United Nations. The International Council for the Exploration of the Sea (ICES), founded in 1902, coordinates fishery research in the North Atlantic and adjacent seas. It is headquartered in Denmark and operates through more than 100 working groups and other symposia with the participation of 1600 scientists.[57] The North Pacific Marine Science Organization (PICES) was created in 1990 to serve as a Pacific version of ICES.[58]

The profusion of fishery conservation organizations has some benefits: each organization can focus on the specific needs of the geographic area and species it manages. But the intersection of these institutions causes problems as well. Conservation measures passed in one RFMO can impact fishing behavior in other fisheries. Those fishing for one species in a given geographic area, for example, may move to a different ocean during closed seasons or when they have reached their quota. One of the causes of overfishing in the Atlantic tuna fishery in the 1970s was the increasingly strict regulation in the Pacific tuna fishery, after which Pacific fishing vessels chose to fish in

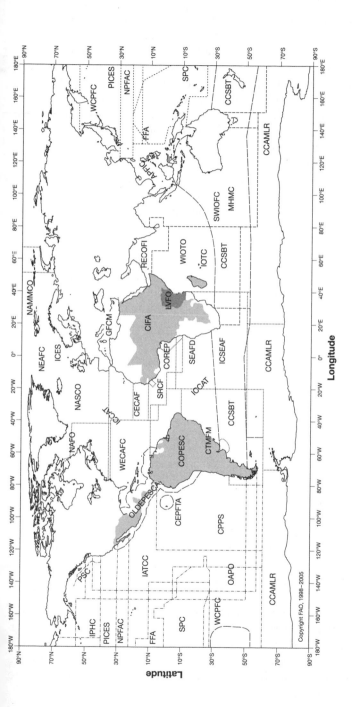

Figure 4.1 The geographic focus of international fishery commissions

the Atlantic instead.[59] Fisheries commissions have begun to coordinate some of their measures with these behaviors in mind.

UNCLOS also impacts the regulation of high-seas fisheries and the institutions that govern it, in several ways. First, it changed the rules on what constituted the high seas. Though some, principally Latin American, states had unilaterally declared management authority (or even outright ownership) of the sea hundreds of miles from their coastlines beginning in the 1950s, this principle was contested internationally and not adopted in a uniform format. UNCLOS endorsed the idea of an "exclusive economic zone" (EEZ) extending 200 miles from the coastline of a state. In this area states could not prevent innocent passage of ships, but they did gain the legal ability unilaterally to manage the natural resources found there. Since up to 90 percent of ocean fish caught are found within 200 miles of coasts,[60] this change had a major impact on fisheries management.

Several different effects were generated by this major change. The first was the impact on fisheries themselves. One underlying argument in favor of this change from a management perspective was that it would essentially privatize (in Hardin's terminology) the management of certain parts of the ocean; if states had unilateral control over resources there, they would gain an incentive to manage these resources well. Most commentators, however, regard the period immediately after the creation of EEZs as disastrous for fisheries management. What happened?

The response by many state governments when given control of this new expanse of marine wealth was to exploit it as fully as possible. Governments subsidized the building of more ships and created other incentives to bring their citizens into the fishing industry. At the same time, the new EEZ system replaced one version of the tragedy of the commons on the international scale with a similar structure domestically. What had previously been individual fishers from multiple countries competing for the same fish stock became multiple individuals licensed by one country competing for the same fish stock. The same incentive to use expensive technology to increase efficiency, combined with domestic subsidies in many states, created an overcapitalized domestic fishery within most EEZs, and dramatic depletion of fisheries within EEZs.[61]

The second type of impact from the creation of EEZs was on the institutions that governed international fisheries. Most had been created to govern fish caught anywhere, with the occasional exception of the (quite small) territorial sea. After UNCLOS, states with large EEZs demanded their right to make use of these resources and to determine the conditions under which others could. A number of long-standing fisheries management institutions had to be renegotiated to take account of the new international rules.[62]

In some cases, the terms of reference of a given institution were simply revised to allow for states to determine fishing practices within their EEZs. Some of the fisheries organizations – the IATTC and the NEAFC – remained in effect but changed their rules to reflect this new jurisdiction. In other cases, fisheries organizations simply ceased to exist and new ones were created in their place. What had been the International Commission for Northwest Atlantic Fisheries was replaced by NAFO, for example.

The third implication of EEZs for fishery management involved those fish species that crossed among EEZs or between EEZs and the high seas. UNCLOS directed states with "straddling stocks" in their EEZs to cooperate with each other and, through the relevant regional fishery management organizations, to manage them.[63] This cooperation was generally lacking, however. The regional fisheries management organizations in their post-UNCLOS incarnations officially abdicated responsibility for fish inside EEZs, and states, both inside and outside of these organizations, resisted efforts to manage straddling stocks.[64] Agenda 21 from the 1992 United Nations Conference on Environment and Development had called for an international conference on straddling and highly migratory stocks, and in December 1992 the United Nations General Assembly officially approved the convening of a UN conference on the topic.[65] The conference met in a number of sessions from 1993 to 1995. During this time some states took unilateral action: Canada, for example, shot warning shots at Spanish vessels taking turbot in NAFO-managed waters just outside of Canada's EEZ, though Spain had taken pains to make its turbot fishing conform to the letter (if not the spirit) of the NAFO regulations.[66] The aftermath of the Turbot War, as it was called, added to the growing call for international agreement to address the issue of straddling stocks.

When the UN conference began, in 1993, it was not yet clear whether it would result in a legally binding international agreement or simply a declaration of principles. There was strong sentiment, however, especially after the Turbot War, in favor of a binding agreement. The result was the Agreement for the Implementation of the Provisions of the United Nations Convention on the Law of the Sea Relating to the Conservation and Management of Straddling Fish Stocks and Highly Migratory Fish Stocks (1995). This agreement does not itself provide the management for straddling stocks, but rather elaborates on the obligations under UNCLOS for states to cooperate to manage such species. All states that have an interest in a given fishery pertaining to these stocks must join existing fishery management organizations (or work to create them where none exist) or must agree to comply with the regulations of these organizations whether or not they are members. There are similar provisions authorizing enforcement of RFMO provisions.[67] This agreement entered into force in December 2001.

In addition, as part of the UNCLOS effort to bring together ocean regulations generally, the straddling stocks agreement elaborated an obligation on the part of states to conduct their international fishing in accordance with the regulations of regional fishery management organizations, and to negotiate international cooperative agreements to protect these resources where none exist. If they do not do so, they lose access to these resources.[68]

The overall success of international institutional efforts to conserve ocean fisheries has been low. The FAO estimates that one-quarter of the world's fisheries are overexploited or depleted, with another half fully exploited.[69] A recent study found that, worldwide, populations of large predatory fishes (those, like tuna and swordfish, that are the subject of international management efforts) are currently at 10 percent of the levels they were before industrial exploitation.[70] Atlantic cod, pollack, halibut, and salmon are nearly commercially extinct, and at least nine of 16 Pacific fish stocks are deemed to be overfished.[71]

Fishery conservation organizations face consistent difficulties in their efforts to manage fishing of these stocks. Most fishery commissions regularly set their catch limits above those recommended by their scientific bodies. Politically, this disconnect is not surprising: decisions in fishery commissions are made by the member states whose domestic fishing industries will suffer in the short term if they are not able to continue their level of fishing. Any uncertainty in the scientific estimates or causes of fish declines increases the pressure not to take drastic action to cut fishing quotas. Non-compliance with fishery rules is reasonably easy to accomplish because it is difficult to detect. Additionally, an increasing amount of fishing is being conducted under flags of convenience. Up to 20 percent of high-seas fishing vessels are registered in states to which they have no other connection, often precisely to avoid having to abide by international fishery agreements.[72]

Bycatch is an increasingly large problem also that is not well addressed in fishery institutions. The FAO estimates that up to 25 percent of the world's catch of fish is composed of species that are not sought and are often simply discarded.[73] Fishery regulations can themselves increase the incentives for bycatch; when catches are limited there is an incentive to "high-grade," or catch the best quality of the limited number of fish allowed. The segmentation of many fishery management institutions by species also means that those seeking one type of fish may not account for the additional species they catch in their efforts to seek the desired fish.

Conclusions

The ocean commons is particularly difficult to manage. It is hard to monitor what is done in this vast and often unfriendly space, owned by no state and far from view. Given this difficulty, international institutions managing maritime issues have done a surprisingly effective job in changing the way ships are built and operated. The IMO has overseen a wide range of international agreements that have led to increased safety on and decreased pollution from ships.

Many of the institutions created under the Law of the Sea are still recent and evolving, but have, for those states that accept their mandates, shown some sign of effective governance. At minimum, they have changed the way the oceans are governed internationally. How well they fare over time, and whether UNCLOS can help remedy some of the difficulties with maritime governance, remains to be seen.

Institutions protecting fisheries have had the most difficulty gaining the participation of relevant actors and persuading states to accept strict limits on their fishing. In the face of uncertainty over stock estimates, causes of declines, and the behavior of others, it can be difficult to accept certain current restrictions for the sake of uncertain future benefits. The many different regional fishery management organizations have varied levels of success in protecting the stocks they manage, but have, over time, evolved strategies for better managing the behavior of fishers. The protection of the oceans will remain a difficult institutional challenge.

Notes

1 Philip E. Steinberg, *The Social Construction of the Ocean* (Cambridge: Cambridge University Press, 2001), 14.
2 Eula McDonald, "A Half Century of Developments in Ocean Shipping," *Towards a World Maritime Organization*, United States Department of State, Publication 3196 (1948), 1.
3 Comité Maritime International, "History," available at http://www. comitemaritime.org/histo/his.html.
4 Treaty of Versailles (1919), Article 379.

5 McDonald, "A Half Century of Developments," 5.
6 McDonald,"A Half Century of Developments," 5–11.
7 Cleopatra Elmira Henry, *The Carriage of Dangerous Goods by Sea: The Role of the International Maritime Organization in International Legislation* (London: Frances Pinter Publishers, 1985), 39.
8 Convention of the International Maritime Consultative Organization, Articles 6 and 8.
9 This was accomplished by Resolution a.400 (X) of 17 November 1977. Henry, The Carriage of Dangerous Goods by Sea, 43.
10 These began as subcommittees but were promoted between 1975 and 1977 to subsidiary bodies of the organization. Henry, *The Carriage of Dangerous Goods by Sea*, 44.
11 Elizabeth R. DeSombre, *Flagging Standards: Globalization and Environmental, Safety, and Labor Regulations at Sea* (Cambridge, Mass.: MIT Press, 2006).
12 IMO Convention, Article 28(a). Note that the original name of the organization was the International Maritime Consultative Organization; the name was shortened in 1982.
13 International Court of Justice, "Case Summaries: Constitution of the Maritime Safety Committee of the Inter-Governmental Maritime Consultative Organization," Advisory Opinion as of 8 June 1960, available at http://www.icj-cij.org/icjwww/idecisions/isummaries/imscsummary 600608.htm; Olav Knudsen, *The Politics of International Shipping* (Lexington, Mass.: Lexington Books, 1973), 81–82.
14 IMO, "Convention on the International Maritime Organization," available at http://www.imo.org/Conventions/mainframe.asp?topic_id = 771.
15 IMO Resolution A.862(20), 1997.
16 IMO Resolution A.647(16), 1989.
17 International Convention for the Prevention of Pollution from Ships (1973), Article 15.
18 IMO, "Summary of Status of Conventions," 31 July 2005, available at http://www.imo.org.
19 IMO, "International Convention for the Safety of Life at Sea (SOLAS) 1974," available at http://www.imo.org.
20 The agreement was completely overhauled by a 1995 amendment that entered into force in 1997.
21 IMO, "Introduction to IMO," available at http://www.imo.org
22 Ronald B. Mitchell, *Intentional Oil Pollution at Sea* (Cambridge, Mass.: MIT Press, 1994).
23 MARPOL 73/78, 1992 Amendments.
24 MARPOL 73/78, Annex II.
25 MARPOL 73/78, Annex IV.
26 International Convention on Oil Pollution Preparedness, Response and Cooperation (1990).
27 Protocol on Preparedness, Response and Co-operation to Pollution Incidents by Hazardous and Noxious Substances (2000) to the International Convention on Oil Pollution Preparedness, Response and Cooperation.
28 London Convention, Article 4.
29 International Convention on the Control of Harmful Anti-Fouling Systems on Ships (2001).

30 International Convention for the Control and Management of Ships' Ballast Water and Sediments (2004).
31 Piers Campbell, Judith Hushagen, and Dipanwita Sinha, *Challenges, Opportunities and Evolution: Review of the Secretariat of the International Maritime Organization, Switzerland*: MANNET (21 March 2001), 13.
32 Campbell, Hushagen, and Sinha, *Challenges, Opportunities, and Evolution*, 3–4, 13.
33 Clyde Sanger, Ordering the Oceans: The Making of the Law of the Sea (London: Zed Books, 1986), 67.
34 UNCLOS, Articles 3 and 17.
35 UNCLOS, Articles 76(1) and 82.
36 UNCLOS, Articles 194(1–2), 205, and 211
37 Stephen D. Krasner, *Structural Conflict: The Third World Against Global Liberalism* (Berkeley: University of California Press, 1985).
38 UNCLOS (1982), Annex III, Article 13; International Seabed Authority Secretariat, "International Seabed Authority" (2005), 2, available at http://www.isa.org.jm/en/default.htm.
39 UNCLOS, Article 161(8).
40 International Seabed Authority Secretariat, "The International Seabed Authority: Structure and Functioning," 1, available at http://www.isa.org.jm/en/default.htm.
41 Bernard H. Oxman, "The 1994 Agreement on Implementation of the Seabed Provisions of the Convention on the Law of the Sea," *American Journal of International Law* 88(4) (October 1994), 687–96.
42 International Seabed Authority Secretariat, "International Seabed Authority," 3.
43 International Tribunal for the Law of the Sea Secretariat, "Proceedings and Judgments," available at http://www.itlos.org/.
44 See, for example, UNCLOS, Preamble and Articles 41 and 238.
45 Bernard H. Oxman, "Environmental Protection in Archipelagic Waters and International Straits: The Role of the International Maritime Organization," *International Journal of Marine and Coastal Law* 10(14) (1995), 462–81.
46 UNCLOS Article 211(5) is one such example.
47 UNCLOS, Article 21(4).
48 Oxman "Environmental Protection," 474.
49 Garrett Hardin, "The Tragedy of the Commons," *Science* 168 (1968), 1243.
50 J. Samuel Barkin and Kashif Mansori, "Backwards Boycotts: Demand Management and Fishery Conservation," *Global Environmental Politics*, 1(2) (May 2001), 30–41.
51 International Convention for the Regulation of Whaling, Preamble.
52 Sean Phelan, "A Pacific Rim Approach to Salmon Management," *Environmental Law* 33 (2003), 248–50.
53 Christopher C. Joyner, "Managing Common-Pool Marine Living Resources: Lessons from the Southern Ocean Experience," in J. Samuel Barkin and George E. Shambaugh, eds., *Anarchy and the Environment* (Albany: SUNY Press, 1999), 70–93.
54 UN FAO Secretariat, "Regional Fishery Bodies," available at http://www.fao.org/fi/body/rfb/chooseman_type.htm.

55 UN FAO Secretariat, "Advisory Committee on Fishery Research," available at http://www.fao.org/fi/body/acfr/acfr.asp.
56 UN FAO Secretariat, "The Coordinating Working Party on Fisheries Statistics," available at http://www.fao.org/figis/servlet/static?dom = org&xml = cwp_inst.xml.
57 ICES Secretariat, "What Do We Do?" available at http://www.ices.dk/aboutus/aboutus.asp.
58 PICES, "History of PICES," available at http://www.pices.int/.
59 Elizabeth R. DeSombre, "Tuna Fishing and Common Pool Resources," in Barkin and Shambaugh, eds., *Anarchy and the Environment*, 56.
60 David A. Colson, "Current Issues in Fishery Conservation and Management," *U.S. Department of State Dispatch* 6(7) (1995), 100.
61 Harry N. Scheiber, "Ocean Governance and the Marine Fisheries Crisis: Two Decades of Innovation and Frustration," *Virginia Environmental Law Journal* 20 (2001), 126–27.
62 M.J. Peterson, "International Fisheries Management," in Peter M. Haas, Robert O. Keohane, and Marc A. Levy, eds., *Institutions for the Earth* (Cambridge, Mass.: MIT Press (1993), 249–305.
63 UNCLOS, Article 63.
64 Julie R. Mack, "International Fisheries Management: How the U.N. Conference on Straddling and Highly Migratory Stocks Changes the Law of Fishing on the High Seas," *California Western International Law Journal* 26 (Spring 1996), 318–21.
65 UN General Assembly Resolution 47/192, 29 January 1993.
66 Christopher C. Joyner and Alejandro Alvarez von Gustedt, "The 1995 Turbot War: Lessons for the Law of the Sea," *International Journal of Marine and Coastal Law* 11 (November 1996), 425–58.
67 Agreement for the Implementation of the Provisions of the United Nations Convention on the Law of the Sea Relating to the Conservation and Management of Straddling Fish Stocks and Highly Migratory Fish Stocks, Articles 8, 13, and 19–23.
66 UNCLOS (1982), Article 118.
69 UN FAO, *The State of World Fisheries and Aquaculture* (Rome: UN FAO, 2004), 28–35.
70 Ranson A. Myers and Boris Worm, "Rapid Worldwide Depletion of Predatory Fish Communities," *Nature* 423 (2003), 280–83.
71 Tim Eichenberg and Mitchell Shapson, "The Promise of Johannesburg: Fisheries and the World Summit on Sustainable Development," *Golden Gate University Law Review* 34 (2004), 592–94.
72 Elizabeth R. DeSombre, "Fishing Under Flags of Convenience," *Global Environmental Politics* 5(4) (November 2005), 74.
73 Ivor Clucas, "Fisheries Bycatch and Discards," *FAO Fisheries Circular* 928 (1997).

5 Atmospheric commons

The institutions addressing atmospheric commons are all reasonably recent but quite well developed. The logic for international approaches to addressing these issues is strong. The atmosphere is not controlled by any one state, and actions taken by states in one location affect the atmosphere in other locations. States thus cannot protect their own populations from environmental problems of the atmosphere simply by controlling their own domestic behavior. And these problems can be dramatic. Acid rain has caused forest damage and the death of lake ecosystems, as well as damaging human health, across Europe and is spreading worldwide with increasing industrialization. A depleted ozone layer leads to increases in skin cancer, cataracts, and immune-system disorders among humans and other species, and damages plant life. The WHO estimates that 150,000 human lives are already lost annually from existing effects of climate change.[1] Rising sea levels will inundate populated areas inhabited by millions of people, and changing patterns of temperature and rainfall will affect food production, disease vectors, and impact the health or even survival of species and ecosystems.

In some cases, such as acid rain and other forms of transboundary air pollution, the effects are directional: where a state lies in the atmospheric currents determines the environmental effects it will have on, or receive from, others. But in other cases, such as ozone depletion and climate change, the impacts do not depend on the location of the emissions. In this kind of pollution problem the atmosphere acts as a true commons, and the need for all potential sources of emissions to be controlled within the institutions to address these problems influences the characteristics of the institutional rules and processes developed to address them.

This chapter discusses the institutions created to address three major problems of the atmospheric commons. Transboundary acid rain has been the focus of regional institutions, most importantly the Convention on Long-Range Transboundary Air Pollution, focusing on Europe. The processes created by the Vienna Convention and Montreal Protocol govern the response to ozone depletion. Most recently the Framework Convention on Climate Change and its Kyoto Protocol attempt to address climate change.

Transboundary acid rain

Acid rain was the earliest issue of the atmosphere to be addressed through international cooperation. It initially became an international problem because of earlier domestic efforts to avoid local impacts of power generation. After serious problems with smog and respiratory problems caused by coal burning, local officials mandated high smokestacks on power plants and other coal-burning facilities to put emissions higher into the air so that they would not fall locally and affect ecosystems near the facilities producing the emissions. This technological approach had the effect of dispersing the pollutants away from the location from which they were generated, sometimes sufficiently long distances that they crossed international borders.[2]

The problem of acid rain was a precursor to the Stockholm Conference in 1972. At the time, Scandinavian states were concerned about problems of acid rain, since they were feeling its effects; Sweden in particular raised the idea of a UN conference to address issues of the human interaction with the environment. Though the conference did not achieve specific remedies to the problem of acid rain, its declaration and action plan included items relevant to, and inspired by, the problem. For instance, Recommendations 72 and 73 of the action plan address the need to limit emissions of pollutants that cross international borders and to assess these pollutants, their pathways, and their effects.[3]

The Convention on Long-Range Transboundary Air Pollution

Another opportunity to address the issue was presented to those states concerned about the problem. In the mid-1970s the Soviet Union, at the height of the Cold War, proposed negotiation on a "low politics" issue as a way to encourage cooperation, and thus further détente, between East and West. The idea was that if states could cooperate on issues not related to security it might lower tensions more generally. The UNECE was charged with finding such an issue on which to negotiate, and suggested the possibility of environmental cooperation, specifically acid rain.[4]

International cooperation on acid rain faced a set of then-common circumstances for international environmental cooperation. People had observed a problem and its effects – lakes in Scandinavia and elsewhere were becoming acidified – but did not have a clear understanding of the causes. At the time the most affected states believed that this acidification was due to transport of sulfur dioxide emissions from elsewhere in Europe, but the idea that these substances could travel such long distances received much skepticism. In 1977 a report by the Organization for Economic Cooperation and Development (OECD) from a study initiated after the Stockholm Conference argued that long-range transport of acidifying substances was happening,[5] supporting earlier studies from the 1960s suggesting that it was possible.

Negotiation of the agreement was unusual in some ways since it took place in a highly politicized Cold War context, yet the primary disagreements in the negotiation took place between the Nordic states, which wanted binding international commitments to reduce acidifying pollution, and the Western European states (especially the United Kingdom and West Germany), which were not especially concerned with the problem and resisted changing their behavior.

The resulting cooperative structure presaged the form of later cooperation on atmospheric issues and other environmental problems about which there was uncertainty and disagreement. The convention negotiated, on Long-Range Transboundary Air Pollution (LRTAP), was a broad framework convention that established the basis for and form of cooperation, without requiring much in the way of substantive mitigation of the problem. States agreed in principle to limit the emissions of acidifying substances.[6]

Most importantly, LRTAP sets up the scientific framework for a better understanding of the environmental problem, its causes, and the extent of its effects. States are required to collect and submit data on their emissions of air pollutants. The institution dictates the format of these data reports, which harmonizes the research and information collected under LRTAP. Because states had to begin collecting this kind of information, states that previously did not have research capacity gained the incentive to develop it.[7] In addition, states must cooperate on research about potential air pollutants, monitoring models for evaluating the levels of air pollutants and, most importantly, the effects of emissions of these pollutions on the environment and on human health.

The parties also agreed to implement and further develop an international monitoring program, the Cooperative Program for Monitoring and Evaluation of Long-Range Transmission of Air Pollutants in

Europe (referred to as EMEP) to monitor emissions and trans-boundary movements of sulfur dioxide and related substances, as well as their effects on ecosystems. Following a 1984 protocol to LRTAP, this program came to be financed by mandatory contributions from member states, based on wealth, population, and other geographic considerations. EMEP was originally formed by the OECD in 1978 (from a network of monitoring stations created earlier in the 1970s that had contributed to its 1977 report) but was brought under LRTAP after the 1979 convention. The program runs nearly 300 monitoring stations throughout Europe, from which it measures pollution levels.[8] States also submit emissions reports to EMEP. It then makes use of meteorological data from the WMO to create emissions trajectories. This allows calculation of where a given state's emissions go.

EMEP's data gathering gives it the ability to monitor compliance with the agreement, since it can compare information given about emissions with measurement of air pollutants in the direction it knows the emissions travel. Though the LRTAP secretariat does not empha-size this capability, it may be responsible for the high level of confidence placed in the self-reported emissions data. Emissions data can also be verified against international energy data.

Other monitoring and research takes place within the LRTAP struc-ture. The Working Group on Effects oversees a set of International Cooperative Programs (ICPs) assessing impacts on natural resources. States participate in these programs on a voluntary basis and they are self-financed, which limits their effectiveness. Current ICPs focus on forests, waters, materials, and vegetation, as well as integrated moni-toring and modeling and mapping. There is also a Task Force on Health as a part of the Working Group on Effects.

In the LRTAP convention the UNECE, and specifically its Air Pollution Unit, became the secretariat for the organization created. The actual staffing of the secretariat is minimal and has not grown despite the growth in number of regulations and parties to the conven-tion.[9] The parties to the agreement constitute the Executive Body, the decisionmaking body for the cooperative process, which meets annu-ally. The Executive Body has established a number of subsidiary working groups that manage collective research and work to draft protocols. The Executive Body makes decision by consensus, on such issues as establishing task forces and extra groups, asking for more information from parties, or following up on non-compliance or facili-tating compliance. These decisions are not considered to be legally binding, however, so the primary substantive changes to behavior come through the negotiation of protocols to the convention.

Because the UNECE existed prior to the creation of LRTAP it retained its previous institutional structure for much of the early period of operation of the agreement. For several years pre-existing UNECE bodies, like a Working Party on Air Pollution Problems, existed alongside the LRTAP-created groups. In 1991 the UNECE did some organizational streamlining to better address these potential duplications of effort.[10] Other structures within the UNECE continue to address other issues of pollution and environmental protection in Europe, and issues beyond environmental protection. There is a shifting number of working groups that operate under the Executive Body. Current working groups include those on Effects and on Strategies and Review. There is also an EMEP Steering Body that oversees the monitoring done through the institution.

The agreement is intended to be regional, only open to member states of, or those with consultative status to, the Economic Commission for Europe. The United States and Canada are allowed to join because of their consultative status. Though some states have been reluctant to take on later commitments, all the negotiating states quickly signed and ratified the 1979 agreement.[11]

The process of monitoring and coordination institutionalized by the LRTAP Convention provided the main impetus for further negotiations of substantive protocols that mandated specific action to reduce the problem of air pollution. A number of states were only reluctant participants in initial LRTAP negotiations because they did not believe their emissions could be causing harm or did not believe that they faced problems themselves from acid rain. Data collected in research processes set up or supported by LRTAP began to demonstrate the extent of the environmental impacts, however. Information presented at a 1982 conference in Stockholm indicated the extent of lake and forest acidification, including the extent of forest death in Germany's famed Black Forest. Germany shortly thereafter became a proponent of binding emissions reductions.[12] Since Germany had previously been strongly opposed to measures for emissions control, this shift proved pivotal in allowing for the negotiation of binding protocols. It is through these protocols that LRTAP's regulatory efforts are implemented. There are currently seven protocols that require specific emissions reductions, along with a 1984 protocol to finance EMEP.

The first abatement protocol is the 1985 Protocol on the Reduction of Sulphur Emissions or Their Transboundary Fluxes by at Least 30 Per Cent, which entered into force in 1987. It is currently referred to as the First Sulphur Protocol. Because acid rain is a directional issue, the idea of states each reducing their emissions by the same amount regardless of where they are situated in the atmospheric currents does not make environmental sense, but from a negotiation standpoint it proved easier for all states to agree to the same reduction level. The ideological pressure to accept emissions reductions, what Marc Levy called "tote-board diplomacy," came from the "30 percent" club of states that committed to reducing their emissions before a specific obligation to do so existed. By 1984 a sufficient number of states had agreed to do so that a protocol could be concluded. The Soviet bloc, however, resisted a requirement for domestic action, and instead insisted that the option be included that states reduce the "transboundary fluxes" of pollutants by that amount instead. In the case of the Soviet Union, this requirement was met not by reducing emissions generally, but rather by changing the location of sulfur-emitting facilities so that their pollutants would no longer cross international borders.[13]

The 1988 Protocol Concerning the Control of Nitrogen Oxides or Their Transboundary Fluxes entered into force in 1991. It first required that states freeze emissions of nitrogen oxides (or their transboundary fluxes) at 1987 levels by the end of 1994. It also required that states negotiate further reductions in nitrogen oxide emissions based on where cuts will have the greatest environmental impact.[14] As of 2006 at least 19 of the 29 parties to the protocol had reached or exceeded the initial goal, leading to a 9 percent total emissions reduction from 1987 levels.[15]

The 1991 Protocol Concerning the Control of Emissions of Volatile Organic Compounds or Their Transboundary Fluxes entered into force in 1997. Volatile organic compounds (VOCs) are a major precursor to the creation of ground-level ozone, which has respiratory and other environmental effects. This protocol allows states to choose from three different reduction obligations at the time of signature or ratification. The first option is to achieve a 30 percent reduction of VOCs (from a base year chosen between 1984 and 1990) by 1999. The second option allows for the reduction by 30 percent of VOC emissions within a specified Tropospheric Ozone Management Area (and provided that total VOC emissions in 1999 do not exceed those in 1988). The third option is for states whose emissions in 1988 were below a specified level (figured in amount, determined by capita and per square kilometer); they may simply choose to stabilize their emissions by 1999 at 1988 levels.[16] Though Bulgaria, Greece, and Hungary had emissions low enough and chose the third option and Norway and Canada chose the second option, most states have taken on the first option for reductions.[17]

A radical shift in the LRTAP approach came with the 1994 Protocol on Further Reductions of Sulphur Emissions (often referred to as the Second Sulphur Protocol), which entered into force in 1998. Unlike previous protocols that mandated identical emissions reductions obligations for all parties, this protocol attempts to implement the concept of "critical loads" as a guiding framework for determining reductions. Because of the different airflow patterns and geographic location, not all states contribute or receive the same amount of air pollutants. In addition, the natural characteristics of the ecosystems where pollutants are deposited – for instance, whether they have natural buffering capabilities – influence what kind of effect the pollutants that do fall will have. UNECE officials endorsed the idea that emissions should be regulated such that no state receives emissions that exceed a "critical load" of the regulated substance, defined as "an exposure to one or more pollutants below which significant harmful effects on specified sensitive elements of the environment do not occur, according to present knowledge." This protocol is an imperfect implementation of the idea of critical loads; it contains a number of provisions that limit the extent to which this approach is followed. First, it indicates that these obligations are to be implemented "as far as possible, without entailing excessive costs."[18] The actual reduction obligations laid out in an annex are generally regarded as representing a compromise between environmental requirements and what states were actually willing to accept in terms of obligations.[19] But it provides an important conceptual advance in linking abatement obligations by states to actual environmental conditions on the ground.

Additional protocols to LRTAP expand the agreement's purview. They address pollutants with long-range transport but which are not the acidifying substances that provided the initial focus for the agreement. Two 1998 protocols entered into force in 2003. The Protocol on Heavy Metals requires parties to reduce their emissions of cadmium, lead, and mercury below the level of emissions of 1990 (though parties have the option to choose an alternate base year between 1985 and 1995). It also gives specific emissions limits from stationary sources, and requires that states cease the use of lead in gasoline. The Protocol on Persistent Organic Pollutants (discussed further in Chapter 6) creates a list of 16 substances (including pesticides, industrial chemicals, and other contaminants), with a goal of eliminating emissions of these substances. Of those on the list, some are banned entirely, others are scheduled for later elimination, and the use of some restricted.

Finally, the 1999 Protocol to Abate Acidification, Eutrophication and Ground Level Ozone entered into force in 2005. This agreement requires further action on pollutants addressed in earlier protocols, creating a ceiling for emissions of sulfur, nitrogen oxides, VOCs, and ammonia. The levels of emissions of the substances by states are determined (as in the Second Sulphur Protocol) in a way that takes into account where the emissions have the greatest impact and where the least expensive reductions can be made. These control measures also signal an important shift in LRTAP policymaking, acknowledging that following a critical-loads approach requires regulating many pollutants simultaneously. In addition, the protocol sets limits for emissions from specific sources (such as power plants and automobiles) and requires the use of "best available techniques" of emission control. The agreement aims, once fully implemented, to achieve an emissions reduction of 63 percent in sulfur emissions, 41 percent in nitrogen oxide (NOx) emissions, 40 percent in VOC emissions, and 17 percent in ammonia emissions from 1990 levels.[20]

It is also important to note the role of one NGO within the operating process of LRTAP. The International Institute for Applied Systems Analysis (IIASA) is a cooperative scientific institute set up in 1972 by science organizations from both Eastern and Western Europe (along with the United States), with the support of the governments of these states. Its focus is on creating and disseminating models and management techniques. One of its research areas has been acid rain, and it created a simulation known as RAINS that evaluates environmental benefits and economic costs of various air-pollution control strategies. IIASA has been involved in LRTAP negotiations and decisionmaking from the beginning, but has had particular influence in the development and adoption of the "critical-loads" concept, which can be modeled under RAINS. IIASA has played the same role more recently in European Union air-quality legislation.

Since LRTAP was negotiated and its various institutional structures made operational, the change in emissions has been dramatic. Emissions of most of the regulated substances have fallen in the major states. Sulfur dioxide emissions (from land-based sources) in Europe fell by 70 percent between 1980 and 2000. Emissions of nitrogen oxides in Europe rose in the decade following 1980 (before the NOx Protocol entered into force) but decreased by 30 percent overall by 2000. Not all of this changed behavior is traceable to the convention and its institutional processes, however. Emissions of sulfur dioxide in the UK decreased as that country changed from coal to gas as a major energy source, for reasons unrelated to LRTAP obligations, and emissions in Eastern Europe decreased with the economic and industrial changes brought on by the disintegration of the Soviet Union. Most recently,

EU policy, rather than LRTAP obligations, has been an influence on the emissions of EU member states. Nevertheless, the behavior of some states in Europe has been changed by the existence of LRTAP, particularly such states as Austria, Finland, the Netherlands, and Swizerland, which learned of their vulnerability from studies undertaken in the context of LRTAP.[21]

There have been some beneficial environmental impacts of these decreased emissions. The area of Europe that receives acid deposition beyond what the environment can buffer has decreased from 34 percent in 1990 to 11 percent in 2000. In 1980 approximately 207 million hectares of European ecosystems were harmed by acidification; by 2000 it was only about 38 million, and the affected area has continued to shrink.[22]

Transboundary air pollution elsewhere

At least in part because the majority of the transport of acidifying substances takes place on the scale of hundreds of kilometers, the international cooperative efforts to address them have largely been regional. The European arrangement is the most institutionally developed and has made the biggest difference in changing the emissions behavior of its member states, but there are arrangements either existing or in the process of being created in other regions.

The most developed of these other acid rain arrangements is in North America. This agreement is not considered at length here because it is bilateral and not highly institutionalized. Though both the United States and Canada are parties to the LRTAP convention, they agreed, after much political disagreement, to negotiate what became the United States–Canada Air Quality Agreement (1991). The agreement contains a set of general obligations to "reduce transboundary flows of . . . acidic deposition precursors,"[23] and to engage in environmental impact assessment, prior notification, mitigation, and a process of cooperative or coordinated scientific, technical, and economic research. In an annex the United States and Canada agree to specific – and separate – emissions reductions for sulfur dioxide and nitrogen oxides. Each state's obligations are given in separate units of measurement, with the United States required to reduce "tons" (English) and Canada required to reduce "tonnes" (metric) of pollutants.

Among other measures, Canada agreed to reduce SO_2 emissions in the seven eastern provinces to 2.3 million tonnes per year by 1994, to maintain that level through 1999 and to not exceed a permanent annual cap of 3.2 million tonnes any time after 2000. The United

States agreed to reduce sulfur dioxide emissions to 10 million tons below 1980 levels by 2000 and to reduce nitrogen oxide emissions to 2 million tons below 1980 levels by 2000.[24] There are a variety of requirements for fuel efficiency standards and other technological requirements as well. Both the United States and Canada have broadly followed the requirements of the agreement, though the United States would have been required to by its own domestic Clean Air Act amendments in 1990, which passed before the Air Quality Agreement was signed.

Institutionally the U.S.–Canada agreement relies on an existing structure, the International Joint Commission (IJC), that was formed under the Boundary Waters Treaty between the two states in 1909. The IJC coordinates public comments on air quality. The agreement also created a bilateral Air Quality Committee to review the implementation of the agreement. There is no specific institutional process for changing obligations under the agreement.

With increasing industrialization elsewhere in the world, problems of acid deposition have emerged as well. Though not entirely new in Asia, the problem has become more acute recently. Japan addressed the issue domestically with strong controls on emissions from power generation and automobiles, but acknowledged that these efforts could not prevent impacts from emissions from elsewhere. At this point the major efforts undertaken have been to monitor air pollutants and ecosystemic effects. The most important of these is the East Asian Acid Deposition Monitoring Network (EANET), which began operations in 2001. Though Japan initially proposed the creation of this network, it now involves states throughout East Asia. It includes a secretariat (housed in UNEP's Regional Office for Asia and the Pacific), a Scientific Advisory Group, and National Focal Points within participating countries.[25] EANET has worked to standardize acid rain monitoring in the region, no small task given that each member state has its own techniques for monitoring and analysis. One of the goals of the organization is to work for the reduction of regional sulfur dioxide emissions, though this step has not yet been attempted and it will likely face political difficulties.[26]

Ozone depletion

Perhaps the most widely heralded institutional process for addressing an international environmental problem is that pertaining to ozone depletion. The Montreal Protocol process has fundamentally changed the worldwide use of a set of environmentally damaging chemicals, leading to initial signs of environmental improvement. It has done so in a way that brought all relevant states into the control processes and provided assistance for developing states to meet the obligations of the underlying international agreements.

Ozone depletion is the destruction of molecules of ozone in the stratosphere that provide protection to the earth from harmful ultraviolet radiation. The primary chemicals initially identified as problematic, chlorofluorocarbons (CFCs) and halons, were important industrial chemicals, used as aerosol propellants and in refrigeration, cleaning of electronics, and fire suppression. The problem of ozone depletion created a new set of difficulties for the creation of a regulatory institution. In previous environmental problems, like acid rain, an effect was observed and then causes for that effect ascertained, and regulations created to address those causes. In the case of ozone depletion the impact was theorized before it was observed, leading to potential difficulties in gaining international cooperation to regulate industrial behavior for which an outcome had not yet been observed. The long atmospheric life of these substances – the most common CFC lasts for 100 years and some can persist for up to 1700 years[27] – meant that waiting for clear signs of environmental damage would extend the period of environmental degradation. States agreed to cooperate in anticipation of the problem.

The Vienna Convention

Initial international efforts on this issue began in the 1970s, led by UNEP. UNEP convened a conference of experts in 1977 to adopt a World Plan of Action on the Ozone Layer, encouraging international cooperation in research and modeling on causes, effects, and trends in ozone depletion, to be undertaken by the United Nations and other international organizations, states, and NGOs. This meeting also established a Coordinating Committee on the Ozone Layer (CCOL) to help oversee this research. This committee met regularly until 1985 and issued reports summarizing the state of knowledge on ozone depletion.[28]

Prior to international negotiations some states had taken domestic action to limit their use of CFCs. Most notable among these was the United States, which passed rules in 1977 phasing out the use of CFCs in non-essential aerosols; even prior to these rules the consumption of these substances in the United States had fallen dramatically because of public environmental concern.[29] The U.S. action alone cut worldwide consumption of CFCs by approximately 25 percent.[30] Sweden and Norway undertook similar action and Canada forbade the use of CFCs in most aerosols.

In 1981 the UNEP Governing Council passed a motion presented by Sweden to authorize negotiations towards a binding international agreement on the protection of the ozone layer and established a working group (to coordinate with the CCOL) to begin this process. International concern about the potential problem was not uniform, however, and the decrease in worldwide consumption of CFCs further decreased pressure for an international agreement. Countries that had controlled their own domestic consumption of CFCs generally proposed international measures that mirrored what they had already taken on, and those that had not yet passed domestic rules were reluctant to take on international obligations. Eventually the "Toronto Group," Canada, the United States, Australia, Switzerland, and the Nordic Countries, together proposed a set of measures that would allow states to choose which form of reductions to take. These measures were opposed by the European Community and Japan, which resisted taking action. Industrial manufacturers and users of CFCs also opposed international action, and warned that international controls would be costly and disruptive to industry; and others pointed to the continuing uncertainty about the scope or magnitude of a potential problem that had not yet made itself apparent.

Because of these continuing disagreements, the working group conceded that the only form of international agreement possible at the time would be a framework convention, without binding emissions reduction obligations. The resulting agreement was the Vienna Convention for the Protection of the Ozone Layer (1985), which entered into force in 1988. The Vienna Convention included the obligation by states to take "appropriate" action to protect the ozone layer, to cooperate in scientific research, and to exchange information. It established an important process of scientific cooperation, to address concerns by reluctant states that the limited knowledge on ozone depletion did not justify strict emissions controls. Institutionally, the agreement established the Conference of the Parties as its decision-making body, and designated UNEP as the organization's secretariat.

The Montreal Protocol

The possible elaboration of abatement obligations was left to the negotiation of future protocols. But as a compromise for dropping insistence on control measures within the Vienna Convention, the negotiators agreed to a resolution to immediately convene a working group to begin negotiations for a protocol, with an aim to complete it by 1987.[31] Official negotiations began in 1986, with the initial negotiating positions reflecting positions taken in the negotiation of the Vienna Convention. One major change, however, was that U.S. producers of CFCs dropped their opposition to international measures, because they feared stronger domestic action if international control of ozone-depleting substances (ODS) was not undertaken, and because they hoped to be able to develop alternative chemicals if international controls created a sufficient market incentive.

Negotiations continued through 1987. The major points of contention involved whether the controls would be on production or consumption of ozone-depleting substances and how deep these cuts would be. UNEP convened a conference of atmospheric modelers, who demonstrated that under any of the proposed plans notable ozone depletion would still occur. UNEP executive director Mostafa Tolba participated in the discussions in an effort to persuade states that current scientific knowledge pointed to the necessity for action. A number of scientific assessments during this period, especially those sponsored by the U.S. National Aeronautics and Space Administration (NASA) in 1984 and 1985, were influential in developing scientific consensus for action.[32] The discovery in 1985 of what came to be known as the "ozone hole," a seasonal thinning in the ozone layer above Antarctica, provided additional impetus to conclude an agreement, though human responsibility for this phenomenon had not yet been ascertained. An eventual agreement was reached just before the original deadline imposed by the conference of the plenipotentiaries already scheduled for September.[33] To enter into force, the protocol required ratification by at least 11 states that collectively represented at least two-thirds of global CFC consumption. It entered into force in January 1989.

The document on which the negotiators agreed was the Montreal Protocol on Substances that Deplete the Ozone Layer (1987). It required that parties freeze consumption (defined as "production plus imports minus exports")[34] of five specified CFCs at 1986 levels by 1990, and then reduce their use by 20 percent by 1994 and 50 percent below 1986 by 1999. States also agreed to freeze consumption of three halons at 1986 levels by 1993.[35] The Protocol uses a system of calculating a substance's "ozone-depletion potential" (ODP), which is an assessment of how much damage a given substance can do to the ozone layer; this regulatory decision allowed for the comparison of different substances in regulatory measures.

Important exceptions to these rules were created, however, for developing states (as defined in the UN system) whose per capita consumption of ozone-depleting substances was less than .3 kg. These states had an additional ten years in which to meet the protocol's obligation, and could even increase their consumption during that period as long as it did not exceed .3 kg/capita. In order to persuade states to join the agreement, especially those states that did not yet produce their own CFCs, the Montreal Protocol mandated that states party to the agreement only trade ozone-depleting substances with other parties.

Institutionally, the main decisionmaking mechanism in the Montreal Protocol is the annual Meeting of the Parties (MOP), which operates alongside the Conference of the Parties to the Vienna Convention, though in practice the major decisions are made in the MOP. All states party to the agreement are represented, with one vote each. The MOP has oversight responsibility for all of the activities that take place under the protocol. It approves the budget and activities of the Ozone Secretariat, and adopts decisions on issues pertaining to compliance, implementation, and review of the agreement.

The subsidiary bodies of the Montreal Protocol are also important parts of the broader institutional structure. The first MOP created four assessment panels, which were later merged. The current structure involves a Technology and Economic Assessment Panel (TEAP) that oversees a number of subsidiary bodies to address specific aspects of TEAP's mandate. Collectively they undertake assessments of substitutes for ozone-depleting substances and evaluate their economic and technological appropriateness. The current committees are those that focus on medical aerosols; chemical uses; rigid and flexible foams; halons; methyl bromide; refrigeration, air conditioning, and heat pumps; and solvents and adhesives.[36] The MOP also established an Open-Ended Working Group (OEWG) that meets between MOP meetings.

The secretariat functions for the Montreal Protocol have been folded into those for the Vienna Convention; the Ozone Secretariat, run by UNEP, is housed in UNEP headquarters in Nairobi, Kenya. The secretariat has played a particularly active role in assisting the implementation of the Montreal Protocol and the negotiation and implementation of its amendments. It also prepares a report on the implementation of the agreement for each MOP.

The most important function of this organization is to decide on amendments and adjustments to the protocol. Major changes in protocol obligations can be negotiated through amendments to the protocol. These require negotiation, signature, and ratification, and are used to significantly alter the phaseout schedule or to add new controlled substances to the obligations. The first set of amendments were negotiated in London in 1990 and took the important step of requiring the eventual complete phaseout of CFCs and some halons, when previously only a reduction had been mandated. The timeline for reductions was also accelerated. Amendments in Copenhagen in 1992 added hydrochlorofluorocarbons (HCFCs), hydrobromofluorocarbons (HBFCs), and methyl bromide (MeBr) to the list of substances controlled under the Montreal Protocol. The regulation of MeBr, an agricultural fumigant, was particularly controversial, and coincided with a new method of determining ODPs that suggested that MeBr reductions would play an important role in reducing ozone depletion. The Montreal amendments in 1997 mandated a phaseout of MeBr for developed states by 2005 and created a process of trade licensing to address the growing problem of illegal trade in ozone-depleting substances. The Beijing amendments in 1999 added bromochloromethane to the list of controlled substances and modified the regulation of HCFCs to include controls on production and tighten controls on consumption.[37]

The other important way that changes to control measures in the protocol can happen is through "adjustments" to the obligations, made by the MOP. Decision to adjust the protocol can be made by approval of two-thirds of the parties, provided that this decision represents a majority of both developed and developing country parties.[38] These adjustments are binding on all parties, even those that do not vote in favor, which is quite unusual for international environmental agreements. The adjustment process has been used to make substantive changes in treaty obligations. The most important of these are the acceptance of a phaseout of methyl bromide consumption by 2010 agreed to in Vienna in 1995, when previously only a freeze at 1991 levels by 1995 had been accepted by the parties. The Vienna adjustments also established dates for developing country freeze and phaseout of HCFCs and phaseout of CFCs, halons, carbon tetrachloride, and methyl chloroform.[39] In all, the Montreal Protocol process now controls 96 different ozone-depleting chemicals.[40]

Because ozone-depleting substances have the same effect on the ozone layer no matter where they are emitted, those who do not participate in phasing them out could undermine the ability of others to protect the ozone layer. For that reason, there were a number of efforts under the Montreal Protocol to encourage participation, especially by developing countries. The trade restrictions with non-parties were intended to lure states without their own production capacity (which in 1987 included most developing states) into the agreement so they could continue to

Table 5.1: Main changes in Montreal Protocol obligations for developed states

	Montreal Protocol (1987)	London (1990)	Copenhagen (1992)	Montreal (1997)	Beijing (1999)
CFCs	50% cut by 1998	phaseout 2000	phaseout 1996	–	–
halons	freeze by 1992	phaseout 2000	phaseout 1994	–	–
carbon tetrachloride	not controlled	phaseout 2000	phaseout 1996	–	–
methyl chloroform	not controlled	phaseout 2005	phaseout 1996	–	–
HCFCs	not controlled	voluntary phaseout 2040	freeze by 1999; phaseout 2030	–	freeze production 2004
MeBr	not controlled	not controlled	freeze by 1999	phaseout 2005	–

Source: Adapted from Edward A. Parson, *Protecting the Ozone Layer: Science and Strategy* (Oxford: Oxford University Press, 2003), 240–41.

buy ozone-depleting substances from the major producer states in the agreement. The ten-year time lag was meant to circumvent developing country concern about being prohibited from using ozone-depleting substances to develop industrially, and the promised technical and financial assistance would help them adapt to alternate technologies when their time to reduce ODS use came.

These attempts were largely unpersuasive, however. As long as some of the developing country producers of ODS – China and India, most importantly – remained outside of the Montreal Protocol system, developing states would have access to these substances. Many ozone-depleting substances also are simple enough to produce that new state production capacity could be created. Ten extra years before having to meet a standard you are not interested in meeting in the first place is not a sufficient incentive to agree to meet it. And the unspecified technical assistance looked too much like a promise that would go unfulfilled, or would divert funding from other development aid. Most developing countries refused to sign the Montreal Protocol initially. Mexico was the only developing country producer of ODS that signed the protocol when it was first open for signature. Other developing states that joined early, such as Malaysia, characterized the agreement as "inequitable," and India and China refused to join until a mechanism for financial assistance was specified.[41]

The Multilateral Fund

In order to bring these reluctant states into the agreement the negotiations towards the London amendments in 1990 focused on specifying the process by which developing states would receive assistance under the agreement. The Technical and Economic Options Committees undertook a synthesis report, confirming that developing states would indeed need assistance to meet their obligations under the protocol. Some developed countries, however, were concerned about the potential cost of such assistance and the institutional process through which it would be provided. Developed states preferred to use existing funding institutions, primarily the World Bank, but developing states were concerned that they would have little control over the allocation of funding if it were distributed through the World Bank. The United States, however, threatened to block creation of a standalone fund specifically for the Montreal Protocol. UNEP executive director Tolba organized working groups to conduct the negotiations, and conducted case studies to determine what the costs of meeting control obligations would be. The pressure of U.S.-based NGOs, developing states, and other Montreal Protocol parties eventually weakened U.S. opposition to the creation of a fund.[42]

The result was the Montreal Protocol Multilateral Fund. It was created as an interim fund in 1991 and was made permanent under the 1992 Copenhagen amendments. It funds projects in developing states (called "Article 5 countries" because it is Article 5 of the protocol that details the special obligations of these states) to assist them in meeting their obligations under the Montreal Protocol and its amendments. The funding, contributed by developed states (non-Article 5 countries), is based on the UN Scale of Assessments for the donor states, which means that the wealthiest contribute the most. Donor states may use 20 percent of their assessed donation to do bilateral projects if they choose. Funding is assessed on a three-year cycle. In the time between when the Multilateral Fund began as an interim entity in 1991 and the end of 2005 it has received pledges of US$2.1 billion in funding.[43]

The funding from the Multilateral Fund is intended to cover the "incremental costs" of projects. Though these are sometimes difficult to calculate, the idea is that developing states should not bear the additional costs of whatever behavior they undertake in order to implement the Montreal Protocol. So if a substitute chemical costs more than an ozone-depleting substance that was being used, those costs would be covered, as would the cost to retrofit a production process with non-ODS technology. Potential cost-savings are calculated as well, so if a process results in some savings those will be used to offset increased costs.

The Montreal Protocol's Meeting of the Parties oversees the broad aspects of the Multilateral Fund, by agreeing on the replenishments of the fund, every three years. The Multilateral Fund itself is run by an Executive Committee (ExCom), which is charged with overseeing the activities of the fund. This process includes creating criteria for project eligibility, monitoring the implementation of projects, creating plans and budgets (on a three-year cycle) for the fund, allocating funding to implementing agencies, and approving country programs and specific projects for funding.

The ExCom is composed of the representatives of 14 states, seven from Article 5 states and seven from non-Article 5 states, elected by the Montreal Protocol MOP. Decisions in the ExCom are made by consensus if possible, but if not they require what has come to be known as "double-majority" voting: a decision requires a two-thirds majority that must also constitute majority votes in each bloc. This voting structure gave a measure of reassurance to developing states that their wishes could not be easily overridden. This voting structure is particularly unusual for a funding organization – in most organizations that distribute development aid (such as the World Bank and the regional development banks) donor states have voting power proportional to the amount of money they donate.

The ExCom has performed a serious oversight function, rather than simply approving all projects and programs put before it. At its third meeting, for instance, it rejected all the work programs of the implementing agencies for duplication and confusion.[44] The ExCom has worked over the years to improve the effectiveness of the Multilateral Fund by modifying problematic policies. For example, developing countries were not initially required to forgo funding during the period when they were allowed to increase their ODS consumption, leading to a situation in which states were able to receive funding to close down old ODS-producing facilities while simultaneously building new ones. The ExCom, however, changed the process to require that states be decreasing their use of any substance for which they were receiving phaseout assistance from the fund.[45]

Central to the operation of the fund are the implementing agencies that do the actual work of proposing and executing projects. These are the World Bank, the UNDP, the United Nations Industrial Development Organization (UNIDO, added as an implementing agency in 1993), and UNEP. The World Bank is responsible for nearly half (45 percent) of the funding disbursement; its focus is on large-scale projects. UNDP, which receives 30 percent of funding, focuses on technical assistance, feasibility studies, and demonstration projects, as well as some direct investment. UNIDO, with 20 percent of funding, focuses on investment projects and plant-level phaseout. UNEP, which is prevented by its charter from implementing investment projects, focuses on institutional strengthening (including the establishment of National Ozone Units in recipient countries) and the preparation of country programs. It is allocated 5 percent of funding.[46] UNEP headquarters in Nairobi serves as fund treasurer.

The Multilateral Fund Secretariat, run by UNEP, is located in Montreal, Canada. In addition to day-to-day administrative tasks, it is responsible for monitoring data on the performance of fund projects, which it reports to the ExCom. The fund secretariat was intentionally set up in a different location from the protocol secretariat to increase the independence of the fund. The ExCom has given the responsibility to the secretariat to comment on proposals before meetings and return to implementing agencies for revisions those it does not feel are adequate. Because the Secretariat sees all the proposals, it is also well placed to put on the policy agenda those issues with broader cross-project implications.

The Multilateral Fund has had a major impact on the phaseout of ozone-depleting substances in developing countries. It has allocated more than $2 billion for the implementation of more than 5,000 projects. One hundred and thirty nine Article 5 states have created National Ozone Units. The Fund estimates that it has phased out 71,000 ODP tonnes of ozone-depleting substances in developing states,[47] and by the time all the projects already approved have been implemented the fund will have removed 204,843 ODP tonnes of ozone-depleting substances that would have otherwise been consumed, and 182,000 tonnes ODP that would otherwise have been produced.[48]

There have been some difficulties in reduction of use of ozone-depleting substances. A reasonably serious black market in controlled substances began once developed states were required to begin phasing out their use of CFCs. While much of this black market has been time-limited in the developed world and the incentive to use these substances decreases with shifts in technology,[49] the process of developing country consumption reductions offers new opportunities for illegal trade in controlled substances. Similarly, the emissions of CFCs and halons in some developed countries, particularly in North America, persist after official use has ended, because of slow replacement of refrigerators, air conditioners, and the use of pre-existing fire extinguishers, as well as leaks from recycling.[50]

Not all states have met their obligations under the Montreal Protocol, but the organization has a robust implementation process to address issues of non-compliance. The first set of states to not fulfill Montreal Protocol requirements were a set of Eastern European states that found that the economic turmoil caused by their transition from communism made it difficult to meet the 1996 deadline for phaseout of CFCs. The treaty secretariat persuaded them to submit themselves to the non-compliance procedure developed by the Montreal Protocol institution. Through this process they were allowed increased flexibility in phaseout dates and access to additional funding.[51] Since then, the Implementation Committee has taken up issues of non-compliance that have ranged from the procedural, primarily non-reporting of required data, to the substantive, such as consumption of controlled substances beyond that allowed by the phaseout schedule of the agreement. The states found to be in substantive non-compliance at the end of 2005 were Azerbaijan, Bangladesh, Chile, China, Ecuador, Micronesia, Fiji, Honduras, Kazakhstan, Kyrgyzstan, Libya, Sierra Leone, and Uruguay.[52] These states were identified through data they reported to the Ozone Secretariat, and are asked by the Implementation Committee to formulate a plan of action to bring themselves back into compliance. The committee works with them to gain the assistance they need to do so. Most states are generally cooperative in formulating a plan, and the non-compliance thus far has been fairly circumscribed.

As suggested by the minimal non-compliance, the Montreal Protocol process has had an impressive impact on state behavior overall. All developed states have now, with small exceptions for essential use, phased out their consumption and production of CFCs, halons, carbon tetrachloride, and methyl chloroform, and developing states have begun their process of doing the same.[53]

And the environmental news is encouraging. Because of the long atmospheric lifetimes of many ozone-depleting substances (with some of the first CFCs released in the 1920s still persisting), even decreasing the concentrations of these substances present in the atmosphere is difficult. But the concentrations of ozone-depleting substances are no longer increasing and are even beginning to decline.[54] Existing substances will continue to have environmental effects far into the future, which explains why the seasonal thinning in the Antarctic in 2005 was among the largest recorded.[55] The level of ozone depletion has probably neared its peak, however. Current estimates suggest that the ozone layer over the Antarctic will recover by 2065.[56] Although this recovery is later than originally estimated by models based on full and successful implementation of all amended Montreal Protocol requirements, it is something that would not have been possible without the creation and implementation of the Montreal Protocol. The international agreement and the institutional structure to implement it have succeeded in changing worldwide behavior in a way that is having a beneficial environmental impact.

Climate change

The institutional process to address climate change mirrors that pertaining to ozone depletion, but it has become much more difficult to achieve effective international governance on climate change or beneficial impact on the environment.

Climate change, more colloquially known as global warming, refers to a set of changes in world climate patterns that result from increased carbon dioxide (and other similar gases, such as methane, ozone, CFCs, and nitrous oxide) in the atmosphere. Though there are many natural causes of these substances, their abundance in the atmosphere increased dramatically with the advent of industrialization and has been continuing to increase. Because these "greenhouse gases" increase the ability of the earth's atmosphere to trap radiation from the sun, an increased average global temperature results. The predicted effects are varied and are not only about temperature, however. Increased ocean temperature leads to a rise in sea level because of the thermal expansion of water, and ocean and atmospheric currents are predicted to change, impacting weather patterns worldwide.

The basic science underlying the greenhouse effect has been understood for more than a century. At the turn of the twentieth century Swedish scientist Svante Arrhenius postulated that human activities responsible for putting increased amounts of carbon into the atmosphere could raise the earth's temperature. Other scientific advances came during the International Geophysical Year (1957–58, declared by the International Council of Scientific Unions) with the creation of permanent CO_2 monitoring stations, followed by the creation of the World Weather Watch and the Global Atmospheric Research Programme, under the WMO. The scientific community began discussing the need for policy action beginning with the First World Climate Conference in 1979.

The Intergovernmental Panel on Climate Change

From an institutional perspective, the most important scientific organization created before international negotiations to address climate change began was the Intergovernmental Panel on Climate Change (IPCC). The WMO and UNEP created this organization in 1988 "to assess on a comprehensive, objective, open and transparent basis the best available scientific, technical, and socio-economic information on climate change from around the world."[57] Though intergovernmental, it is not a standard international organization. States appoint eminent climatologists and researchers in relevant fields to the organization, but they serve as individuals rather than as representatives of states. The organization was charged with reporting on the status of climate science and issuing policy guidance. Each state appoints an IPCC "focal point" that coordinates IPCC involvement of the state.

Governmental representatives to the IPCC meet annually in a plenary session. This group makes decisions on the structure and procedures and budget of the organization, as well as the mandate of working groups and the timing of new reports. The IPCC Bureau has 30 members elected by the IPCC as a whole who serve for the duration of the preparation and presentation of an Assessment Report. The bureau is chaired by the chair of the IPCC. The IPCC Secretariat is supported by UNEP but hosted by the WMO at its headquarters in Geneva.

The IPCC operates via three working groups, the focus of which changes slightly with each assessment undertaken. For the present assessment, Working Group I focuses on science and evaluates the scientific understanding of the climate system and of climate change generally. Working Group II focuses on socioeconomic issues, examining the consequences of climate change and options for adapting to it. Working Group III evaluates options for reducing greenhouse gas emissions or otherwise preventing the problems of climate change. The IPCC also operates a Task Force on National Greenhouse Gas Inventories that examines practices and methods for undertaking inventories of greenhouse gas emissions. Each working group and task force has two co-chairs, one from a developing country and one from a developed country. The working group and the task force are also supported by Technical Support Units, located in (and supported by) the state of the developed country party whose national co-chairs a given working group. The co-chairs of the working group and the task force also serve on the bureau.

The most important output from the IPCC is the assessment reports it issues, on each of the topics the working groups focus on. Each assessment report is written by several hundred scholars and experts. The sections of the reports also undergo an intensive process of peer review, in which their findings and arguments are evaluated by qualified scholars not involved in the writing of the report. Each report also contains a Summary for Policymakers. This document is approved by the plenary session of the IPCC, which involves a negotiation of every line in the report. The lead authors of the full report also must approve the summary to make sure it is consistent with the science in the full report.

The First Assessment Report came out in 1990, before the major negotiations for an international agreement on climate change. It determined that there was a scientific reason to be concerned about climate change. After this report was issued, the UN General Assembly agreed to begin negotiations towards a climate treaty. The Second Assessment Report was issued in 1995. It is best known for the finding that "the balance of evidence suggests a discernible human influence on the global climate."[58] The Third Assessment Report was completed in 2001 and supported the assertion that humans are impacting the climate and will continue to do so through the twenty-first century. It predicted a continued increase in global average temperature and sea level. The fourth report is scheduled for 2007.

In addition to these broad assessments, the IPCC has prepared other reports on issues related to climate change. IPCC Working Groups I and III worked with the Montreal Protocol's Technology and Economic Assessment Panel on a Special Report on Safeguarding the Ozone Layer and the Global Climate System, focusing on HCFCs and perfluorocarbons. This report was requested by both the Conference of the Parties to the Framework Convention on Climate Change and the Meeting of the Parties to the Montreal Protocol, to address the fact that some common substitutes for ozone-depleting substances could contribute to climate change.

The United Nations Framework Convention on Climate Change

The scientific understanding of climate notwithstanding, the political problem of how to respond to climate change followed the new, but increasingly common, model of ozone depletion, in which a problem is hypothesized before its effects are felt. Scientists could measure the increasing concentrations of carbon dioxide in the atmosphere and could predict the likely consequences, but there had been no environmental impacts that people experienced as a result of this increase in greenhouse gases that could be unambiguously linked to climate change.

There were a number of early international efforts to address climate change politically. A variety of international conferences were held in the 1970s and 1980s, sponsored by international scientific groups, the WMO, and others, prior to the creation of the IPCC in 1988. Also in 1988 was an international conference in Toronto on "The Changing Atmosphere: Implications for Security" that called for states to cut their emissions of CO_2 by 20 percent by 2005, and a resolution in the United Nations General Assembly that called for "protection of the global climate for present and future generations."[59] The following year, the UNEP Governing Council requested that UNEP and the WMO begin negotiations for a framework convention to address climate change,[60] and the UN General Assembly recommended negotiation of a climate change agreement as well.[61] When the first IPCC report came in 1990, along with the WMO's Second World Climate Conference, pressure for a global agreement intensified.

Despite the fact that initial negotiations began under UNEP and the WMO, the United Nations General Assembly took over the negotiation process, with the creation of an Intergovernmental Negotiating Committee. The decision was also made to reach agreement on a convention in time to sign it at the already planned 1992 United Nations Conference on Environment and Development.

Though the agreement was conceptualized from the beginning as a framework convention, states had different views about the extent to which the agreement would include substantive abatement commitments for developed or developing states. There were many cleavages in the negotiations on this issue: between states more and less vulnerable to climate change, between richer and poorer states, between states that are larger or smaller emitters of greenhouse gases, and between those whose income comes primarily from the production of fossil fuels and those less economically dependent on world consumption of these substances. Even within developed states there were disagreements on the best types of instruments (taxes versus emissions requirements, overall rules versus those calculated per capita) to use to minimize environmental damage.

The extent of disagreement during the negotiation meant that no actual abatement obligations were included. States committed themselves to "stabilization of greenhouse gas concentrations in the atmosphere at a level that would prevent dangerous anthropogenic interference with the climate system."[62] They also agreed to conduct national inventories of greenhouse gas emissions and cooperate in scientific analysis of the issue.

Negotiations on the United Nations Framework Convention on Climate Change (UNFCCC) were completed in time for the agreement to be signed at UNCED in 1992. The agreement entered into force in March 1994. Developing countries are promised funding to meet the "full costs incurred . . . in complying with their obligations," indicating as well that the extent to which developing countries would be responsible for any action under the convention would depend on the developed countries meeting their obligations to provide funding and technology.[63] The Global Environment Facility (discussed further in Chapter 7) is designated as the institution to coordinate this funding process.

The Kyoto Protocol

Negotiations towards a protocol were initiated by the first Conference of the Parties in Berlin in 1995. The Ad Hoc Committee on the Berlin Mandate, as the negotiating committee was called, held eight negotiating sessions between 1994 and 1997. The negotiation was predicated on creating actual limits on emissions, but states disagreed on which states would be required to take them on. Another major discussion was on the possibility and extent of emissions trading. The final negotiations centered on the specific levels of emissions limits.[64]

The Kyoto Protocol requires actual reductions in emissions of greenhouse gases by developed countries (those listed in Annex I of the UNFCCC) by the time period 2008–12. These reductions are based on a 1990 emissions baseline and average about 5.2 percent, but differ by state, based largely on what individual states were willing to agree to, rather than any specific environmental or economic logic. Following the precedent set in the Montreal Protocol for special consideration for developing countries (listed in Annex II of the UNFCCC), there was no real consideration of obligations for these states in the negotiation of the agreement. They have no emissions abatement obligations under the Kyoto Protocol and are granted funding and technology transfer to support their activities (such as national reporting) under the UNFCCC.[65] There is opposition to this exemption of developing states from abatement obligations, particularly on the part of the United States. It is certainly true that in the long run developing states (some of whom are currently among the largest emitters of greenhouse gases) will need to reduce their greenhouse gas emissions for any significant impact to be made.

The protocol includes three "flexibility" mechanisms that give states options for meeting their reduction obligations. The first is emissions trading. States that reduce their emissions more than required may sell the spare reductions to other states for them to use to meet their obligations. The second is known as joint implementation. Developed country parties can receive credit for projects done in other developed country parties to reduce greenhouse gas emissions. Finally the agreement creates the Clean Development Mechanism (CDM), which allows developed country parties to receive emissions reductions credit for projects done in developing countries.

The protocol featured a double ratification rule, requiring that 55 states, representing 55 percent of developed country emissions of greenhouse gases in 1990, ratify the agreement before it could enter into force. Because the United States declared its intention not to ratify the agreement, meeting that emissions threshold required ratification by almost all other developed country parties. U.S. non-participation gave great bargaining leverage to those who had not yet ratified, and a number of conferences subsequent to the negotiation of the agreement modified the requirements in ways that appeased the concerns of those that had not yet ratified, particularly Japan, Canada, Russia, and Australia.

In a set of negotiations that took place at UNFCCC COP meetings (including an expanded COP-6, Part 2, when the issues had not been decided by the deadline the parties had set), states discussed the way the Kyoto obligations would be interpreted and implemented. One of the most important aspects of these Marrakesh Accords, as these understandings are known, concerns the extent to which states can count the removal of carbon from the atmosphere by "atmospheric sinks" (also called land use, land-use change, and forestry; or LULUCF) towards meeting their obligations. The parties agreed that human-created atmospheric sinks created since 1990 can count, and created a formula to define the amount that can be counted per year. They also agreed that these measures could be used under the CDM with some limitations on amount. Under these arrangements states gained the ability to make use of sinks to fulfill their obligations more than had been previously envisioned. This development represented acquiescence to the concerns of those states whose ratification of the protocol was necessary for it to enter into force. The accords also indicate that domestic emissions reductions should constitute a "significant element of the effort" each party makes in meeting its obligations, and that only states that have fulfilled the procedural requirements of the agreement may do projects under Joint Implementation and the CDM. In addition, the accords called for an increase in GEF funding for climate change and created three additional funds to help least developed countries and help countries adapt to climate change.[66]

Russia, which has already met its obligations under Kyoto simply because of the economic changes that followed the collapse of the Soviet Union, maintained that it would not ratify. It argued variously that climate change could be beneficial to the state in such a cold climate and (more persuasively) that the market for its excess emissions reductions was diminished without U.S. participation in the agreement. Russia eventually ratified in November 2004, causing the protocol to enter into force in February 2005.[67]

The same institutional structure oversees both the UNFCCC and the Kyoto Protocol. The secretariat is located in Bonn, Germany. The main decisionmaking body for the protocol is the MOP, which meets annually, in conjunction with the COP for the UNFCC. The institutional structure also includes a Subsidiary Body for Scientific and Technological Advice and a Subsidiary Body for Implementation, which meet twice a year and advise the MOP. The Marrakesh accords also added a CDM Executive Board to oversee implementation of the CDM, with representation from states with different concerns about climate change.[68]

While many states have changed their emissions behavior in the wake of the UNFCCC and the Kyoto Protocol, many Annex I states are likely to fall short of their Kyoto obligations. There are some optimistic overall trends. Between 1990 and 2003 the greenhouse gas (GHG) emissions by Annex I parties decreased collectively by between 5.9 percent (not taking LULUCF into consideration) and 6.5 percent (including LULUCF). Individual emissions practices vary considerably, however, ranging from an increase of 57.5 percent (Canada) to a decrease of 77.5 percent (Lithuania).[69] Some European states, like Britain, France, and Germany, are on target to be able to meet their obligations, but others, such as Italy and Spain, are much further behind.[70] Moreover, the enormous emissions decreases from the former Soviet bloc countries are mostly attributable to the dramatic economic changes these states went through at the end of communism. While beneficial from the perspective of GHG emissions, these decreases are not attributable to the Kyoto Protocol and emissions in these states are likely to begin to increase with increased economic prosperity.

The emissions of the largest emitters of greenhouse gases, however, continue to increase dramatically. These states do not have obligations under the Kyoto Protocol: the United States (the largest emitter), as long as it has not ratified the agreement, and China (second largest), along with all other developing countries, because they are not Annex I states. The worldwide increase in GHG emissions suggests that the problem of climate change is nowhere close to being ameliorated; indeed, the IPCC acknowledges that many of the impacts of climate change are inevitable at this point.[71]

The important question is what will happen after what Kyoto calls the "first commitment period." In December 2005 the organization began the negotiation process for action beyond 2012, and created a working group to discuss commitments for future reductions.[72] Others are less certain that the existing institutional structure is capable of undertaking sufficient action to slow climate change, especially without U.S. participation and with developing countries strongly resistant to taking on emissions reductions. An important, and unresolved, question is thus whether the UNFCCC and the Kyoto Protocol will be the institutional structure within which future obligations on climate change are negotiated.

Conclusions

The institutions addressing problems of the atmospheric commons have been among the most successful global environmental institutions. The institutions governing all three of these issues followed a similar process, beginning with general framework conventions that set out the goals and processes of cooperation, followed, as new information clarified the environmental problem, by increasingly strict protocols mandating substantive emissions reductions.

LRTAP has progressively tightened restrictions on emissions of acidifying substances in Europe and expanded the substances it regulates, and environmental conditions on the ground have improved. The Montreal Protocol governance process has changed industrial activity with respect to chemicals previously considered safe, and is beginning to result in environmental improvement. Though the problem of climate change is more controversial and more difficult to address, the institutional process to address it is following many of the successful processes put into place by earlier atmospheric institutions. It remains to be seen whether (and how), as increasingly dire predictions of the impacts of climate change are borne out by scientific research, states will be willing to act to address this problem.

Notes

1 WHO, *Climate Change and Human Health* (Geneva: WHO, 2003).
2 Pamela Chasek, *Earth Negotiations* (Tokyo: United Nations University Press, 2001), 80.
3 UNCHE, *Action Plan for the Environment*, 1972.
4 Gregory S. Wetstone and Armin Rosencranz, *Acid Rain in Europe and North America* (Washington D.C.: Environmental Law Institute, 1983).
5 OECD, *The OECD Programme on Long-Range Transport of Air Pollutants*: *Summary Report* (Paris: OECD, 1977).
6 LRTAP, Articles 2–5.
7 Marc A. Levy, "European Acid Rain: The Power of Tote-Board Diplomacy," in Peter M. Haas, Robert O. Keohane, and Marc A. Levy, eds., *Institutions for the Earth* (Cambridge, Mass.: MIT Press, 1993), 88.
8 EMEP, "Site Descriptions," available at http://www.nilu.no/projects/ccc/network/index.html.
9 Henrik Selin and Stacy D. VanDeveer, "Mapping Institutional Linkages in European Air Pollution Politics," *Global Environmental Politics* 3(3) (August 2003), 23.
10 Levy, "European Acid Rain," 85–86.
11 UNECE, "Status of Ratification of the 1979 Geneva Convention on Long-Range Transboundary Air Pollution as of 5 September 2005," available at http://www.unece.org/env/lrtap/status/lrtap_st.htm.
12 Barbara Connolly, "Asymmetrical Rivalry in Common Pool Resources and European Responses to Acid Rain," in J. Samuel Barkin and George E. Shambaugh, *Anarchy and the Environment* (Albany: SUNY Press, 1999), 130.
13 Levy, "European Acid Rain," 92–94.
14 LRTAP Protocol Concerning the Control of Emissions of Nitrogen Oxides, Article 2; The United States negotiated a different base year of 1978.
15 UNECE, "Protocol Concerning the Control of Emissions of Nitrogen Oxides," available at http://www.unece.org/env/lrtap/nitr_h1.htm.
16 LRTAP, Protocol Concerning the Control of Emissions of Volatile Organic Compounds or Their Transboundary Fluxes, Article 2(2).
17 UNECE, "The 1991 Geneva Protocol Concerning the Control of Emissions of Volatile Organic Compounds or Their Transboundary Fluxes," available at http://www.unece.org/env/lrtap/vola_h1.htm..
18 Protocol to the 1979 Convention on Long-Range Transboundary Air Pollution on Further Reduction of Sulphur Emissions, Articles 1(8), 2(1), and 2(5)(b).
19 Connolly, "Asymmetrical Rivalry," 129.
20 UNECE, "1999 Gothenburg Protocol to Abate Acidification, Eutrophication and Ground-Level Ozone," available at http://www.unece.org/ env/lrtap/ multi_h1.htm.
21 Levy, "European Acid Rain," 119.
22 Swedish NGO Secretariat on Acid Rain, "Acidification," available at http://www.acidrain.org/pages/acidEutrophications/sub3_1.asp#Areas.
23 Agreement between the Government of Canada and the Government of the United States of America on Air Quality (hereafter AQA), Article IV (2).
24 AQA, Annex I.

25 EANET Secretariat, "East Asian Acid Deposition Monitoring Network," available at http://www.eanet.cc/eanet.html.
26 Anna Brettell, "Security, Energy, and the Environment: The Atmospheric Link," in In-taek Hyun and Miranda Schreurs, eds., *The Environmental Dimensions of Asian Security: Conflict and Cooperation Over Environment, Energy and Natural Resources* (Washington, D.C.: United States Institute of Peace Press, forthcoming).
27 U.S. Environmental Protection Agency, "Class I Ozone-Depleting Substances," available at http://www.epa.gov/docs/ozone/ods.html.
28 Edward A. Parson, *Protecting the Ozone Layer: Science and Strategy* (Oxford: Oxford University Press, 2003), 47–50.
29 William C. Clark and Nancy M. Dickson, "America's Encounter with Global Environmental Risks," in The Social Learning Group, Learning to Manage Global Environmental Risks (Cambridge, Mass.: MIT Press, 2001), 266.
30 Parson, *Protecting the Ozone Layer*, 43–50.
31 Resolution on a Protocol Concerning Chlorofluorocarbons, Final Act of the Conference of Plenipotentiaries on the Protection of the Ozone Layer, 22 March 1985.
32 Parson, *Protecting the Ozone Layer*, 103.
33 Pamela S. Chasek, *Earth Negotiations* (Tokyo: United Nations University Press, 2001), 106–7.
34 Montreal Protocol, Article 1.
35 Montreal Protocol, Article 2; in the protocol the dates are given from the time of entry into force of the agreement; they have been translated into specific years here.
36 Ozone Secretariat, "Subsidiary Bodies of TEAP," available at http://hq.unep.org/ozone/teap/subsidiary_bodies.asp.
37 Parson, Protecting the Ozone Layer, 205–42. Under the London amendments states were required to report data on HCFCs but other controls were voluntary.
38 This latter provision was added in the London amendments; it mirrors the decisionmaking process in the Multilateral Fund.
39 Parson, *Protecting the Ozone Layer*, 230–32.
40 Ozone Secretariat, "Control Measures and Phase Out Schedule Under the Montreal Protocol," available at http://hq.unep.org/ozone/Treaties_and_Ratification/control_measures.asp.
41 Richard Benedick, *Ozone Diplomacy* (Cambridge, Mass.: Harvard University Press, 1991), 99–101.
42 Elizabeth R. DeSombre and Joanne Kauffman, "The Montreal Protocol Multilateral Fund: Partial Success Story," in Robert O. Keohane and Marc A. Levy, eds., *Institutions for Environmental Aid* (Cambridge, Mass.: MIT Press, 1996), 97–98.
43 Multilateral Fund Secretariat, "About the Multilateral Fund," available at http://www.multilateralfund.org/about_the_multilateral_fund.htm.
44 United Nations Environment Program, Draft Report of the Third Meeting of the Executive Committee of the Interim Multilateral Fund, UNEP/OzL.Pro/ExCom3(18) (1991).
45 Elizabeth R. DeSombre, "The Experience of the Montreal Protocol: Particularly Remarkable and Remarkably Particular," *UCLA Journal of Environmental Law and Policy* 19(1) (2000/2001), 74–75.

46 Multilateral Fund Secretariat, "Implementing Agencies," available at http://www.multilateralfund.org/implementing_agencies.htm.
47 Multilateral Fund, *Creating a Real Change for the Environment* (Montreal: Multilateral Fund Secretariat, 2005), 2–7.
48 Multilateral Fund for the Implementation of the Montreal Protocol, available at http://www.multilateralfund.org/.
49 DeSombre, "The Experience of the Montreal Protocol," 62–69.
50 "Editorial: New Ozone Findings Temper Success Story," *Minneapolis Star-Tribune* (3 January 2006).
51 Edith Brown Weiss, "The Five International Treaties: A Living History," in Edith Brown Weiss and Harold K. Jacobson, eds., *Engaging Countries* (Cambridge, Mass.: MIT Press, 1998), 154–55.
52 UNEP, "Report of the Seventh Meeting of the Parties to the Vienna Convention for the Protection of the Ozone Layer and the Seventeenth Meeting of the Parties to the Montreal Protocol on Substances that Deplete the Ozone Layer" (16 December 2005), 58–69.
53 UNEP, "Backgrounder: Basic Facts and Data on the Science and Politics of Ozone Protection" (August 2003), available at http:// hq.unep.org/ozone/ pdf/Press-Backgrounder.pdf.
54 Ozone Secretariat, "2002 Findings of Assessment Panel," available at http:// hq.unep.org/ozone/Public_Information/4Av_PublicInfo_Facts_assessment.asp.
55 British Antarctic Survey Bulletin (19 December 2005), available at http:// www.theozonehole.com/ozonehole2005.htm.
56 Alexandra Witze, "Antarctic Ozone Hole Set to Take 60 More Years to Recover," *Nature News* (online, 8 December 2005), available at http://www. nature.com/news/2005/051205/full/051205-9.html.
57 IPCC, "Why the IPCC Was Created," available at http://www.ipcc.ch/ about/about.htm.
58 IPCC, *Climate Change 1995: The Science of Climate Change* (Cambridge: Cambridge University Press, 1995).
59 UN General Assembly Resolution A/RES/43/53, 6 December 1988.
60 UNEP Governing Council Resolution 15/36, 25 May 1989.
61 UN General Assembly Resolution A/RES/44/207, 22 December 1989.
62 UNFCCC, Article 2.
63 UNFCCC, Article 4(3) and (7).
64 Pamela S. Chasek, David L. Downie, and Janet Welsh Brown, *Global Environmental Politics*, 4th edn. (Boulder: Westview Press, 2006),121–22.
65 Kyoto Protocol, Article 11.
66 David A. Wirth, "The Sixth Session (Part Two) and Seventh Session of the Conference of the Parties to the Framework Convention on Climate Change," *American Journal of International Law* 96 (July 2002), 648–60.
67 UNFCCC Secretariat, "Kyoto Protocol Status of Ratification," available at http://unfccc.int/essential_background/kyoto_protocol/status_of_ratification/items/2613.php.
68 Michele M. Betsill, "Global Climate Change Policy: Making Progress or Spinning Wheels?," in Regina S. Axelrod, David Leonard Downie, and Norman J. Vig, eds., *The Global Environment: Institutions, Law and Policy* (Washington, D.C.: CQ Press, 2005), 116.

69 UNFCCC Secretariat, "Greenhouse Gas Emissions Data for 1990–2003," available at http://unfccc.int/essential_background/background_publications_htmlpdf/items/3604.php.
70 "EU Industry Must Cut CO2 to Meet Kyoto Targets," *Planet Ark* (Reuters Environmental News Service) (11 January 2006).
71 IPCC, "16 Years of Scientific Assessment in Support of the Climate Convention" (December 2004).
72 UNFCCC Secretariat, "Press Release: United Nations Climate Change Conference Agrees on Future Critical Steps to Tackle Climate Change," available at http://unfccc.int/meetings/items/2654.php.

6 Transboundary movement of hazards

International action is needed, and institutions have been created, to address environmental problems that cross national borders. Often this border crossing is unintentional. Sulfur dioxide in the air travels with the prevailing winds; CFCs reach and deplete the ozone layer in places unrelated to where they are released. While the environmental harm caused by these substances is unintentional, they are used and released in the course of intentional industrial activity. Alternately sometimes the resource of concern is itself transboundary. Migratory species move across national jurisdictions in ways that suggest that they, or the habitats on which they depend, must be protected in multiple places. Harm to these species requires protecting them in all locations to which they travel.

Another set of institutions, examined in this chapter, addresses the movement of – and often trade in – hazardous substances. In some cases (as with trade in hazardous waste) these substances are themselves the byproducts of other industrial activity, but the trade is not incidental: this waste is transported intentionally to locations where disposing of it is cheaper or easier than in the location in which it was generated. In other instances (such as with pesticides or persistent organic pollutants (POPs)) the substances in question are themselves useful, but have been discovered to be harmful to human and ecological health to an extent not initially anticipated. Their movement across borders, either intentionally as substances banned in one location are traded to others where they are not, or through ecological cycles and movement within the food chain, transmits them to locations where people and organisms that did not choose exposure to them may be harmed.

The first of the global agreements created to address these problems were those that focused on international trade in hazardous waste, through the Basel Convention on the Transboundary Movement of

Hazardous Wastes and Their Disposal, with other regional agreements created to implement bans on transboundary waste disposal. The next focus was on trade in hazardous chemicals and pesticides intentionally traded, organized by the Rotterdam Convention on the Prior Informed Consent Procedure for Certain Hazardous Chemicals and Pesticides in International Trade. From there the logical expansion was to regulate the movement of other types of chemical hazards – POPs – that move at least partly in an involuntary manner. The Stockholm Convention on Persistent Organic Pollutants forms the core of the institutional process for addressing this issue.

These efforts share a number of similar approaches. The first is the idea of prior informed consent (PIC), the principle that states should have the right to know what they (or their residents) might be allowing across their borders and what dangers it could cause. Based on this knowledge they should be able to refuse import. (This principle, renamed advanced informed agreement (AIA), is the same approach that was later applied to the Biosafety Protocol, considered in Chapter 3). An extension of this approach allows states to categorically refuse specified imports of hazards; to indicate that they should never be contacted even to request permission to move something across their borders. Finally, the concerns about more diffuse harms from toxic substances have been approached by restricting trade even to states that have not banned the use of these substances, unless it is for environmentally sound disposal.

The second major similarity is that all of these agreements achieve their main regulatory objectives through restricting trade. This restriction, moreover, applies in some cases to states that have not taken on the obligations of the treaties in question, requiring that states refuse to trade in these substances with states that are not members of the agreement. There have been concerns expressed that these processes may run afoul of the World Trade Organization (WTO) prohibition on restricting trade for purposes other than trade policy.[1] This concern is greater in cases where trade prohibitions affect trade with non-parties, since they have not consented to the trade-restrictive regulatory structure. The agreements, particularly the more recent ones, have been negotiated with the knowledge of the potential intersection between the two sets of principles, but have chosen not to address the issue head on. The Stockholm Convention on Persistent Organic Pollutants, for instance, simply notes that "this Convention and other international agreements in the field of trade and the environment are mutually supportive."[2] Such a statement neither indicates an intention to supersede WTO rules when conflict arises nor subsumes Stockholm provisions to WTO standards.

These agreements and the institutions they create are focused at least partly on giving developing states practical control over their borders that they already have in principle as sovereign states. One might wonder why states need to have the right to refuse to accept hazardous substances elaborated in a treaty. But in practice developing states have often had little knowledge of what passed across their borders. The negotiation of agreements to address transfer of hazardous substances began after a number of high-profile examples of this lack of developing country control.

Transboundary movement of hazardous wastes

Though there is no universally accepted definition of hazardous waste, it is generally understood as unwanted material that poses a threat to human health and the environment. The question of what constitutes waste is as difficult as that of what should be considered hazardous; what is unwanted by some is useful to others, further complicating efforts to define or measure hazardous waste. The vast majority of what is generally considered to be hazardous waste (nearly 500 million tons per year) is currently generated by states in the developed world. Estimates suggest that about 90 percent of hazardous waste is currently produced by developed states and 80 percent of the world's total comes from the United States. In many of the states in which this waste is produced increasingly strict regulations about how it can be disposed of have increased costs of local disposal dramatically. States have thus looked for disposal opportunities elsewhere. Approximately 10 percent of hazardous waste generated is transported across international borders.[3]

The popular press often refers to these international disposal processes as "dumping." But although there certainly have been efforts to deposit hazardous waste in locations without the knowledge of the officials of the state in which it has been left, for the most part this transfer happens as a commercial transaction with financial compensation. States (or commercial entities) with waste pay other states (or commercial entities) to dispose of it. In theory this situation might not be a bad one: disposal states may choose whether the income they gain from agreeing to dispose of such waste offsets the potential environmental dangers it causes. In the best of circumstances waste could be disposed of in a location that is safer for it – away from population centers and water sources, in geologically stable areas – than the location in which it was generated. In practice, however, these efforts have functioned in a less than ideal manner. States that agree to take in waste may do so without the resources or knowledge to dispose of it safely, acquiescing either because they do not know the extent of the hazards or because their economic situation is sufficiently dire that they will take the risk for the promised income. Often these transactions are not taking place between states. A commercial enterprise in one state that needs to dispose of its waste in a cost-effective manner may contact individuals in another state who agree to take it in, without the knowledge of either side's state. Among the most frequently mentioned examples of this kind of transaction is the Nigerian citizen who rented his backyard to an Italian company for the storage of 8000 barrels of toxic and carcinogenic wastes.[4] Though most of the hazardous waste trade takes place between industrialized countries,[5] the aspect of this trade that provided the impetus for international negotiations was that between rich and poor states. This trade was increasing by the mid-1980s.[6]

There is concern not only about the disposal location but also about the process of moving the waste. The long-distance transport of hazardous substances increases the possibility that accidents along the way will create environmental damage, and increases the geographic range in which such a disaster could happen. Being able to transport waste elsewhere to dispose of it can also be responsible for decreasing the pressure on those who generate it to change their practices. Requiring states to dispose of waste within their own borders (or industrial actors to bear the cost of local disposal) helps to internalize some of the externalities of waste disposal and increases the incentives to find better ways to store it or avoid its generation in the first place.

The Basel Convention

It was concerns about these types of problems, and the dangers to the environment and to human health that could result, that prompted international attention to the issue of hazardous waste trade and the eventual negotiation of an international agreement to address it. The first efforts to manage hazardous waste trade internationally came from the Organization for Economic Cooperation and Development (OECD). In the 1980s the OECD developed a set of principles to control the movement of hazardous waste among countries in the OECD and created a system to classify and control such waste. The organization also proposed, in 1985, a draft for an international agreement to regulate movement of hazardous waste across state borders. The OECD yielded its involvement to UNEP once it became clear that UNEP was seriously pursuing an international agreement.[7]

UNEP first took up the issue in 1981, and the Governing Council created a working group to focus on the disposal of hazardous waste in 1982.[8] In 1985 this working group produced the Cairo Guidelines and Principles for Environmentally Sound Management of Hazardous Wastes, which the UNEP Governing Council adopted in 1987. These guidelines specified that exporting states should notify recipient states of the content of shipments of hazardous materials and should receive the consent of the recipient state before export. The exporting state should also verify that the recipient state has disposal requirements as stringent as those in the exporting state. These guidelines did not legally bind states, however.

The adoption of the Cairo Guidelines included a process (already planned at the time of the Governing Council decision) for the negotiation of an international, legally binding, agreement on the control of these substances.[9] The initial negotiating meetings took place in Budapest, with the adoption of the binding agreement in Basel, Switzerland, in 1989. UNEP executive director Mostafa Tolba played a central role in the negotiations, insisting that it be a substantive agreement rather than a framework convention.[10]

Negotiations were contentious. Developing states, particularly those in Africa, along with NGOs lead by Greenpeace, wanted to create a system in which developed states could not export hazardous wastes at all, or at least not to developing states. But the primary waste-generating states in the industrialized world, especially the United States, refused to agree to a system in which waste trade was prohibited. Developing states eventually acquiesced to a PIC system, believing it to be better than creating no agreement at all. The specification of the notification and consent scheme was controversial as well. Developing and industrialized states disagreed over how stringent the consent requirements would be, the extent of economic assistance for developing states, and the extent of liability requirements.[11] One rejected provision, for instance, would have required that the standards for the handling of hazardous wastes in countries of import be at least as stringent as those in the country that was exporting waste. African states initially proposed that United Nations inspectors verify the compliance of disposal sites with treaty requirements, but this provision was also voted down.[12] Other controversies concerned the right of transit through states and how to consider dependent territories and territorial waters.

The Basel Convention on the Control of Transboundary Movement of Hazardous Wastes and Their Disposal was opened for signature in 1989 and entered into force in 1992. The convention is organized around a set of principles. First, generation of hazardous waste should be minimized. Second, hazardous waste should be disposed of in a location as close to where it is generated as possible. Finally, transboundary movement of such waste should be tightly regulated. Annex I of the convention specifies categories of wastes controlled under the agreement, Annex II lists wastes not controlled (such as household waste) but that nevertheless require "special consideration," and Annex III defines "hazardous characteristics."

The specific rules embodied in the agreement make use of the idea of prior informed consent. Each state must appoint at least one "competent authority" and designate one as the recipient of information about the transfer of hazardous waste. Any state wishing to export hazardous wastes must notify (in writing) the competent authority of a recipient state. The recipient state is supposed to respond in writing within 60 days, either consenting to the shipment or denying permission. States may, however, waive their need to respond; under these circumstances, if no reply is received during the 60-day period exporting states may carry through with the export.[13] This latter provision has been suggested by some to be a weakening of the PIC principle. Developing states lacking capacity may have difficulty responding within 60 days, and not requiring an affirmative answer before shipping hazardous waste could lead to undesired receipt by developing states. While exporters are charged with ensuring that any waste they export only goes to states that are able to dispose of in an environmentally sound manner, there is no actual definition of what constitutes "environmentally sound," nor any clear process for ensuring that disposal meets that requirement once it has been sent.

States are allowed to prohibit the import of hazardous waste entirely. After they inform the secretariat of this decision other states may not allow export of hazardous wastes to them. By 1994 nearly 100 states had chosen to refuse all imports of hazardous waste.[14] In addition, any waste that is exported illegally, or waste that is exported within the requirements but that cannot be safely disposed of by the state that imports it, must be taken back by the state from which it originated.

Other obligations, such as the requirement to ensure that "the generation of hazardous wastes . . . is reduced to a minimum," are technically legally binding but almost impossible to enforce or even measure. Transport of waste to the Antarctic is also forbidden. In addition, states may not trade in hazardous waste with states that are not members of the agreement unless the waste shipment takes place under an international agreement that provides protections that are as strict as those required by the Basel Convention and are compatible with it.[15]

Amendments to the agreement are to be proposed and voted on at meetings of the COP. In order to be adopted an amendment must receive a three-fourths majority vote (of all parties present and voting). After an amendment has been adopted it must be ratified by individual states that voted in favor of the amendment originally, in order to bind them. When three-fourths of those states that voted in favor of the amendment have ratified it, the amendment enters into force.

The convention creates the COP as its decisionmaking body. This group meets at irregular intervals that have thus far ranged from one year to three. An Open-Ended Working Group meets in between COP meetings and works to implement and review COP decisions and convention effectiveness. Other working groups for the agreement include one for implementation (that existed previously in an ad hoc version), an ad hoc Working Group for the Protocol, and separate Legal and Technical Working Groups. Secretariat services for the agreement are provided by UNEP, headquartered in Geneva. The secretariat organizes itself into four programs – technical and capacity building; legal and compliance; partnerships, resource mobilization, and outreach; and resource management and conference services – in order to oversee the needs of treaty governance.

A 1999 Protocol on Liability and Compensation (adopted at COP-5) creates a framework for providing compensation for illegal dumping or spills of toxic wastes transported internationally, and for assigning liability for these problems. This issue was omitted from the original agreement and instead included as a protocol. As of late 2005 it had received a mere seven of the 20 ratifications required for it to enter into force, however.[16]

The sixth COP in 2002 adopted a compliance mechanism. This process created a Compliance Committee consisting of 15 member states drawn from five different UN regional groups. Parties may submit information about non-compliance – their own or that of another party – to this committee. The secretariat may also submit information to this committee when there is evidence in national reports that states may be having difficulty meeting their obligations under the agreement. The committee primarily focuses on assisting parties, through technical assistance, rather than on punishing infractions. Its terms of reference explicitly state that it is to be non-confrontational and that its objective is to "assist Parties to comply with their obligations under the Convention and to facilitate, promote, monitor and aim to secure the implementation of and compliance with" the agreement.[17] As of early 2006, the process had not been invoked.

Among the most important decisionmaking work of the COP has been the adoption of what is known as the Basel Ban. This process originated at the first meeting of the COP in 1992, in a proposal from UNEP executive director Tolba that the parties ban trade in hazardous waste between developed and developing countries. At this point his proposal was widely supported by developing states, and some European states – Finland, Denmark, Norway, Switzerland, Italy, and Sweden – supported it as well. But the opposition of the other major industrialized states was enough to block adoption of the proposal at that point. The issue was brought up again in the COP in 1994, where it received majority support to prevent the shipment from states that are members of the OECD, a group of developed states, to those that are not. This agreement would have taken effect in 1997. But some states argued that such a measure could not be passed by COP decision, since it would have the effect of amending the convention. Instead, in the third COP in 1995, a majority of parties voted in favor of amending the convention to accomplish the same end.[18] As an amendment, the Basel Ban requires ratification by three-fourths of the states that accepted it initially. This has not yet happened; as of early 2006 there were 61 ratifications of a required 62,[19] suggesting that the amendment might soon enter into force.

An additional controversy under the agreement has been the status of waste transport for recycling. During the negotiation of the convention it was initially uncertain whether waste destined for recycling would be subject to regulation, but it was eventually included. Once the Basel Convention and other regulations in developed countries to restrict trade in hazardous waste came into being, the international shipment of waste for "recycling" increased noticeably.[20] There was disagreement in the negotiation of the Basel Ban over whether to include waste intended for recycling in the ban. Some of the major industrialized states (including the United States, the United Kingdom, and Japan) argued that waste for recycling should be exempted from a ban on trade. Developing states, however, wanted the ban to cover all waste trade, and pointed to a study by Greenpeace indicating that much waste had been falsely labeled as recyclable or simply not recycled after being transported to developing states.[21] The eventual compromise allowed the trading of waste between North and South for "resource recovery, recycling reclamation, direct re-use, or alternative uses"[22] until 1997, but not thereafter.

Finally, while much of the international trade in hazardous waste is now indeed conducted under the system of prior informed consent that the Basel Convention oversees, it is much less clear that the institutional processes under the agreement have had a major impact in reducing the extent of international trade of such substances. A compilation of the first decade of country reports from Basel Convention members (which excludes large waste-trading states like the United States) finds cumulative trade increasing dramatically in the first ten years of the agreement. Of additional relevance is the fact that the collective reports of hazardous waste imports are, in each year, higher – sometimes dramatically so – than the collective reports of hazardous waste exports,[23] suggesting that reports of trade are inaccurate and exports likely understated.

More importantly, the institution has had little impact on the other main objective of the agreement: reducing the generation of hazardous waste overall. A 2004 secretariat report suggested that immediately following the entry into force of the agreement the global generation of hazardous waste decreased by a small amount, but the report attributed this diminution to the changes in activities of former Soviet-bloc countries transitioning to market economies, rather than to any effect from the Basel Convention. Moreover, hazardous waste generation has been increasing consistently since a low in 1996.[24] The fifth COP in 1999 decided that a focus for the first decade of the new century would be on waste minimization, itself an acknowledgment that the first decade of the agreement had had little impact on this aspect of the problem of hazardous waste. More importantly, the agreement is not set up to achieve a reduction in hazardous waste generation. It contains only vaguely worded obligations to reduce generation, does not have a uniform definition of hazardous waste, and does not require states to even calculate their level of generation of regulated wastes, thus providing no point of comparison for behavior over time.

As of the end of 2005 there were 166 members of the agreement.[25] The United States has signed but not ratified the agreement. It participated in the negotiation as the center of the coalition of developed states that refused to participate if a ban on waste trade from North to South was enacted. The United States has also actively opposed the Basel Ban and worked hard, through indirect methods (since it is not a party to the treaty and thus cannot participate in its decisionmaking processes directly), to gather opposition to it. The possibility that the United States might ratify the Basel Convention without the ban amendment has caused major controversy sufficient that some environmental activists would prefer that the United States remain outside of the agreement altogether.[26] If the United States joined the agreement without the ban it would be allowed to trade hazardous waste with other member states and yet not be bound by the prohibition against sending waste to developing states. Though the United States disposes of the vast majority of the hazardous waste it generates within its own borders, its share of the world's generation of hazardous waste is so large that even the 1 percent of waste it does send abroad makes it one of the important exporters of such waste.[27]

The Bamako Convention

African states had agitated for a much stronger regulatory system under Basel that would ban waste trade between developed and developing countries. When the initial negotiation failed to include such a provision, the Organization of African Unity (OAU) immediately began negotiations on an African agreement that would go further. OAU Resolution 1199, calling for this new agreement, argued that the inadequacies of the Basel Convention with respect to monitoring, technical and financial support, and especially its continued acceptance of hazardous waste trade, required a "common African position" on the issue of hazardous waste and its transport.[28] As a result, OAU members remained initially apart from the Basel Convention.[29] Only after the negotiation of a separate African agreement did some choose to join Basel as well.

The OAU created a working group of experts in law and environmental issues to draft a negotiating text. Negotiations were completed on the Bamako Convention on the Ban of the Import Into Africa and the Control of Transboundary Movement and Management of Hazardous Wastes Within Africa in 1991, and the agreement entered into force in 1998.

The Bamako Convention uses a broader definition of hazardous waste than does Basel, holding household waste to the same standards as other hazardous wastes. Unlike Basel it applies as well to radioactive waste. It also defines as hazardous any substance that has been banned, canceled, or not accepted for (or withdrawn from) registration in the state in which it was manufactured. Annex I of the agreement lists the categories of wastes that are controlled under the agreement, and Annex II specifies the characteristics of wastes considered to be hazardous.

The primary obligation of the agreement is for states to forbid the import of hazardous wastes, into any jurisdiction they control, from non-contracting states. Since only OAU (now African Union) member states can join the agreement, this provision prohibits imports of hazardous wastes from any state outside of Africa. States that are party to Bamako also agree not to dump or incinerate hazardous wastes in internal waters or on the high seas.[30]

The actual institutional function of the Bamako Convention has been almost non-existent, however. The decisionmaking body for the agreement is the COP, in which all member states are represented. The African Union (the successor organization to the OAU) has taken over secretariat responsibilities and is responsible for calling meetings of the COP. While the treaty stipulates that the first COP meeting should happen within a year of entry into force, no such meeting had happened as of mid-2006, despite the treaty's entry into force seven years earlier. The African Ministerial Conference on the Environment in 2004 urged "the African Union and the United Nations Environment Programme to revitalize the Bamako Convention" and establish the first COP.[31] The UNEP documentation in preparation for the 2005 African Ministerial Conference on the Environment notes that the agenda was to include an update on a proposed COP-1 for the convention.[32] The convention has served an important role, allowing African states to indicate, pursuant to the Basel Convention, that they will not accept shipments of hazardous wastes. But ensuring that these wishes are fully respected will require a governance process that Bamako and the African Union have been slow to implement.

Other regional agreements

Additional regional organizations have taken the opportunity that exists under the Basel Convention to negotiate regional agreements that expand upon the obligations of states to restrict hazardous waste trade. States of Central America created the Acuerdo Regional sobre Movimiento Transfronterizo de Desechos Peligrosos in 1992, which requires that Central American states ban the import to and transit through their territory of hazardous waste. Members of the South Pacific Forum negotiated the Waigani Convention to Ban the Importation into Forum Island Countries of Hazardous and Radioactive Wastes and to Control the Transboundary Movement and Managements of Hazardous Wastes within the South Pacific Region in 1995. It requires that states ban the import of hazardous (including radioactive) waste. The hallmark of the regional agreements negotiated along these lines is that they create a complete ban on hazardous waste imports from outside the region. The Regional Seas and related agreements (see Chapter 2) have negotiated post-Basel Protocols addressing wastes, following a strategy of minimizing waste generation and creating rules for better managing the trade in hazardous substances that exists. The states party to the Barcelona Convention for the Protection of the Mediterranean Sea Against Pollution, for example, added the Izmir Protocol on the Prevention of Pollution of the Mediterranean Sea by Transboundary Movements of Hazardous Wastes and their Disposal in 1996.

Other traveling toxics

Wastes are not the only hazards traded across borders. As rules to address trade in hazardous waste were being developed, international attention turned to addressing additional types of hazardous materials that might move across borders but would not necessarily be regulated by rules pertaining to waste. Chemicals and pesticides were increasingly exported internationally, and the 1970s and 1980s saw an enormous expansion of these exports to developing states, which by 1980 received a quarter of all trade in chemicals and one-third of all trade in pesticides.[33] This trade was not without consequences: the WHO estimated that between 1.5 and 3 million people are accidentally poisoned by these substances annually, the vast majority of these poisonings taking place in developing countries.[34] Initially some harmonization of national rules pertaining to the regulation of chemicals was undertaken by the OECD, but these rules did not attempt to regulate the transboundary movement of chemicals when states did not already have strong existing legislation.

The issue of international chemical safety had been taken up by a variety of UN bodies, most prominently UNEP and the FAO. Both initially focused on increasing the availability of information about the hazards of chemicals traded internationally. In 1985 the FAO, focusing on chemicals used as pesticides, adopted an International Code of Conduct for the Distribution and Use of Pesticides. UNEP had begun to address the issue of trade in hazardous chemicals as in the 1970s, in a decision recommending that governments work to prohibit export of chemicals that have been banned domestically, at least without the consent of the importing countries.[35]

One of the central processes for the regulation of chemicals existing at this time was the International Registry for Potentially Toxic Chemicals (IRPTC), created in 1976, following a recommendation from the Stockholm Conference in 1972. This registry, headquartered in Geneva, compiles information on regulations already in place in states that export chemicals, including limits and bans. A 1982 General Assembly resolution, at the behest of developing states, created the UN Consolidated List of Products Whose Consumption and/or Sale Have Been Banned, Withdrawn, Severely Restricted or Not Approved by Governments,[36] a similar mechanism, to which IRPTC contributes. In 1984, prompted by the Dutch government, the UNEP Governing Council created a Provisional Notification Scheme for Banned and Severely Restricted Chemicals, an expansion of IRPTC's mandate (again with IRPTC contributing, by developing a database of decisions by states to restrict specific chemicals.) Under this system states were to choose Designated National Authorities (DNAs) to notify IRPTC of any national actions controlling chemicals.

In 1987 the UNEP Governing Council adopted the London Guidelines for the Exchange of Information on Chemicals in International Trade,[37] in an effort to create a permanent system. The guidelines call upon states that export or import chemicals to exchange information and establish regulatory mechanisms to better manage chemicals, including by creating national registers of toxic chemicals.

Additional intergovernmental processes for the management of chemicals came out of preparations for the 1992 Rio Conference. Chapter 19 of Agenda 21, which addresses the "Environmentally Sound Management of Toxic Chemicals Including Prevention of Illegal International Traffic in Toxic and Dangerous Products," specifically calls for the creation of an intergovernmental forum on chemical safety. As a follow-up, UNEP, the International Labour Organisation (ILO) and the WHO jointly convened an International Conference on Chemical Safety in Stockholm in 1994. This conference created the Intergovernmental Forum on Chemical Safety (ICFS) and was considered to be its first meeting.[38] This forum has met every three years since then. Despite its designation as "intergovernmental," its structure includes both public (state-based) representation and participation from industry actors.

A related approach is the work towards developing a Strategic Approach to International Chemicals Management (SAICM). The UNEP Governing Council took up this issue beginning in 1995, with UNEP Governing Council Decision 18/12 suggesting that the UNEP executive director organize a group of experts to recommend international measures to reduce the risks of a set of chemicals. UNEP convened such a group in 1996. It pointed to four sets of problems with chemicals management that deserved attention: the lack of capacity in developing countries to deal with hazardous chemicals and pesticides, the problem of disposing of chemicals and pesticides that werc no longer wanted, the inadequacy of information for decision-making on chemical management, and the possibility that some chemicals should be phased out altogether.[39]

Environmental organizations had been pushing, in the creation of these various chemicals management schemes, for a system that would require actual notification before hazardous chemicals were traded. Though they did not succeed in including a PIC system or even one that required simple notification in any of the initial international regulatory processes, they had pressured individual governments to adopt such policies. Some, most notably the Netherlands, the United States, Canada, Japan, and eventually the European Community, were developing national regulations that restricted international trade of domestically banned substances, required notification to importing parties, and, in some cases, actually would require PIC. These environmental groups joined developing states in pressuring UNEP and the FAO to create a standard system, building from existing regulations, that would better regulate trade in chemicals internationally. In 1989 these two UN institutions worked together to create a voluntary PIC system. This system was officially integrated into existing schemes by amendment to the FAO Code of Conduct and the UNEP London Guidelines.

This voluntary process worked by creating a list of chemicals subject to PIC; anyone trading them across borders was encouraged – but not required – to obtain informed consent before shipping. For each of the listed chemicals, the secretariat of the process prepared a Decision Guidance Document (DGD) that summarized the available scientific information on the hazards of that substance. The DNAs were then charged with creating an "Importing Country Response," indicating whether that state allows imports of that substance. This information was disseminated to all DNAs.

The list of chemicals was created by the FAO/UNEP Joint Group. While existing regulatory processes and databases should have been useful for this process, they were not used for a variety of reasons: industry opposed the use of the UN Consolidated List and IRPTC had not used consistent definitions in collecting its information. The list was therefore created from scratch, based on chemicals that were subject to bans, severe restrictions, rejection, and withdrawal in individual countries. Under the system an initial list of chemicals subject to PIC was created, and after that point any time any one state enacted control measures for a new chemical it would be added to the list requiring PIC. By the late 1990s there were 38 substances listed in the PIC list.[40]

The Rotterdam Convention

There are some advantages to a non-binding regulatory system. David Victor argues that the voluntary PIC system allowed for flexibility. Since states knew they could avoid using the system if it produced regulations with which they disagreed, they were willing to leave the specifics of the process to experts.[41] Pesticide and chemical manufacturers also resisted regulation of any sort, particularly any binding international rules, so the designation of the rules as non-binding lessened potential opposition. But many of the non-state actors that pushed for the creation of the non-binding system really hoped for a binding agreement, and many developing countries agreed. Even as the process of regulation under the voluntary system was being created, preparations were underway for negotiation of a binding agreement.

In 1994, shortly after the Rio Conference, the FAO Council delegated to the FAO secretariat the job of preparing a draft Prior Informed Consent Convention. UNEP's Governing Council decided in 1995 to authorize the UNEP executive director to work with the FAO to convene an Intergovernmental Negotiating Committee (INC) to work towards a legally binding PIC agreement for chemicals management.[42]

The negotiations to move towards a binding agreement were held between 1995 and 1998. The negotiating process centered on how extensive the trade prohibitions would be. Developing states argued that chemicals prohibited domestically in developed countries should not be allowed to be sold or transported to developing countries, regardless of the domestic regulations in the importing countries, a provision others successfully opposed. There was also a question of whether, as proposed by the European Union, the agreement should take a convention/protocol format, allowing for protocols to address specific chemicals later. Many of the non-European industrialized states, foremost among them the United States, Canada, and Australia, argued against, and prevailed. Additional disagreements arose over the extent of information that would be required to be sent with a traded chemical.[43] The final decision was that the agreement would not create a set of harmonized rules for transmission of information, but exporters would "ensure adequate availability of information with regards to risks and/or hazards"[44] and would follow restrictions applicable in their own states. Negotiations that produced the Rotterdam Convention on the Prior Informed Consent Procedure for Certain Hazardous Chemicals and Pesticides in International Trade were completed in 1998.

The Rotterdam Convention essentially made the previous voluntary PIC process into a binding one, though there are a few changes. Unlike the voluntary agreement, under Rotterdam two (rather than one) state control actions, from states in different regions, are required for a chemical to be included in the list of substances requiring PIC.

Under the agreement, states may only export a chemical from the list of controlled chemicals (in Annex III) upon receiving consent from the importing state. All parties must inform the convention secretariat of any domestic regulations they have pertaining to toxic chemicals. All member states also declare, for each listed substance, whether they refuse under any conditions to accept shipments of that chemical, consent in general to imports of that substance, or consent under certain circumstances. States that wish to export chemicals must abide by the decisions of potential importers about whether to accept these chemicals.

In an interesting effort to ensure consistency with WTO rules against discriminatory trade, the agreement requires that states that refuse all imports of a specific substance under the agreement also stop producing it domestically (and may not import the substance from a state not party to the convention).[45]

The agreement also calls for states with advanced regulatory programs to provide technical assistance and help with capacity building in those states with less advanced regulatory programs, but it does not specify a process for this assistance. The lack of a specific funding mechanism in the agreement was controversial.[46]

The agreement entered into force in February 2004.[47] UNEP and the FAO together provide secretariat services for the agreement; as a result the secretariat for the Rotterdam Convention is located both in Geneva and in Rome. The COP is the main decisionmaking body for the institution, but the bulk of the regulatory work is conducted in committees. An Open-Ended Working Group has been created to work towards a non-compliance procedure.

The most important of the committees in the institution is the Chemical Review Committee, which recommends to the COP whether chemicals will be listed in Appendix III. Members of this committee are "government-designated experts in chemicals management" appointed by the COP. States propose the listing of chemicals or pesticides in Appendix III by submitting specified documentation. The secretariat also collects information on how states have regulated the proposed chemical, what evaluations of its risks have been done, and other information specified by the Chemical Review Committee. The Committee reviews this information in order to make a recommendation to the COP about whether a chemical should be listed, based on a set of criteria specified in Appendix II (for chemicals) and Appendix IV (for pesticides). The COP chooses, by consensus, whether to accept the committee's recommendation.[48] Before the agreement entered into force an Interim Chemical Review Committee, created by the negotiation process, was designated so that the process of reviewing chemicals for inclusion in the list could begin. In 2004, after the treaty entered into force, the first COP made the interim decisions binding.[49]

There are some concerns about how well the system set up under Rotterdam will function in reality. For instance, the trade provisions require much less documentation than do other efforts (such as CITES; see Chapter 3) to regulate trade for environmental purposes. There is no requirement that the manufacturer of the chemical be identified, nor the exporter, shipper, route, state of import, or importer. Unlike many international agreements (including others, like the Basel Convention, addressing trade in hazards) it does not prohibit trade with non-parties, and it does allow for export without prior informed consent in a set of circumstances deemed "exceptional;" these primarily involve the presumption of consent based on previous behavior.[50] For chemicals banned or severely restricted domestically but not listed in Annex III, the PIC requirements are also relaxed, requiring export notification but not actual consent.

An additional fear is the central involvement of the chemical industry (in developed countries) in the evaluation process of the regulated chemicals and pesticides. Much of the information about the hazards of chemicals comes from the producers of these substances, whose interests do not lie in restricting their use. Similarly, the chemicals are often tested under climatic and operational conditions in the developed countries in which the manufacturers operate, conditions that may not be relevant to the developing countries to which these substances may be exported.[51] The agreement has only begun to operate, however, so it remains to be seen how these fears play out in practice.

The Stockholm Convention

Some chemical pollutants are particularly dangerous because they are long-lived in the environment. Of special importance are those that bioaccumulate – that concentrate in the fatty tissue of organisms and become more concentrated as they are ingested continually up the food chain. They can cause cancer, disruptions of the immune and endocrine systems, birth defects, and other health problems. A set of these chemicals, called persistent organic pollutants (POPs) because of these characteristics, have been discovered to travel long distances in the environment from where they are manufactured or used. One of the major signals of the severity of this environmental problem came with the discovery that Inuit peoples in the Arctic Circle had concentrations of polychlorinated biphenyls (PCBs) in their tissues far exceeding safety standards, though these people had never used such substances. POPs also impact wildlife. These substances travel both in the food chain and in the air in vapor form (when exposed to higher temperatures) and are particularly likely to be deposited in cold areas.[52]

The efforts to regulate POPs built on many of the preceding regulatory processes for chemicals that also produced the Rotterdam Convention, as well as domestic regulatory efforts in some states. Beginning in the 1990s some individual states and regional organizations had taken steps to regulate the use of some POPs. The Convention for the Protection of the Marine Environment of the North-East Atlantic (the OSPAR Convention) included a ban on dumping POPs into the North Sea. The Helsinki Commission, overseeing the Convention on the Protection of the Marine Environment of the Baltic Sea Area (1992), made a number of recommendations that states limit their discharges of a number of POPs.[53] The United States and Canada agreed to control POPs in an effort to protect the great lakes from chemical pollution, and Mexico joined the other two in a Resolution on Sound Management of Chemicals as part of the North American Agreement on Environmental Cooperation (the environmental side agreement to the North American Free Trade Agreement).

UNEP Governing Council Decision 18/32 in 1995 called for a process involving the Inter-Organization Program on the Sound Management of Chemicals (IOMC), the IFCS, and the International Program on Chemical Safety to begin a process of assessing 12 initial POPs. The IFCS then convened a special ad hoc working group to create a process for evaluating these chemicals. This working group held a meeting of experts in 1996 in the Philippines, which concluded that there was enough evidence to regulate these substances internationally.[54]

The official process of creating the treaty came with a UNEP Governing Council resolution in 1997 accepting the findings on POPs from the 1996 IFCS special session.[55] The Governing Council resolution included the direction to form an INC to negotiate a treaty specifically on POPs with an initial focus on the 12 previously identified substances. The goal was to negotiate a treaty by 2000.[56]

Before negotiations began, UNEP held regional workshops in eight locations, focusing on concerns of developing countries about what a

POPs agreement could mean for them. These workshops are credited with increasing awareness of the problems of these substances and making negotiators aware of the concerns of states that would be impacted by the regulations.[57] UNEP also made sure to provide funding for developing country officials to attend the negotiation sessions, and held two of the five negotiating sessions in Africa to increase the involvement of developing countries. The negotiations themselves were held beginning in 1998. The Stockholm Convention on Persistent Organic Pollutants was open for signature in 2001 and entered into force in 2004. As with the Rotterdam Convention, the INC continued to meet after the agreement was completed to oversee the transition to a functioning agreement before it entered into force.

The negotiations were more contentious than anticipated, in part due to different approaches to management. Developed states, influenced by the POPs Protocol to the Convention on Long-Range Transboundary Air Pollution (discussed on pp. 150–51), considered the issue to be primarily about long-range transport. Developing states were more concerned about issues of local management.[58] The major controversy, however, came over the regulation of dichlorodiphenyltrichloroethane (DDT). Some developing countries in malaria-prone areas were especially concerned about the inclusion of DDT, the most effective insecticide used against mosquitoes, on the list of substances to be controlled under the agreement. NGOs were also deeply involved in the negotiations; they were officially included as observers in the negotiations, which gave them access to the decisionmakers involved in the process. A number of health and environmental NGOs organized themselves into the International POPs Elimination Network (IPEN) in order to coordinate efforts, and were joined by other major environmental NGOs. IPEN and most of the other environmental NGOs advocated the principle that the convention should seek to eliminate rather than to manage POPs.[59]

The treaty initially addresses the 12 substances that had been the focus during the negotiations. Eight of them are pesticides: aldrin, endrin, dieldrin, chlordane, DDT, heptachlor, mirex, and toxaphene. Two are industrial chemicals: PCBs and hexachlorobenzenes. The final two, dioxins and furans, are the byproducts of industrial activity or waste incineration.

The substances to be controlled under the treaty are listed in annexes. Annex A lists the substances whose use and production are scheduled to be eliminated. (There are special procedures for PCBs, listed in this annex, to account for the extent of their use in existing electronic equipment, allowing a phase down rather than requiring immediate elimination of equipment in which they are a component part.) Annex B lists substances whose use and production are restricted but not prohibited altogether. Initially the only substance listed in Annex B is DDT (though others could eventually be added), and some specific arrangements are made in this annex for DDT. Annex C lists regulated chemical byproducts. The other annexes elaborate information on the persistence and other chemical properties of regulated chemicals and socioeconomic considerations for regulation.

Under the agreement states are required to prohibit or eliminate production and use of substances listed in Annex A. States are, however, allowed to designate "specific exemptions" for use of substances listed in this annex. Parties must restrict production and use of substances listed in Annex B. States can register for exemptions to these restrictions as well. The secretariat maintains a list of the exemptions, which must specify the country, purpose, and length of time for the exemptions. These exemptions are subject to review by the COP and are scheduled to end five years after the treaty's entry into force. In addition, states may only register exemptions at the point of becoming a party to the agreement (or before); states are thus not free to create new exemptions at any point in time. In another move to limit the use of the exemptions process, once all exemptions have been removed for a specific substance and purpose no new ones may be entered. The agreement creates a separate process of exemption for DDT, listed in Annex B. This chemical may only be used for disease-vector control following WHO guidelines, and only then "when locally safe, effective and affordable alternatives are not available to the Party in question."[60] A separate register of DDT exemptions is kept. The process allows for flexibility in obligations (including differentiation between obligations of states) without having to formally write the differentiation into the agreement or create a process for amending the agreement to account for it. The agreement also includes a controversial provision for other exemptions from obligations for certain critical uses of POPs, such as for research and development or use in location-limited production of other substances.

The convention limits trade in controlled substances. For those chemicals for which a relevant trading partner has not registered an exemption, parties may not export chemicals listed in Annex A or B to any state, whether it is a party or not, unless the export is for "environmentally sound disposal."[61]

Parties must also undertake measures to decrease or prevent releases of listed chemicals unintentionally produced (listed in Annex C), by developing national plans to identify current and projected releases of these substances and elaborating strategies to minimize the release into the environment of these substances. Though some in the negotiations had proposed creating specific timetables for reductions of these byproducts by certain amounts, others opposed this and such a measure was not included in the final agreement. Similarly, states must ensure that existing stockpiles of chemicals listed in Annex A or B (including wastes) are properly disposed of, though the treaty does not create a specific process by which this would be ensured.

There are a number of obligations for parties to gather and report information. States are required to develop their own implementation plans within two years of joining the agreement, which must be reported to the secretariat of the agreement and periodically reviewed and updated. They must also provide regular reports on their production, import, and export of controlled substances and lists of states to which these substances have been exported or from which they have been imported. Though the agreement creates no standing scientific body, states are required to conduct research, including cooperatively, and to report the results and data from this research.

The agreement is administered by a secretariat under the auspices of UNEP. The headquarters of the agreement are in Geneva. The treaty process is governed primarily by the COP, with all member states represented and having equal voting rights. Any party may propose the addition of a substance to one of the annexes. These proposals are given to the Persistent Organic Pollutants Review Committee, consisting, as specified in the convention, of "government-designated experts in chemical assessment or management," with equitable geographic distribution.[62] Decisions in the committee can be made by approval of two-thirds of the members voting. If the committee is satisfied that the pollutant meets the criteria elaborated in Annex D, it forwards the proposal and its evaluation to the parties to the agreement and asks for information specified in Annex E on the socioeconomic impacts of control measures and alternatives. The committee may then decide to submit the chemical and all gathered information to the COP, which will decide whether to include it in one of the annexes.

A decision by the COP to add a substance to the appendices requires a three-fourths majority vote. The treaty specifies that the COP should make this decision in a "precautionary manner." Once the COP has decided to add a substance, the parties are all bound by its inclusion, unless they opt out. To do so they must give notification within a year of the adoption that they do not intend to be bound by the new provision. In an unusual process, however, states may instead declare, when joining the agreement, that any changes to the annexes require its affirmative ratification rather than becoming binding if the state does not opt out.

One of the contentious issues in the negotiation process was the specification of a funding mechanism. Under the agreement, developed states agree to "provide new and additional financial resources to enable developing country Parties and Parties with economies in transition meet the agreed full incremental costs" of implementing the agreement. Developing states preferred a funding process focused solely on the problem of POPs, out of concern that the GEF had too broad a focus and that funding would become diluted across the many issues for which it provides funding. Nevertheless, the treaty specifies the GEF as the interim funding mechanism,[63] and the first meeting of the COP in 2005 affirmed the continuing status of the GEF as the funding mechanism for the agreement. At the same time, however, the COP asked for the creation of a memorandum of understanding between the GEF Council and the Stockholm Convention COP to assist cooperation.[64]

Initial worries that the treaty would take a long time to enter into force did not come to pass. Concerns expressed about the lack of documentation for trade under the Rotterdam Convention apply to an even greater extent to Stockholm. The agreement does not require any uniform documentation with shipments of regulated substances.[65] As of mid-2006 there were 120 states that had ratified the convention, the United States (which signed in 2001) not among them.[66] Lack of U.S. participation is worrying because of its major role in producing POPs.

Additional regulation of persistent organic pollutants

The Convention on Long-Range Transboundary Air Pollution (see Chapter 5) has also addressed the regulation of POPs, via a protocol. The Protocol on Persistent Organic Pollutants was first discussed within LRTAP beginning in 1989. Negotiations began on a protocol in 1994 and entered into force in October 2003. As of mid-2006 there were 25 parties.[67] Because it is a protocol to an existing convention, it is governed by the LRTAP decisionmaking process rather than creating its own institutional structure.

The protocol lists controlled substances. An initial 16 were included in the agreement, and a process was created to evaluate substances for possible future inclusion in this list. Substances are listed in three different annexes. Annex I includes pesticides and industrial chemicals that are to be eliminated completely, including existing stockpiles, which need to be destroyed in an environmentally friendly way. Annex

II lists pesticides and industrial chemicals the use of which is restricted. There are some exceptions to the restrictions for those substances listed in Annexes I and II if they exist in small quantities.

Relations among toxics institutions

There is overlap among the major agreements pertaining to international movement of hazardous substances, in terms of substances regulated and the processes by which they are regulated. Cooperation across the major institutions to address these issues (Basel, Rotterdam, and Stockholm) has been informal rather than structured. Many of the same actors within governments (or in NGOs) work towards implementing the agreements, and involvement of UNEP in providing secretariat services for all three creates opportunities for communication across them that might not otherwise happen.

UNEP in particular makes the argument that these three agreements provide "a framework for lifecycle management" of hazardous chemicals, especially POPs (which are addressed in all three agreements). A UNEP brochure gives an overview of "the hazardous chemicals and waste conventions,"[68] and discussions under the UNEP Intergovernmental Group on International Environmental Governance considered whether these three agreements should be clustered. In practice, however, there is little actual coordination across agreements.

Conclusions

Institutions governing the transboundary movement of toxics are relatively new and involve potentially conflicting concerns of developed and developing states. Early experience suggests that these institutions have thus far had some impact on the ability of developing states to implement their complex preferences – to avoid receiving hazardous waste or to continue to use DDT for malaria control – but have not, as yet, fundamentally changed the way developed states generate waste or work with toxic chemicals and pesticides. Both the Rotterdam and Stockholm Conventions have only recently begun to operate, however. Whether these institutions can change the way chemicals and pesticides are used and moved across borders remains the central challenge.

Notes

1 Jonathan Krueger, *International Trade and the Basel Convention* (London: Earthscan, 1999).

2 Stockholm Convention on Persistent Organic Pollutants. Preamble.
3 Pamela S. Chasek, David L. Downie, and Janet Welsh Brown, *Global Environmental Policitics*, 4th edn. (Boulder: Westview Press, 2006), 129.
4 Jim Vallette and Heather Spaulding, eds., *The International Trade in Wastes: A Greenpeace Inventory* (Washington, D.C.: Greenpeace USA, 1990).
5 Kate O'Neill, *Waste Trading Among Rich Nations* (Cambridge, Mass.: MIT Press, 2000).
6 David J. Abrams, "Regulating the International Hazardous Waste Trade: A Proposed Global Solution," *Columbia Journal of Transnational Law* 28(3) (1990), 807–11.
7 Krueger, *International Trade and the Basel Convention*, 22–23.
8 UNEP Governing Council Resolution 10/24, 31 May 1982.
9 UNEP Governing Council Resolution 14/30, 17 June 1987.
10 Mostafa K. Tolba, with Iwona Rummel-Bulska, *Global Environmental Diplomacy: Negotiating Environmental Agreements for the World, 1973–1992* (Cambridge, Mass.: MIT Press, 1998), 101.
11 Krueger, *International Trade and the Basel Convention*, 30–31.
12 Abrams, "Regulating the International Hazardous Waste Trade," 830–31.
13 Basel Convention, Articles 5 and 6.
14 Chasek, Downie, and Brown, *Global Environmental Politics*, 131.
15 Basel Convention (1989), Articles 4 and 11.
16 Basel Convention Secretariat, "Basel Protocol on Liability and Compensation . . . ," available at http://www.basel.int/ratif/frsetmain. php# protocol.
17 Secretariat for the Basel Convention, "Mechanism for Promoting Implementation and Compliance: Terms of Reference," available at http://www.basel.int/legalmatters/compcommitee/index.html.
18 David Downie, Jonathan Krueger, and Henrik Selin, "Global Policy for Hazardous Chemicals," in Regina S. Axelrod, David Leonard Downie, and Norman J. Vig, eds., *The Global Environment: Institutions, Law and Policy* (Washington, D.C.: CQ Press, 2005), 130. There are some differences between the original decision and the ban amendment. The OECD categorization is not used, instead prohibiting trade between states that are listed in Annex VII and those that are not.
19 Secretariat of the Basel Convention, "Status of Ratification: Ban Amendment," available at http://www.basel.int/ratif/frsetmain.php?refer = ban-alpha.htm.
20 Jennifer Clapp, *Toxic Exports: The Transfer of Hazardous Wastes from Rich to Poor Countries* (Ithaca: Cornell University Press, 2001).
21 Jim Puckett, "The Basel Ban: A Triumph Over Business-as-Usual" (Amsterdam: Basel Action Network, 1997), available at http://www.ban. org/about_basel_ban/jims_article.html.
22 Basel Convention, Annex IV(B); Ban amendment.
23 Secretariat of the Basel Convention, *Global Trends in Generation and Transboundary Movement of Hazardous Wastes and Other Wastes: Analysis of the Data Provided by Parties to the Secretariat of the Basel Convention* (UNEP: Basel Convention Series, No. 14, April 2004).
24 Secretariat of the Basel Convention, *Global Trends*.
25 Secretariat of the Basel Convention, "Status of Ratification" (22 August 2005), available at http://www.basel.int/ratif/frsetmain.php.

26 Basel Action Network, "Why the US Must Ratify the Entire Basel Convention (or Not at All)," *Briefing Paper* No. 2 (December 1999).

27 Marian Miller, The Third World and Global Environmental Politics (Boulder: Lynne Rienner Publishers, 1995), 89–90.

28 OAU Resolution 1199, February 1989.

29 J. Wylie Donald, "The Bamako Convention as a Solution to the Problem of Hazardous Waste Exports to Less Developed Countries," *Columbia Journal of Environmental Law* 17 (1992), 430.

30 Bamako Convention, Articles 4 and 22.

31 African Ministerial Conference on the Environment, "The Sirte Declaration on the Environment for Development and the Decision on a Strategic Approach to International Chemicals Management,", SAICM/PREPCOM.2/INF/13 (4 August 2004), available at http://www.chem.unep.ch/saicm/meeting/prepcom2/saicm2_infs/saicm2_inf13/INF13.pdf.

32 UNEP, African Ministerial Conference on the Environment Extraordinary Meeting of the Expanded Bureau of AMCEN (21 October 2005).

33 David Victor, "'Learning by Doing' in the Nonbinding International Regime to Manage Trade in Hazardous Chemicals and Pesticides," in David G. Victor, Kal Raustiala, and Eugene B. Skolnikoff, eds., *The Implementation and Effectiveness of International Environmental Commitments: Theory and Practice* (Cambridge, Mass.: MIT Press, 1998), 226

34 Robert L. Paarlberg, "Managing Pesticide Use in Developing Countries," in Peter M Haas, Robert O. Keohane, and Marc A. Levy, eds., *Institutions for the Earth* (Cambridge, Mass.: MIT Press, 1996), 309–50.

35 UNEP Decision 85(V), 25 May 1977.

36 UN General Assembly Resolution 37/137, 17 December 1982.

37 UNEP Decision 14/27, 17 June 1987.

38 International Institute for Sustainable Development, "Summary of the Fourth Session of the Intergovernmental Forum on Chemical Safety: 1–7 November 2003," *Earth Negotiations Bulletin* 15(87) (9 November 2003), 1–2.

39 International Institute for Sustainable Development, "Summary of the First Session of the Preparatory Committee for the Development of a Strategic Approach to International Chemicals Management: 9–13 November 2003," *Earth Negotiations Bulletin* 15(92) (16 November 2003), 1.

40 Victor, "Learning by Doing," 236–44.

41 Victor, "Learning by Doing," 257.

42 UNEP Governing Council Decision 18/2, 26 May 1995.

43 Jenifer Ross, "Legally Binding Prior Informed Consent," *Colorado Journal of International Environmental Law and Policy* 10 (1999), 522.

44 Rotterdam Convention, Article 13.

45 Rotterdam Convention, Article 10(9).

46 Paula Barrios, "The Rotterdam Convention on Hazardous Chemicals: A Meaningful Step Towards Environmental Protection?," *Georgetown International Environmental Law Review* 16 (Summer 2004), 737–39.

47 Rotterdam Convention Secretariat, http://www.pic.int.

48 Rotterdam Convention (1998), Articles 5 and 18.

49 IISD, "Second Meeting of the Conference of the Parties to the Rotterdam Convention on the Prior Informed Consent Procedure for Certain Hazardous Chemicals and Pesticides in International Trade: 27–30 September 2005, Report 1," *Earth Negotiations Bulletin* 15(125) (27 September 2005).

50 Rotterdam Convention, Article 11(2).
51 Barrios, "The Rotterdam Convention," 739–40.
52 Arctic Monitoring and Assessment Project, *Arctic Pollution Issues: A State of the Arctic Environment Report 1997*, available at http://www.amap.no.
53 Henrik Selin and Stacy VanDeveer, "Baltic Sea Hazardous Substances Management: Results and Challenges," *Ambio* 33(3) (2004), 153–60.
54 IISD, "Report of the Conference of Plenipotentiaries on the Stockholm Convention on Persistent Organic Pollutants: 22–23 May 2001," *Earth Negotiations Bulletin* 15(57) (25 May 2001).
55 Peter Lallas, "The Stockholm Convention on Persistent Organic Pollutants," *American Journal of International Law* 95 (July 2001), 695.
56 UNEP Governing Council Decision 18/32, 25 May 1995.
57 Erin Perkins, "The Stockholm Convention on Persistent Organic Pollutants: A Step Towards the Vision of Rachel Carson," *Colorado Journal of International Environmental Law and Policy*: 2001 Yearbook (2001), 196.
58 Henrik Selin and Noelle Eckley, "Science, Politics, and Persistent Organic Pollutants," *International Environmental Agreements: Politics Law and Economics* 3 (2003), 17–42.
59 Andrew J. Yoder, "Lessons from Stockholm: Evaluating the Global Convention on Persistent Organic Pollutants," *Indiana Journal of Global Legal Studies* 10(2) (Summer 2003), 133–34.
60 Stockholm Convention, Articles 3 and 4 and Annex B.
61 Stockholm Convention, Article 3(2). These prohibitions do not apply to "laboratory-scale" amounts of controlled substances.
62 Stockholm Convention, Article19(6)(a).
63 Stockholm Convention, Article 13(2) and 14.
64 IISD, "Summary of COP-1 to the Stockholm Convention: 2–6 May 2005," *Earth Negotiations Bulletin* 15(117) (2005), 8.
65 Richard W. Emory, Jr., "Transposing to Enforceable National Law the Obligations of the PIC and POPs Conventions for Imports and Exports," *Colorado Journal of International Environmental Law and Policy Yearbook* (2001), 38.
66 Stockholm Convention Secretariat, "Participants," available at http://www.pops.int/documents/signature/signstatus.htm#notes.
67 United Nations Economic Commission for Europe, LRTAP Secretariat, "Protocols to the Convention," available at http://www.unece.org/env/lrtap/status/lrtap_s.htm.
68 UNEP, "The Hazardous Chemicals and Wastes Conventions," available at http://www.basel.int/pub/threeConventions/pdf.

7 Emerging issues and future directions

This volume concludes by discussing three issues that are becoming increasingly important in global environmental institutions. These are the role of funding in the negotiation and implementation of international environmental agreements; the efforts to gain participation by all relevant states (especially the United States, which has become increasingly reluctant) in international environmental institutions; and the broader question of whether, or how, the system of global environmental governance should be fundamentally reshaped.

Funding

One of the major issues facing international environmental cooperation is how to pay for it. In some circumstances, environmental action can save money, through avoiding the costs of environmental degradation. These cost savings, however, tend to be in the aggregate and in the long term. In the short term, making use of different technologies, forgoing development opportunities not considered to be environmentally damaging, and undertaking other environmentally beneficial behaviors requires costly investment. Similarly, even if environmental behavior can benefit a country in the aggregate it may not benefit all sub-state actors. The costs that are avoided from ensuring clean water do not benefit the company that must pay to dispose of its toxic waste somewhere other than the local water supply. Most environmental problems are externalities of other economic activities – the unintended (and unpriced) effects of industrial activity. That means that, at least initially, changing behavior in order to make it less environmentally damaging is likely to have a cost.

There are a variety of costs to undertaking environmental activities. These include indirect costs such as the costs of setting up and running international organizations (paying for permanent staff and running an office, and travel to meetings) and supporting international scientific research. For most states, however, the primary costs pertain to their own domestic implementation.

Developing countries have been hesitant to accept the expenses of international environmental agreements. This reluctance is understandable. They are not primarily responsible for most of the international environmental problems that currently exist. They fear that richer states, which were the ones to create many of the current problems in their process of industrialization, now want to prevent them from industrializing using the same inexpensive and tested technologies developed states used. And developing states, often with growing populations, have many pressing problems of poverty on which their initial attentions are focused. If these states are to join international environmental agreements, they need to be persuaded that doing so is worth their while. Funding may make that possible.

Global Environment Facility

The most prominent institution for international funding to address global environmental issues is the GEF. It was established at roughly the same time as the Montreal Protocol Multilateral Fund (discussed further in Chapter 5), to serve as a more general funding institution for environmental aid. Although there had been calls for an institutional structure for channeling funding for the environment in the World Commission on Environment and Development and in UNEP in the 1980s (see Chapter 2), the initial creation of the GEF came out of discussions in the World Bank beginning in 1989. The bank had been asked to look into the usefulness of an open-ended funding mechanism for international environmental issues by the German and French finance ministers.[1] The GEF began as a pilot program in November 1990, housed in the World Bank but with involvement from other international funding institutions. The United States, which had opposed the creation of a new open-ended funding obligation, was assuaged by the promise that the new organization would not immediately be made permanent.[2]

What differentiates this institution from previous World Bank lending is that the aid is given primarily as grants rather than loans. World Bank funding has traditionally been premised on supporting projects that could eventually generate income so that the loans may be repaid. This approach has been problematic for issue areas such as the environment in which problems are the result of unpriced externalities, and many useful reforms would not be economically profitable. In

addition, states may not be eager to take out loans to accomplish benefits that accrue primarily to the global environment. As with the
Multilateral Fund, the funding is intended to cover the incremental
costs to developing countries of undertaking environmental activities
that do not generate net economic benefits.

The initial approach was to focus on four areas where environmental impacts are decidedly international: biodiversity, climate
change, ozone depletion, and international waters. At UNCED in Rio
in 1992 the organization was named as the interim funding mechanism
for both the UN Framework Convention on Climate Change and the
Convention on Biological Diversity.

The pilot phase of the GEF was reviewed in 1993 by an independent panel commissioned by the organization (that included critics of
the bank and the GEF). This panel pointed to a lack of participation
by affected communities in GEF decisionmaking, noted a lack of
accountability, and found that the implementing agencies were not
cooperating sufficiently.[3] Some NGOs, most prominently Conservation
International and the Natural Resources Defense Council, undertook
their own evaluations of the pilot GEF. They commented on the
unsuitability of general World Bank operating procedures, which had
traditionally focused on large infrastructure projects, to the GEF
mission and criticized the bank for its lack of local capacity building and
oversight and for projects that were "too big." They nevertheless
expressed optimism that a reformulated GEF could play an important
role.[4]

Responses to the official evaluation and other criticisms were
mixed, but the World Bank engaged countries in negotiations about
the reorganization of the GEF for its permanent, "operational" phase.
As was the case in the initial creation of the mechanism, it was the
tensions between the developing countries and the United States that
were the most prominent in efforts to reform the GEF. Even prior to
the 1993 evaluation the developing countries had won concessions for
their agreement to allow the GEF to become the interim funding
mechanism for the UNFCCC and the CBD, with promises that the
organization would be made more democratic and transparent.

In an effort to achieve greater representation, a "participants
assembly" was created to oversee GEF operations. This assembly
includes representatives from all member states and from the implementing agencies and the conventions that make use of the GEF. It
operates by consensus and can approve potential amendments to the
underlying GEF agreement and make statements about GEF policies

and goals. It meets only every four years and some have questioned its usefulness, arguing that it has no clear governance purpose.

In addition, the renegotiation created a reformed GEF Council. The new council was created with 32 members, 16 from developing countries, 14 from developed countries, and two from the former Soviet bloc, with each group allowed to determine how representatives would be chosen. It meets twice a year to approve GEF work programs and projects. Decisions require a double-majority vote, requiring the support of three-fifths of the countries on the council as well as three-fifths of votes as weighted by contributions, although consensus is sought and generally obtained. Decisions thus require the support of the largest donors and some developing country agreement. The secretariat was created as functionally independent from the World Bank. In addition, the mandate of the organization was broadened, to include land degradation. Agreement on these reforms and on making the GEF permanent came in March 1994.

Though housed in the World Bank, the GEF also uses UNDP and UNEP as implementing agencies for projects. In addition, it cooperates with the regional development banks as well as UNIDO and the FAO, called executing agencies, in establishing projects. The organization also has a Scientific and Technical Advisory Panel, composed of 15 experts in its focal areas, whose task it is to give advice on all scientific and technical aspects of the GEF's work and priorities.

The funding is contributed by donors every four years in what is known as a "replenishment." The amount of the replenishment is decided in difficult negotiations between the organization and donor states. The GEF began operations with pledges of just over $1 billion. The first replenishment in 1994 was in the amount of $2 billion, the second in 1998 was $2.75 billion, and the third in 2002 came to $3 billion,[5] with a fourth negotiated in 2006. Funding donated for GEF projects is supposed to be "new and additional," meaning that it represents funding from donors that would not have already been given in a different context. But the GEF has not given clear guidelines on what that means and it can be difficult to determine whether states are indeed giving the GEF funding they would not otherwise have given.

Another element of GEF funding is that it is intended to work to leverage other funding, as governments, international organizations, and private entities are asked to give additional support to GEF projects. The GEF claims that it has leveraged $14.5 billion to augment the $4.5 billion in direct funding it has given as grants during its operations.[6]

The involvement of NGOs in global environmental governance has been generally controversial, and nowhere more so than in funding mechanisms. The GEF resisted NGO involvement, but in 1995 decided that the advantages outweighed the disadvantages and began to allow NGOs as observers in GEF meetings.[7] NGOs are now also involved in implementing GEF projects. A small grants program under UNDP funds projects that are administered partly or wholly by NGOs.

GEF funding has contributed to important projects in its focus areas, funding more than 1300 projects in 140 states since its inception. The largest portion of its funding has gone to address issues of biodiversity, with $1.89 billion given in GEF grants for biodiversity-related projects.[8] GEF biodiversity projects have worked to increase the ability of states to implement the CBD, for which it serves as official funding mechanism, and have focused on conservation and sustainable use of particular types of ecosystems.

The GEF is also the funding mechanism for the UNFCCC and Kyoto Protocol. It has thus far provided $1.74 billion in grants for this issue area, for projects focusing on energy efficiency and conservation, the use of renewable energy, the adoption of technologies with low greenhouse gas emissions, and sustainable transport.[9] It has also played an important role in supporting developing countries in conducting emissions inventories and planning adaptation programs.

Funding for the protection of international waters is not connected to any particular global agreement and, as such, has involved a smaller degree of GEF funding than some other areas. The organization has given grants of $767 million to fund projects designed to help states work together to protect shared water resources.[10] The GEF funding goes to address issues of pollution, invasive species management, and quantity of fresh water available for use. At least in part because there is no existing global agreement on this issue, this funding has gone to help states to cooperate internationally. Efforts in this area have been praised for increasing scientific understanding of threats to water quality, but criticized for not requiring clear ecological improvement.[11]

Most international funding to address ozone depletion takes place through the Montreal Protocol Multilateral Fund (discussed in Chapter 5). The GEF role in ozone depletion filled an important gap in Multilateral Fund operations that emerged because of the political and economic transition in Eastern Europe and the Former Soviet Union. Because the Multilateral Fund's rules require that it only fund Article 5 (developing) countries and these former Soviet-bloc states were considered to be developed countries, they were stuck in the awkward position of owing money to the Multilateral Fund for the use of developing countries while not being able to finance their own phaseout. The GEF, working within its original mandate to address ozone depletion, was able to fill this institutional gap, by providing financing for phaseout projects in these countries. It has allocated $177 million towards projects of this type.[12]

Since the GEF was created, additional issue areas have been added to its purview – most prominently land degradation and persistent organic pollutants. It has become the interim funding mechanism for the Stockholm Convention on Persistent Organic Pollutants. Thus far it has put $141 million towards this issue. Most recently the Convention to Combat Desertification has come under the rubric of the GEF.

Some are concerned about the increasing scope of GEF activities. For instance, developing countries resisted naming the GEF as interim funding mechanism for the Stockholm Convention for fear that with finite amounts of funding allocated to more and more issues and treaty processes each individual agreement would gain less.

The GEF has undertaken or commissioned official evaluations throughout its operations. In addition to the evaluation of the pilot phase, a second evaluation, to examine the functioning of the restructured GEF once the pilot phase was past, was commissioned by the organization in 1996 and completed by 1998. A third study (called the *Second Overall Performance Study*)[13] was outlined in 2001 and completed in 2002. The GEF now also has its own Office of Monitoring and Evaluation that reports to the GEF Council. This office has conducted evaluations of clusters of projects, such as of certain types of projects in Eastern European countries addressing phaseout of ozone-depleting substances.[14]

Overall assessments of the GEF's accomplishments from both inside and outside of the organization are mixed. The institution certainly had a rocky start. The implementing agencies themselves in 1998 declared 12 percent of GEF projects unsatisfactory.[15] Some early critics pointed to lack of support from both donors and recipients, and to political battles that constrained operating effectiveness.[16] Some criticisms are structural: funding to support incremental costs and specific convention agendas does not address the underlying political causes of environmental degradation in developing countries.[17] Others argue that projects undertaken by the World Bank outside of the environment realm (such as the construction of an energy pipeline that can increase the use of fossil fuels) undermine the positive results from GEF funding.[18] And, importantly, the amount donor states have been willing to pledge to the organization is vastly less than what most analysts believe is necessary to make real headway against global environmental problems.

The GEF has been praised, however, for being "innovative and adaptable."[19] And even if the funding is insufficient, it is far more than has been contributed to address most of these issues or than would likely be contributed in the absence of the GEF. Early concerns that the organization was not focusing on issues of importance to developing countries should be mollified by the expansion in focus areas. Even critics generally express optimism for the potential of the GEF, a potential its more recent activities seem headed towards fulfilling.

Global participation

A second major issue in global environmental institutions is how to gain participation by all relevant actors. Most of the environmental problems addressed in this volume are global, or at least international, in scope. Ecosystems rarely reflect political boundaries, and activity undertaken in one state has effects in others. Most environmental problems are (in game-theoretic terms) issues of common pool resources (CPRs).[20] The first defining characteristic for such issues is that they are non-excludable, meaning that actors cannot be excluded from the good, such as the fish on the high seas. The second is that they are subtractable, meaning that the resource can be diminished by use. If one person catches a fish it is not available for someone else to catch, and the more fish that are caught the fewer remain in the ocean to reproduce.

The issue of non-excludability means that all states can potentially affect an environmental problem. It is for that reason that environmental institutions are generally global – any state may join. If a problem can be caused by (or can affect) any state, the solution should be open to participation by any state. The issue of subtractability is even more important. It means that a state that remains outside of global environmental governance has the potential to undermine the ability of cooperative institutions to successfully mitigate an environmental problem. If most states agree to cooperate to protect fisheries, their restricting of their fishing behavior can be ineffective if a state with a large fishing fleet continues to catch large numbers of fish. In this circumstance cooperating states lose doubly: they make use of less of a resource than they would prefer to and (if others remain outside the cooperative agreement) also fail to protect the resource.

In this way environmental issues differ from other issues addressed through global institutions. Consider the international institution governing international trade. The WTO operates by requiring that "most favored nation" status be given to all members of the organization – in other words, all members of the WTO must treat all members as favorably (with respect to trade access) as they do any other members. This approach is possible because agreements about trade are not diminished by those who do not participate in them. Those within the organization are not negatively impacted by the fact that not everyone is in it. That is due in large part to the characteristic of the issue area itself, but there are elements to how the institution is designed that could reinforce or alternately undermine the issue structure.

The CPR nature of international environmental problems means that it is essential to include all states that might contribute to an environmental problem in the institutions to address it. There are different approaches that are used to attempt to gain universal participation. One important one is funding, as provided through the GEF (described on pp. 155–161) or the Multilateral Fund. Donors fund the "incremental costs" that developing states incur in taking on environmental obligations, so that fear of the costs does not prevent them from undertaking environmentally beneficial actions.

A second approach is for institutions to provide advantages to members while excluding non-members from benefits. The Montreal Protocol prohibits member states from trading ozone-depleting substances with any state that is not a party. The Basel Convention allows member states to send hazardous waste only to other member states (or those who agree to follow the rules of the convention). The Convention on International Trade in Endangered Species allows trade in regulated species only with other states that follow the CITES documentation procedures. More recently, a number of regional fisheries management organizations have required that members conduct trade in regulated species only with those states that are members of the relevant regional fisheries management organization or can otherwise prove they have caught the fish within its rules.[21]

Another tool used in the effort to achieve widespread participation is the requirement for entry into force of international environmental agreements. Most recent international agreements on any issue require a certain threshold of ratifications (and then a short lag time) before they enter into force. Environmental agreements have generally increased the number of ratifications required for entry into force over time. The Convention on Wetlands of International Importance Especially as Waterfowl Habitat required ratification by only seven states before it entered into force,[22] and the World Heritage Convention by only 12.[23] The Convention to Combat Desertification (1994) required 50 ratifications before it entered into force.[24] The requirement for a certain number of states to ratify makes sense: if a treaty entered into force for a state as soon as it ratified, without consideration for the behavior of others, that state could find itself bound by an agreement that no (or few) others took on. Since the problem would not be successfully addressed under these circumstances, the small number of states that took on the responsibilities of the agreement would suffer the costs of changing their behavior without receiving the benefit of successfully mitigating the environmental problem. Under these circumstances states might be reluctant to ratify agreements.

One of the novelties recently in international environmental agreements is that they have also moved to requiring certain thresholds of behavior. If 50 states ratify agreements pertaining to emissions of an industrial chemical but they are all small states that rarely emit the substance, the group of states in the agreement is not sufficient to make a difference in the environmental problems caused by its use. Similarly, if a large number of developing states ratify an agreement that exempts them from substantive obligations, they will not have an impact on the overall condition. So international agreements under the International Maritime Organization generally require ratification by a certain number of states that account for a certain percentage of registered shipping tonnage. The Montreal Protocol requires ratification by 11 states that represent "at least two-thirds of global consumption of controlled substances" from 1986,[25] and the Kyoto Protocol requires ratification by 55 states that account for 55 percent of the 1990 emissions of CO_2 (or its equivalents) by those states that have initial obligations under the agreement.[26] For the Kyoto Protocol the threshold was designed so that it would be extremely difficult, but not impossible, for the treaty to enter into force without the United States, which accounted for 36 percent of 1990 emissions.

The difficulties gaining a sufficient ratification threshold for the Kyoto Protocol to enter into force are evidence of a broader recent trend in international environmental institutions: the non-participation of the United States in global environmental governance. This trend is obviously not unique to the issue area of the environment. The unilateralism of the United States is well known across issue areas, particularly pertaining to security and human rights. And it is not as recent as popular discussions of the U.S. failure to ratify the Kyoto Protocol might suggest. The United States has remained apart from major environmental institutions beginning in the 1980s. It is important to understand both the implications of the lack of strong U.S. involvement in global environmental institutions and possible reasons for it.

The first large-scale environmental agreement the United States refused to ratify was the United Nations Convention on the Law of the Sea, the negotiation of which was concluded in 1982. The United

States expressed concern over the provisions to oversee deep-seabed mining, especially those that transferred resources to developing countries. The United States has also remained apart from international arrangements pertaining to transboundary movement of hazards. Despite being the largest producer of hazardous waste it has not ratified the Basel Convention. It has also not signed or ratified the Convention on Biological Diversity or the Biosafety Protocol, though it is the largest producer of genetically modified crops. While it has signed both the Stockholm and Rotterdam Conventions it had not, as of early 2006, ratified either.

This U.S. relationship with global environmental institutions is reasonably new. The United States was a willing participant in early resource treaties (such as fisheries agreements) of the first half of the twentieth century, and was a leader in the first wave of negotiations of the major international environmental institutions in the 1970s. The Convention on International Trade in Endangered Species was negotiated at the behest of the United States, and the creation of the World Heritage Convention was proposed by the United States at the Stockholm Conference. The United States also initiated the negotiations that created the London (Dumping) Convention and played an important role in the negotiation of the Montreal Protocol.

The United States also has a reputation for actually living up to the international obligations it takes on,[27] unlike some other states. And there are other agreements (both environmental and otherwise) that it does not ratify but nevertheless does not abrogate either, most human rights treaties being prominent examples. Nevertheless, its non-participation in a number of international environmental agreements causes consternation.

What is the effect of the United States' non-participation in these agreements? On a broader level the implications of the United States' non-participation are both less and more serious than they might initially appear. The United States is still more fundamentally protective of the environment than many other states, and its behavior on many agreements in which it does not participate is often largely in accord with the requirements of the agreement. It exports only a small portion of its hazardous waste (and most of the exports go to Canada), and it is acting within the requirements of all major provisions of UNCLOS, for example.

In addition, non-ratification may mean official non-participation, but the United States is nevertheless clearly involved in most of these institutions, albeit in an unofficial capacity. The United States was represented at all of the meetings about how to implement the Kyoto

Protocol before it entered into force and has been at the meetings of the parties since then. Its involvement comes in part because the states in the agreement hope to be able to persuade the United States to participate and for that reason do not want to exclude it from relevant discussions.

But this version of participation points to the major negative impact of lack of U.S. participation as well. Other states hope to be able to lure the United States to fully join the agreements in question. The effort to bring the United States (or other important states) into international governance processes can lead to a weakening of institutional obligations in order to appease those states.

The Kyoto Protocol is a perfect example. In early 2002 there were still five Annex I states that had not ratified: the United States (responsible for 36 percent of 1990 emissions), Australia, (2 percent), Russia (17.4 percent), Japan (8.5 percent), and Canada (3.3 percent).[28] Some combination of these five states would have to ratify the agreement for it to meet the threshold to enter into force. In order to persuade these states to ratify, negotiations continued over how to interpret the agreement. As discussed in Chapter 5, the rules were changed in ways that substantially weakened the agreement in order to lure the recalcitrant states into the agreement.[29] Japan, Canada, and Russia, the latter two with large forest areas, pushed for a redefinition of how carbon sinks (land-use practices, such as forestry, that keep carbon out of the atmosphere) would be counted under the agreement. This redefinition increases the extent to which they could use and count these practices against their required reductions. Warwick J. McKibben and Peter J. Wilcoxen estimate that this change alone "reduced the overall stringency of the protocol by 54.5 million metric tons of carbon." These obligations were relaxed even further (to an estimate of 70 million metric tons) when Russia's sink allowance was further increased at the seventh COP.[30] Japan and Canada ratified in 2002; Russia's ratification at the end of 2004 cleared the way for the agreement to enter into force in 2005, but not before Russia had wrested additional aid and support in its bid to join the WTO from the European Union as a condition of its ratification.[31] The lack of U.S. participation in Kyoto thus clearly led to the weakening of an already limited agreement.

Why does the United States choose to remain apart from so many global environmental obligations? Uncertainty – about the severity of the problem, the costs of proposed solutions, or even whether an anticipated problem will materialize – is frequently given as a reason for U.S. reluctance. This explanation seems unlikely, however. While it is true that some of the issues the United States has declined to address internationally – such as climate change – have large degrees of legitimate uncertainty, some (such as UNCLOS or Basel) do not. And there are issues with high uncertainty – such as ozone depletion or international fisheries management – in which the United States has actively participated.

Perhaps the United States is simply concerned about the cost of regulatory action, an argument made for why it remains outside the Kyoto process. On the other hand, a comparison of the relative costs of the international environmental obligations the United States takes on with those it does not indicates no clear pattern of cost. The predicted costs of implementing the Montreal Protocol or CITES (which requires complex border control measures) were likely to be much greater than those of implementing the Biosafety Protocol or even the Basel Convention.

Another possibility is that that United States is simply making a rational assessment of the likelihood that it will be the harmed by the environmental problem and prioritizing those issues that would have the greatest impact domestically. But it is not clear that the United States would suffer more damage from ozone depletion than from climate change, or from extinction of endangered species than from loss of biodiversity.

There is no clear answer to what determines U.S. resistance to international environmental agreements, but aspects of domestic politics are likely to play an important role. More important than the overall cost of action to protect the environment may be action that would be costly to politically powerful industries within the United States that have the ability to influence the political process. Many attribute the U.S. reluctance to act on climate change to the political power of domestic energy producers.[32] A more nuanced view of the impact of industry on U.S. willingness to take on international environmental obligations comes from considering the U.S. domestic political process and noting that the separation between the executive and legislative branches requires a supermajority of the Senate plus presidential approval to take on international obligations. The U.S. Senate is particularly prone to pressure from special interest groups, with senators responsive to issues that affect their individual states rather than the country as a whole. The international environmental obligations that the United States takes on tend to be those on which the country has already acted domestically, for which international action does not pose entirely new regulatory burdens and may even create competitive advantage for regulated industries.[33] In other words, those concerned with the U.S. unwillingness to participate fully in international environmental institutions and the international problems this non-participation causes may be advised to focus on persuading it to regulate domestically, which then gives it an incentive to act internationally.

Many institutions or one: towards a World Environment Organization?

As should be clear by this point in the volume, institutions addressing global environmental institutions are numerous and overlapping. Within a given issue area there are multiple institutions that address different aspects of a problem or focus on different types of solutions. There are some advantages to this diffuse structure of global environmental governance. Redundancy in international environmental institutions provides a check against ineffectiveness in any one institution.[34] Innovation, a hallmark of global environmental governance, may be greater when there are many institutions addressing environmental issues in different ways.[35] The presence of multiple institutions focusing within an issue area may itself be a sign that they are fulfilling different roles, since each was negotiated with awareness of previously existing institutions.

But this structure creates problems as well. There is overlap in the mandates and missions of existing organizations. There is competition for scarce resources, be they money or time. Many of the institutions discussed in this volume face shortages of assessed funding, and even assessed funding falls short of needs. Professionals who address global environmental institutions have to attend too many meetings that address similar issues. The creation of a new agreement or institution may serve to appease domestic constituencies and deflect attention, without effectively addressing the underlying problems that caused concern.

Given the difficulties that come from having so many specialized and sometimes overlapping institutions to address global environmental issues, some scholars have argued for a World (or Global) Environment Organization.[36] Such an institution might accomplish what UNEP cannot, in terms of international coordination of all environmental research and action. The promotion of UNEP into a more powerful institution might be the most obvious route for creating such an organization.

There are a number or arguments in favor of the creation of a single global environmental organization. One of the most prominent reasons given for such an institution is to counterbalance the influence of the WTO in conflicts between trade and the environment. As noted throughout this volume, many existing environmental institutions use trade restrictions to accomplish environmental goals. And although the WTO has shown a general acceptance of trade restrictions when undertaken in support of multilateral environmental protection goals,[37] scholars and activists fear the possibility that it will disallow these measures or that environmental impacts from trade will be overlooked internationally because of the primacy of the WTO.[38]

Another reason to consider the advantages of an overarching environmental institution is the concern that existing institutions create incompatible rules or the potential to counteract each other. One early example of these kinds of difficulties came in the context of atmospheric issues. The Montreal Protocol mandated reductions in ozone-depleting substances, but some of the most promising early substitutes had high global warming potentials, meaning that while they did not harm the ozone layer they did contribute to climate change. There was no requirement under the Montreal Protocol process to take environmental impacts beyond those on the ozone layer into consideration, but the MOP did eventually work to phase out substitute chemicals that contributed to climate change. While this particular issue was resolved successfully, the potential for overlap or incompatibility is large.

There are numerous arguments against the creation of a World Environment Organization, however. Environmental issues across the range of existing institutions are sufficiently different from each other that the advantages of addressing them together may not materialize.[39] The specialized knowledge needed to protect fisheries is vastly different from that pertaining to persistent organic pollutants. Even the incentive structures facing regulators in these diverse issues (resources that could be sustainably harvested versus hazardous externalities) are profoundly different. A larger central organization might also face intransigent governance issues that can be avoided in organizations with a smaller focus, with macropolitical issues such as disagreements between North and South preventing action on unrelated issues, and decisions held up by fear of the precedents created.[40]

Perhaps the most persuasive of the arguments against creating an overarching institution is the current impossibility of doing so. At some point in the past it might have been possible to create one central environmental institution. But even if that could have happened after the Stockholm Conference it would be increasingly difficult now, when existing institutions each fulfill functions that at least some states find useful. In addition, international efforts at large-scale institutional coordination in environmentally relevant issues do not have a good track record. The third United Nations Conference on the Law of the Sea (which focused only on oceans) demonstrated the difficulty of attempts to achieve global coordination within an issue area, producing vague rules that often resulted from least-common-denominator agreements, and even then failing to gain the approval of the most powerful state in the system. And at least in the current structure when a state opts out of participation in one global environmental institution it may be actively engaged in another. An all-or-nothing system might run the risk of excluding states that wish to be involved in governance of some, but not all, environmental issues.

The major factor undermining such an institution is political will. It is no accident that the global environment is governed by a segmented set of small institutions, overseen (to the extent that oversight exists) by a weak United Nations program, working at the margins to modestly improve environmental conditions without changing the fundamental economic structures that underpin global environmental problems. States have been unwilling to commit to anything further. One of the most persuasive scholars arguing this point is Adil Najam. He suggests that calls for a single global institution amount to no more than "organizational tinkering" and miss the underlying lack of political interest in addressing the environmental problems.[41] States have yet to be persuaded that their behavior must fundamentally change in order to protect the global environment, and that doing so is worthwhile. As Sebastian Oberthür and Thomas Gehring point out, institutional reform "cannot substitute for lack of political interest in and support for environmental protection."[42]

Though critics disagree on the desirability of a centralized global environmental institution, there is widespread agreement that some kind of reform of the international governance of global environmental issues is necessary. Perhaps the answer to ineffective global environmental governance is to improve the governance in existing institutions, rather than to substitute a new centralized organization. Most suggest better coordination across the range of institutions. Peter Haas advocates a multiplicity of institutions that focus on different functions of environmental governance, consolidating (for example) the work of multiple monitoring organizations.[43] How this consolidation would happen is left unspecified, however. Konrad von Moltke similarly suggests that existing institutions should be "clustered" in like-groupings, coordinated by issue area, instead of creating new institutions.[44]

Ultimately, however, this reform will inevitably be driven, or prevented, by states. As the European acid rain experience demonstrates, institutions can play an important role in redefining states' interests and persuading them to be concerned about problems they were not previously interested in addressing. But states create international organizations and their decisionmaking structures, and they can – and do – choose not to participate in those they do not believe reflect their interests.

International environmental problems are difficult to address internationally. Many environmental problems appear as externalities of other economically beneficial activities undertaken by actors with power in domestic political processes. Though there are long-term advantages to preventing or mitigating environmental damage, there are also short-term costs to doing so, and there is often legitimate uncertainty about the causes or effects of environmental problems. Policymakers seeking re-election fear accepting certain costs in the present to accomplish uncertain gains that might appear long after their political careers end. States that benefit from environmental protection could benefit more from free riding on the cooperation of others, and the fear that others may free ride (and thereby undermine successful international cooperation) may prevent states from creating strong international institutions.

It is thus not surprising that global environmental institutions are, for the most part, weak and underfinanced. Multiple institutions exist because states create those they feel will be most advantageous to their concerns and decisionmaking priorities. That some of these institutions have had the degree of success they have – in protecting some endangered species and ecosystems, preventing ocean pollution, phasing out ozone-depleting substances and lessening acid deposition, and decreasing the transboundary movement of hazards – is a testament to their effectiveness. Reform that can increase the efficiency of existing organizations and can help them undertake the scientific research to persuade states of the necessity of agreeing to substantial environmental protection will help increase this effectiveness over time.

Conclusions

The trends examined in this chapter are representative of the state of global environmental governance. The structure of many environmental issues gives negotiating power to developing countries, without whose participation global environmental institutions will not be fully able to address the environmental problems they attempt to ameliorate. Since most current global environmental problems were primarily caused by the industrializing process of developed states, and developing states are concerned about the increased cost of industrializing without using the environmentally harmful approaches followed by currently developed states, their plea for financial assistance to meet the obligations of global environmental institutions has been persuasive. The GEF has taken the concerns of these states into consideration, reforming its decisionmaking process and expanding its mandate to provide funding for developing states to join and to implement the obligations of global environmental institutions.

At the same time that developing states are accepting more global environmental obligations, the United States, previously a leader in global environmental politics, is accepting fewer. While there are many domestic political explanations for its reluctance, this also comes in a context in which global environmental governance is demanding greater sacrifices of states, frequently moving beyond what they have already undertaken domestically. Apart from the difficulty U.S. non-participation causes for global environmental governance on a number of issues, it also suggests that, as the actions required to mitigate environmental problems become more costly and more complicated, gaining the participation of states that have benefited from the status quo may become increasingly difficult.

Finally, the call for a centralized institution to address environmental governance, while not politically realistic, reflects the concern that the proliferation of institutions to address global environmental problems creates a haphazard international approach that is not ideal for effective governance. As this volume demonstrates, environmental problems requiring international attention have grown in number and complexity, and new institutions have been created to address issues as they emerge. These institutions have had varying degrees of success – from the truly effective institutions focusing on ozone depletion and ocean pollution to the more modest accomplishments of institutions to protect endangered species and conserve fishery resources. The variation in their success depends, however, at least partly on the interests of states and the underlying incentive structures created by the environmental problems themselves, rather than primarily on inefficient institutions. Though better coordination of existing institutions to avoid overlap and inconsistency would be useful, the variety of approaches and institutional structures at least allows those that are able to gain widespread participation and create sufficient environmental concern to successfully govern. These successful institutions stand as models for further efforts to address emerging environmental issues.

Notes

1 David Fairman, "The Global Environment Facility: Haunted by the Shadow of the Future," in Robert O. Keohane and Marc A. Levy, *Institutions for Environmental Aid* (Cambridge, Mass.: MIT Press, 1996), 55–87.
2 Zoe Young, *A New Green Order? The World Bank and the Politics of the Global Environment Facility* (London: Pluto Press, 2002), 53–54.
3 Young, *A New Green Order*, 82, 84–86;
4 Ian A. Bowles and Glenn T. Prickett, *Reframing the Green Window: An Analysis of the GEF Pilot Phase Approach to Biodiversity and Global Warming and Recommendations for the Operational Phase* (Washington, D.C.: Conservation International and Natural Resources Defense Council, 1994).
5 GEF Secretariat, "Replenishment," available at http://thegef.org/Replenishment/replenishment.html.
6 GEF Secretariat, "GEF Funding," available at http://thegef.org/What_is_the_GEF/what_is_the_gef.html#Funding.
7 Fairman, "The Global Environment Facility," 78.
8 GEF Secretariat, "Focal Areas," available at http://thegef.org/Projects/Focal_Areas/focal_areas.html.
9 GEF Secretariat, "Focal Areas."
10 GEF Secretariat, "Focal Areas."
11 Andrea K. Gerlak, "The Global Environment Facility and Transboundary Water Resource Management," *Global Environmental Politics* 13(4) (December 2004), 400–434.
12 GEF Secretariat, "Focal Areas."
13 Global Environment Facility, "Focusing on the Global Environment Facility: The First Decade of the GEF," *Second Overall Performance Study* (25 January 2002).
14 G. Victor Buxton and Risto Ciconkov, GEF-Financed Non-Investment Ozone-Depleting Substance Projects for Countries with Economies in Transition, mid-term evaluation, Evaluation and Oversight Unit (4 July 2004).
15 Cited in Rob Edwards and Sanjay Kumar, "Dust to Dust," *New Scientist* (6 June 1998), 818.
16 Fairman, "The Global Environment Facility," 77–83.
17 Michael P. Wells, "The Global Environment Facility and Prospects for Biodiversity Conservation," International Environmental Affairs 6(1) (Winter 1994), 79–80.
18 Edwards and Kumar, "Dust to Dust," 1818.
19 Alan S. Miller, "The Global Environment Facility and the Search for Financial Strategies to Foster Sustainable Development," *Vermont Law Review* 12 (Summer 2000), 1243.
20 J. Samuel Barkin and George E. Shambaugh, eds., *Anarchy and the Environment* (Albany: SUNY Press, 1999).
21 Elizabeth R. DeSombre, "Fishing Under Flags of Convenience," *Global Environmental Politics* 5(4) (November 2005), 73–94.
22 The Convention on Wetlands of International Importance Especially as Waterfowl Habitat, Article 10(1).

23 Convention Concerning the Protection of the World Cultural and Natural Heritage, Article 33.
24 Convention to Combat Desertification, Article 36(1).
25 Montreal Protocol on Substances that Deplete the Ozone Layer, Article 16(1).
26 Kyoto Protocol to the Framework Convention on Climate Change, Article 25(1).
27 Michael J. Glennon and Alison L. Stewart, "The United States: Taking Environmental Treaties Seriously," in Edith Brown Weiss and Harold K. Jackobson, eds., *Engaging Countries: Strengthening Compliance with International Environmental Accords* (Cambridge, Mass.: MIT Press, 1998), 173–213.
28 UNFCCC, "Kyoto Protocol, Status of Ratification," available at http://unfccc.int/files/essential_background/kyoto_protocol/application/pdf/kpstats.pdf.
29 Robert N. Stavins, "Forging a More Effective Global Climate Treaty," *Environment* 46(10) (2004), 22–30. While the protocol laid out specific emissions obligations, the operational details of implementation were left to be decided by meetings of the COP.
30 W.M. McKibben and P.J. Wilcoxen, "Estimates of the Costs of Kyoto: Marrakesh versus the McKibben–Wilcoxen Blueprint," *Energy Policy* 32(4) (2004), 467–79.
31 Nick Paton, "Putin Throws Lifeline to Kyoto as EU Backs Russia Joining WTO," Guardian (22 May 2004).
32 Sebastian Oberthür and Herman E. Ott, The Kyoto Protocol (New York: Springer, 1999), 18.
33 Elizabeth R. DeSombre, "Understanding United States Unilateralism: Domestic Sources of U.S. International Environmental Policy," in Regina S. Axelrod, David Leonard Downie, and Norman J. Vig, eds., *The Global Environment: Institutions, Law and Policy* (Washington D.C.: CQ Press, 2005), 181–99.
34 Peter M. Haas, "Addressing the Global Governance Deficit," *Global Environmental Politics* 4(4) (November 2004), 3.
35 Steve Charnovitz, "A World Environment Organization," *Columbia Journal of Environmental Law* 27 (2002), 329.
36 Frank Biermann, "The Case for a World Environment Organization," *Environment* 42(9) (November 2000), 22–31.
37 Elizabeth R. DeSombre and J. Samuel Barkin, "Turtles and Trade: the WTO's Acceptance of Environmental Trade Restrictions," *Global Environmental Politics* 2(1) (February 2002), 12–18.
38 Charnovitz, "A World Environment Organization," 337–38.
39 Konrad von Moltke, "Clustering International Environmental Agreements as an Alternative to a World Environment Organization," in Frank Biermann and Steffen Bauer, eds., *A World Environment Organization* (Aldershot, UK: Ashgate, 2005), 176.
40 J. Samuel Barkin, "The Environment, Trade and International Organizations," in Peter Dauvergne, ed., *Handbook of Global Environmental Politics* (Cheltenham, UK: Edward Elgar, 2005), 343.
41 Adil Najam, "Neither Necessary, Nor Sufficient: Why Organizational Tinkering Will Not Improve Environmental Governance," in Biermann and Bauer, eds., *A World Environment Organization*, 235.

42 Sebastian Oberthür and Thomas Gehring, "Reforming International Environmental Governance: An Institutional Perspective on Proposals for a WEO," in Biermann and Bauer, eds., *A World Environment Organization*, 228.

43 Haas, "Addressing the Global Governance Deficit," 7–13.

44 Von Moltke, "Clustering International Environmental Agreements," 175–204.

Bibliography

Books

Regina S. Axelrod, David Leonard Downie, and Norman J. Vig, eds., *The Global Environment: Institutions, Law and Policy* (Washington, D.C.: CQ Press, 2005). This edited volume has individual chapters on many of the institutions discussed here, as well as chapters that cover broader aspects of global environmental governance.

J. Samuel Barkin and George E. Shambaugh, eds., *Anarchy and the Environment: The International Relations of Common Pool Resources* (Albany: SUNY Press, 1999). This volume lays out the theoretical implications of the issue structure of environmental problems, evaluating the arguments with cases from among the most prominent international environmental institutions.

Frank Biermann and Steffen Bauer, eds., *A World Environment Organization* (Aldershot, UK: Ashgate, 2005). A collection of the major scholarly arguments for and against a central institution to govern the global environment.

Edith Brown Weiss and Harold K. Jacobson, eds., *Engaging Countries: Strengthening Compliance with International Environmental Accords* (Cambridge, Mass.: MIT Press, 1998). This study examines five international agreements – CITES, the London (Dumping) Convention, the Montreal Protocol, the World Heritage Convention, and the International Tropical Timber Agreement – and looks at their implementation by a representative set of states and organizations worldwide: the United States, the European Union, Japan, the Soviet Union, Hungary and its successor states, China, India, Cameroon, and Brazil.

W. Bradnee Chambers and Jessica F. Green, eds., *Reforming International Environmental Governance: From Institutional Limits to Innovative Reforms* (Tokyo: United Nations University Press, 2005). Chapters by individual authors assess different ways – such as strengthening UNEP, clustering multilateral environmental agreements, creating a World Environment Organization, and others – to address the difficulties caused by the multiplicity of global environmental institutions.

Pamela S. Chasek, *Earth Negotiations: Analyzing Thirty Years of Environmental Diplomacy* (Tokyo, New York, and Paris: United Nations University Press, 2001). This volume considers the negotiations of the major environmental agreements negotiated between 1972 and 1992, as well as the context before and after this period.

Pamela S. Chasek, David L. Downie, and Janet Welsh Brown, *Global Environmental Politics*, 4th edn. (Boulder: Westview Press, 2006). This concise overview of the evolution of the international politics of the environment includes 11 case studies of environmental issues and the institutions negotiated to manage them.

Jennifer Clapp, *Toxic Exports: The Transfer of Hazardous Wastes from Rich to Poor Countries* (Ithaca: Cornell University Press, 2001). Discusses the creation and evolution of the Basel Convention on the Transboundary Movement of Hazardous Wastes and Their Disposal.

Michael Grubb, Matthias Koch, Abby Munson, Francis Sullivan, and Koy Thomson, *The Earth Summit Agreements: A Guide and Assessment* (London: Earthscan, 1993). The definitive overview of the agreements that came out of the 1992 United Nations Conference on Environment and Development.

Peter M. Haas, Robert O. Keohane, and Marc A. Levy, eds., *Institutions for the Earth* (Cambridge, Mass.: MIT Press, 1993). An early work considered essential in giving an overview of the negotiation of global institutions addressing ozone depletion, acid rain, pollution of regional seas, ocean pollution, fisheries management, and other emerging issues.

Robert O. Keohane and Marc A. Levy, eds., *Institutions for Environmental Aid* (Cambridge, Mass.: MIT Press, 1996). Coverage of efforts to provide funding to address international environmental issues. Includes important discussion of the GEF and the Montreal Protocol Multilateral Fund.

Millennium Ecosystem Assessment, *Ecosystems and Human Well-Being*, vols. 1–5 (Washington, D.C.: Island Press, 2005). This comprehensive assessment undertaken by more than 1300 scientists from nearly 100 states evaluates human impacts on the global (and local) environment.

Marian A. L. Miller, *The Third World in Global Environmental Politics* (Boulder: Lynne Rienner Publishers, 1995). An early overview of the role of developing states in creating global environmental institutions, with a focus on ozone-layer protection, biodiversity conservation, and hazardous waste trade.

Edward A. Parson, *Protecting the Ozone Layer: Science and Strategy* (Oxford: Oxford University Press, 2003). The essential source for everything relating to international efforts to protect the ozone layer.

Clyde Sanger, *Ordering the Oceans: The Making of the Law of the Sea* (London: Zed Books, 1986). An overview of the negotiations and results of the United Nations Convention on the Law of the Sea.

The Social Learning Group, *Learning to Manage Global Environmental Risks*, vols. 1 and 2 (Cambridge, Mass.: MIT Press, 2001). An examination of the process of creating domestic and international action to address acid rain, ozone depletion, and climate change that traces the action from initial scientific studies and domestic responses across a variety of countries.

Mostafa K. Tolba, with Iwona Rummel-Bulska, *Global Environmental Diplomacy: Negotiating Environmental Agreements for the World, 1973–1992* (Cambridge, Mass.: MIT Press, 1998). Tolba, the executive director of UNEP between 1976 and 1992, discusses the environmental issues negotiated during his time at UNEP.

David G. Victor, Kal Raustiala, and Eugene B. Skolnikoff, eds., *The Implementation and Effectiveness of International Environmental Commitments: Theory and Practice* (Cambridge, Mass.: MIT Press, 1998). This volume examines the processes by which global environmental institutions succeed (or fail) in holding states to their commitments and lead to environmental improvement.

World Commission on Environment and Development, *Our Common Future* (Oxford: Oxford University Press, 1987). This report by the commission headed by Gro Harlem Brundtland assesses the relationship between environment and development, makes recommendations for improving the condition of both, and was influential in leading to the 1992 United Nations Convention on Environment and Development and other forms of global environmental governance.

Websites

IISD, *Linkages: A Multimedia Resource for Environment and Development Policy Makers*, available at http://www.iisd.ca/. An indispensable resource for reports on negotiations of ongoing meetings of international environmental agreements and the institutions they create; home of the *Earth Negotiations Bulletin*.

United Nations environmental machinery

United Nations Environment Programme (UNEP), http://www.unep.org.
UNEP Regional Seas Programme, http://www.unep.org/regionalseas/.
Commission on Sustainable Development, http://www.un.org/esa/sustdev/csd/csd.htm.
Millennium Development Goals, http://www.un.org/millenniumgoals/index.html.

Species and biodiversity institutions

CITES Secretariat, http://www.cites.org/.
Convention on Migratory Species Secretariat, http://www.cms.int/.
Ramsar (Wetlands) Secretariat, http://www.ramsar.org/.
World Heritage Convention Secretariat, http://whc.unesco.org/.
Secretariat for the Convention on Biological Diversity, http://www.biodiv.org/.
The World Conservation Union (IUCN), http://www.iucn.org/.
World Conservation Monitoring Centre, http://www.unep-wcmc.org/.

International ocean institutions

International Maritime Organization, http://www.imo.org.
United Nations Convention on the Law of the Sea, http://www.admiralty-lawguide.com/conven/unclostable.html.
International Seabed Authority, http://www.isa.org.jm/.
International Tribunal for the Law of the Sea, http://www.itlos.org/.

UN Food and Agriculture Organization's information page on regional fishery
    bodies, http://www.fao.org/fi/body/rfb/index.htm.

Fisheries commissions

IATTC, http://www.iattc.org/.
ICCAT, http://www.iccat.es/.
IOTC, http://www.iotc.org.
CCSBT, http://www.ccsbt.org/.
NASCO, http://www.nasco.int/.
NPAFC, http://www.npafc.org/.
NEAFC, http://www.neafc.org/.
GFCM, http://www.fao.org/fi/body/rfb/GFCM/gfcm_home.htm.
WCPFC, http://www.wcpfc.org.
IBSFC, http://www.ibsfc.org/.
NAFO, http://www.nafo.ca/.
CCAMLR, http://www.ccamlr.org/.
IWC, http://www.iwcoffice.org/.

Atmospheric commons institutions

LRTAP Secretariat, http://www.unece.org/env/lrtap/welcome.html.
Ozone Secretariat, http://hq.unep.org/ozone/.
Multilateral Fund Secretariat, http://www.multilateralfund.org/.
UN Framework Convention on Climate Change Secretariat, http://unfccc.int/.
Intergovernmental Panel on Climate Change, http://www.ipcc.ch/.

Institutions addressing transboundary movement of hazards

Basel Convention Secretariat, http://www.basel.int/.
Rotterdam Convention Secretariat, http://www.pic.int/.
Stockholm Convention Secretariat, http://www.pops.int/.

Additional institutions

Global Environment Facility, http://www.gefweb.org/.

Index